CITY EXECUTIVES

SUNY Series in Leadership Studies

Barbara Kellerman, editor

CITY EXECUTIVES

Leadership Roles, Work Characteristics,
and Time Management

David N. Ammons
Carl Vinson Institute of Government
University of Georgia

and

Charldean Newell
Department of Political Science
University of North Texas

State University of New York Press

Pages 75–77 were taken from CHALLENGE TO THE CITIES by Henry Maier. Copyright © 1966 by Random House, Inc. Reprinted by permission of Random House, Inc.

Two tables and approximately three pages were from THE NATURE OF MANAGERIAL WORK by Henry Mintzberg. Copyright © 1973 by Henry Mintzberg. Reprinted by permission of Harper & Row, Publishers, Inc.

Some material previously appeared in "Can the Best Mayor Win?" by Richard Ben Cramer. Reprinted by permission of Sterling Lord Literistic, Inc. Copyright © 1984.

Published by
State University of New York Press, Albany

© 1989 State University of New York

All rights reserved

Printed in the United States of America

No part of this book may be used or reproduced
in any manner whatsoever without written permission
except in the case of brief quotations embodied in
critical articles and reviews.
For information, address State University of New York
Press, State University Plaza, Albany, N.Y., 12246

Library of Congress Cataloging-in-Publication Data

Ammons, David N.
   City executives : leadership roles, work characteristics, and time management / David N. Ammons and Charldean Newell.
     p. cm. — (SUNY series in leadership studies)
   Includes notes and index.
   ISBN 0-88706-957-6. ISBN 0-88706-958-4 (pbk)
   1. Mayors—United States. 2. Municipal government by city manager—United States. 3. Time management—United States.
I. Newell, Charldean. II. Title. III. Series.
JS356.A46 1989
352'.000474'0973—dc19   88-15380
                                                                             CIP

10   9   8   7   6   5   4   3   2   1

CONTENTS

Figures and Tables	ix
Preface	xiii
Chapter One: Introduction	1
Scope and Purpose	3
Method	5
What the Book is Not	6
Organization of the Book	7
Chapter Two: An Executive is an Executive is An Executive?	9
Leadership: What It's All About	9
What is a Leader?	10
What Do Executives Do?	11
In What Environment Do They Do It?	14
Good Genes and the "Right Stuff": Dimensions of Effectiveness	18
It All Depends on the Situation	25
Summary	29
Chapter Three: Contemporary Views of Local Government Executive Roles	33
Reformism in American Government	33
City Manager Role Perceptions	46

Political Leadership	52
Chief Executive Roles in the Mid-1980s	59
Comparison with Wright's 1965 Findings	65
Conclusions about the 1985 Study	67
Summary	68
Chapter Four: Not Enough Hours in a Day	**71**
Long Hours	71
Time Allocation	72
Varied Roles and Fragmented Activities	78
Demands, Foci, and Activities in Executive Work	85
Control over Time	99
Summary	101
Chapter Five: Analysis of Time Allocation Patterns	**103**
Correlation	103
Demands	104
Foci of Work	105
Work Activities	110
Relationships across Work Dimensions	111
Summary	115
Chapter Six: Explaining Variations in the Work of Local Government Executives	**117**
Level of the Job	118
Public versus Private	121
Organization Size	122
Managerial Level	125
Managerial Dyads	126

Alternate Explanations for Work Variations	131
Summary	140
Chapter Seven: Time Management	143
Where Does the Time Go?	144
Is There a Better Way?	146
Stress: The Product of Failed Time Management	156
A Matter of Style	159
Summary	160
Chapter Eight: Conclusions	161
Aspects of Managerial Work	163
Prospects for Time Management	165
The Future	170
Appendix	173
Notes	189
Index	219

FIGURES AND TABLES

Figures

Figure 2–1:	The Managerial Grid	23
Figure 2–2:	The 3-D Style Model	27
Figure 2–3:	Continuum of Leadership Behavior	28
Figure 3–1:	Four Forms of Local Government: Hypothetical Organization Charts	38
Figure 4–1:	The Manager's Roles	79
Figure 6–1:	Information Coming from a City	136
Figure 6–2:	Ideal Agenda-City Relationship	137
Figure 6–3:	Different Cognitive Orientations of Mayors	138
Figure 6–4:	Ideal City-Mayor Relationship	139
Figure 6–5:	People/Technical Orientations Demanded by Communities	140
Figure 6–6:	Managerial Types in Terms of People Orientation Versus Technical Orientation	141

Tables

Table 2–1:	Definition of Managerial Behaviors in Yukl's Taxonomy	30
Table 3–1:	Mean Percentage of Time Devoted to the "Management," "Policy," and "Political" Roles by Persons in Various Executive Positions in City Government	62
Table 3–2:	Municipal Officials' 1985 Designation of Most Important Role Compared with Wright's 1965 Findings (Populations Greater than 100,000)	66
Table 4–1:	Eight Managerial Job Types	80
Table 4–2:	Concurrence Rankings: Administrator Versus Governing Body Role Perceptions	84
Table 4–3:	Percentage of Managerial Workweek Claimed by Various Demands	89

Table 4–4:	Focus of Managerial Work in City Government, by Positions—Percentage of Time Devoted to Various Foci	90
Table 4–5:	Percentage of Executive Time Devoted to Various Activities—Comparison with Previous Managerial Time Allocation Studies	97
Table 6–1:	Time Allocations in Executive Work: Apportioned by Demands, Foci, and Activities	120
Table 6–2:	Percentage of Executive Time Devoted to Various Activities, by Organization Size—Comparison with Previous Managerial Time Allocation Studies	123
Table 6–3:	Percentage of Internal Administrative Time Devoted to "Managerial," "Mentor," and "Specialist/Technologist" Roles: Comparison with Previous Research	130

Appendix

Table A–1:	Profile of Respondents, by Form of Government, Position Category, and City Populations	173
Table A–2:	General Linear Model (GLM) Tables for Reported Time Allocations of Mayors, Mayoral Assistants, City Managers, and Assistant City Managers	174
Table A–3:	Summary of Significant Explanatory Variables Identified through Stepwise Regression for Working Hour and Time Allocation Variation among Mayors and City Managers	176
Table A–4:	Pearson Correlation Coefficients for Sources of Demand on Executive Workweek in City Government	177
Table A–5:	Pearson Correlation Coefficients for Foci of Municipal Executive Work	178
Table A–6:	Pearson Correlation Coefficients for Activities in Municipal Executive Work	179
Table A–7:	Pearson Correlation Coefficients for Work Activities, Foci, and Demands on Executive Time in City Government	180
Table A–8:	Pearson Correlation Coefficients for Population, Working Hours, Perceived Executive Control of Time, and Characteristics of Municipal Executive Work	181

Table A–9:	Focus of Executive Work in City Government, by Position and City Size—Percentage of Time Devoted to Various Foci	182
Table A–10:	Pearson Correlation Coefficients for Time Allocation by Chief Executives and Assistants in the Same City	184
Table A–11:	Percentages of Executive Respondents in Specified Age Categories, by Position Held and Population of Jurisdiction Served	185
Table A–12:	Percentages of Executive Respondents Possessing Graduate Degrees, by Position Held and Population of Jurisdiction Served	186
Table A–13:	Percentages of Executive Respondents Possessing MPA Degree, by Position Held and Population of Jurisdiction Served	187

PREFACE

This book is about city executives—what they do, how they spend their time, which of the many demands on their days (and nights!) receive the most attention. It is about executive leadership in the public sector, for the effective mayor or city manager must blend personal time and talents with those of subordinates and marshal the cooperative energies of city council members, business leaders, and interested citizens to have any hope of mastering the problems of the modern city.

The book is written for several audiences—local government practitioners; students of leadership, local government, and public administration; and citizens. City executives can compare time allocation information against their own experiences. While some may be startled to find that their own time allocation priorities differ from those of their counterparts, many will feel their perceptions of uniqueness dissolve as they learn just how similar their own demands, priorities, and work patterns are to those of many of their colleagues in city government. Persons who deal with city executives or who hope one day to become a city executive can get a glimpse of what it is like to be a mayor, a city manager, or one of their key assistants—a glimpse that should prove useful in understanding executive behavior and in preparing either for future interactions or for a career. All may benefit from a chapter focusing on personal time management.

Students in university courses on leadership, local government, or public administration will find in this book a detailed focus that is impossible in more general, introductory texts on those subjects. Advanced scholars will find an empirical data base against which to test their hypotheses that is far more satisfactory than the more common anecdotal treatment of executive leadership in local government.

The interested citizen may also benefit from an improved

understanding of city government and its key actors. The development of current forms of local government, the nature of the various demands on city executives in "unreformed" and in "reformed" cities, and the work load of the "typical" city executive are all explained in terms that the lay reader will appreciate.

The ideas of many writers are incorporated into this book to provide perspective, history, and comparison. However, we take full responsibility for interpretations of those ideas, as well as for any errors of omission or commission in the analysis of our own data and the presentation of our conclusions.

We acknowledge and appreciate the support provided to this project by the University of North Texas through a Faculty Research Grant to the authors and by the Carl Vinson Institute of Government at the University of Georgia. We also express a special word of appreciation for the secretarial assistance of Joan Bertsch, Erma L. Glaze, Karen Hewatt, and Kim Kelley; the graphics work of Anne Huddleston and Reid McCallister; and the research assistance of Victor M. Boyer.

David N. Ammons
Charldean Newell

Chapter One

INTRODUCTION

Among many other characterizations, chief executives have been depicted flatteringly as orchestra conductors and sympathetically as puppets on a string.[1] The public sector management literature, scholarly and otherwise, suggests that the characterizations are no less applicable to executives in local government, notably mayors and city managers, than to their corporate counterparts.[2] Each depiction—even as contradictory as the images of conductor and puppet are—may be supported logically, and, perhaps, anecdotally by its respective author.

Surprisingly little empirical research delving into the nature of the executive role has been conducted, despite popular fascination with the subject. One of the few exceptions is the landmark work of Canadian scholar Henry Mintzberg, who carefully observed, recorded, and analyzed the work activities of three business executives, a hospital administrator, and a school superintendent.[3] Mintzberg argues that, absent empirical data, our answers to perhaps the most basic of management questions, "What do managers do?," are inadequate.[4] After all, what did we really learn about managerial work when Henri Fayol told us that managers plan, organize, coordinate, command, and control, or when Luther Gulick suggested that the essence of the executive's role was reflected in a simple acronym, POSDCORB, memorized by management students through the years?[5] Telling someone who wants to know what managers do that they plan, organize, staff, direct, coordinate, report, and budget (hence, POSDCORB) is a useful beginning, but it is really no more satisfying than telling a baseball fan who wants to know what it is like to be a superstar that his favorite hero hits, fields, throws, and runs. Management writers tend to address managerial functions in one or the other of two unsatisfactory ways: (1) abstractly or (2) concretely but out of context. When examined abstractly, managerial functions appear lifeless and void of the nuances and subtleties that define their essence. When concretely addressed, they tend to be considered singly—providing a stage on which each function appears larger than life, as if that function commands absolute priority, with no serious challengers for the manager's time and attention.

Mintzberg's research gives the serious student of management the context that is otherwise missing from most of the literature on managerial roles. His time analysis places each role in context with the others. In so doing, he provides an empirical basis for challenging many of the conclusions found in other works.[6]

While the literature on municipal executives has been rich in anecdotal approaches to the study of executive roles and, to stretch a financial metaphor, reasonably well-to-do when it comes to behavioral studies, it is clearly the poor cousin to the none-too-wealthy private sector literature in the realm of executive time-allocation studies. Students of municipal management are treated to an array of colorful characterizations of the roles of mayors and city managers, often paralleling and sometimes outstripping similar analogies depicting private sector executives. Consider, for example, the following five descriptions of life as a chief executive, the first three focusing primarily on private sector executives but offering noticeably different points of view, the fourth a self-portrait drawn by a former mayor of Dallas, and the fifth a statement of frustration by a former mayor of Baltimore who chose not to seek reelection:

> The manager has the task of creating a true whole that is larger than the sum of its parts, a productive entity that turns out more than the sum of the resources put into it. One analogy is the conductor of a symphony orchestra, through whose effort, vision and leadership individual instrumental parts that are so much noise by themselves become the living whole of music. But the conductor has the composer's score; he is only interpreter. The manager is both composer and conductor.[7]

> The achievement of . . . stability, which is the manager's objective, is a never-to-be attained ideal. He is like a symphony orchestra conductor, endeavoring to maintain a melodious performance in which the contributions of the various instruments are coordinated and sequenced, patterned and paced, while the orchestra members are having various personal difficulties, stage hands are moving music stands, alternating excessive heat and cold are creating audience and instrument problems, and the sponsor of the concert is insisting on irrational changes in the program.[8]

> Before we made the study, I always thought of a chief executive as the conductor of an orchestra, standing aloof on his platform. Now I am in some respects inclined to see him as the puppet in the puppet-show

> with hundreds of people pulling the strings and forcing him to act in one way or another.[9]
>
> Being a mayor is like walking on a moving belt while juggling. Right off you've got to walk pretty fast to stay even. After you've been in office a short time people start throwing wads of paper at you. So now you've got to walk, juggle, and duck too. Then the belt starts to move faster, and people start to throw wooden blocks at you. About the time you're running like mad, juggling and ducking stones, someone sets one end of the belt on fire. Now if you can keep the things you are juggling in the air, stay on the belt, put out the fire, and not get seriously injured, you've found the secret to the job. You have managed to put it all together into something that works.[10]
>
> You know what this job is? You come in in the morning, and they bring you a big plate of crap to eat. So you grit your teeth, and just when you got it finished . . . they're at the door with a bigger plate of crap.[11]

Colorful depictions of the frenetic pace and frustrations of mayors and city managers are easily drawn, but relatively few studies of municipal executive roles have ventured far beyond such caricatures. Those that have are generally considered to be classics in the field.[12] None from this select few, however, has focused more than tangentially on time allocation—i.e., the question of how key actors in city government actually spend their time. Yet, time allocation by mayors, city managers, and key assistants potentially can reveal a great deal about the nature of managerial work in city government. The absence of such data reduces the ability to generalize the experiences of select mayors and managers to municipal executives as a whole, and unfortunately renders a substantial portion of the more conceptual work on municipal executive roles to be little more than conjecture. Without a broader base of information on the activities of a large number of mayors and city managers, it is impossible to know whether the work pace and array of challenges facing the highly publicized few are unusual or typical.

Scope and Purpose

The objective of this book is the presentation of a clearer picture of the work of city executives than has previously been presented through anecdotes alone. It is not our purpose to discredit the use of anecdotes;

indeed, we use them extensively and believe they enrich the points we attempt to make. It is our contention, however, that anecdotes alone satisfy only the most casual or the most gullible reader. The casual reader enjoys the good story; the gullible reader assumes that every mayor operates like, say, Richard Daley.[13] The more serious student of local government wants to know, "Is this typical?" The study that serves as this book's foundation was undertaken with the intent of developing an improved understanding of the nature of executive roles and managerial work in city government. An endeavor of this sort, supported by empirical data, potentially provides a basis for reconsidering previous work in the fields of leadership and municipal management, and furnishes a benchmark for future research.

Conceivably, the "municipal executive" label could be applied generously to a wide array of department heads, administrative assistants, and other assorted officials sprinkled across the upper ranks of City Hall. Ours, however, is a narrower focus, including only the chief executives and their principal assistants in cities of 50,000 population or greater. In cities with the mayor-council or commission form of government, mayors serve as chief executive; in cities with the council-manager form, the city manager does. Cities with populations less than 50,000 were excluded simply to permit the concentrated use of limited resources. Accordingly, generalizations of the study's findings to smaller cities, as well as to municipal occupations other than those examined, should be approached with caution.

Several research questions provided structure to the study and, therefore, to the book. Chief among those questions are the following: In what ways is the work of executives in municipal government similar to, or different from, that of their counterparts in the private sector? Are the anecdotal images of long working hours confirmed by the executives themselves? What are the principal demands placed on the time of municipal executives? Where is their work focused? How do they divide their time among various activities? How do these allocations compare with the findings of Mintzberg for a mix of executives weighted toward the private sector? How much of the workweek of municipal executives is under their own control, and how much is under the control of others? How is their time divided among principal roles? Has the allocation among roles changed over time? How do all of these factors differ between the four categories of municipal executives being examined in this study (i.e., mayors, mayoral assistants, city managers, and assistant city managers)? What are the ramifications for executive time management?

Method

In contrast to narrow, unidimensional works dealing with city executives' roles or functions, this study concentrates on time allocation not only as evidence of conflicting demands and responsibilities but also as an indication of executive emphases. While it will not be argued here that the percentage of an executive's time devoted to a particular role or activity is a precise measure of its priority *vis-à-vis* other roles or activities, it is at least a rough gauge. A mayor or city manager who spends twice as much time cultivating intergovernmental relations as is spent on city council relations has revealed a great deal about personal priorities, despite possible protests to the contrary or rhetoric about "the great importance" of some function which "inadvertently" has been short-changed in the press of events. Actions, so they say, often speak louder than words.

Despite our view that time allocations provide a rough gauge of the relative priorities assigned to various roles and activities, we recognize the imperfections of that gauge. As we will discover in Chapter Three, the reported time allocations of municipal executives are not in perfect harmony with the relative importance they assign to three executive roles. Most city mangers, for example, consider the "policy role" to be most important for job success; yet, the typical city manager spends more time on the "management role." Such a finding suggests either (1) a disparity between what an executive wishes to *think* is top priority and what in reality (i.e., subconsciously) *is* top priority, as argued above, or (2) the existence of a serious problem of time management. If, for instance, the management role is draining time more productively spent on policy matters, the executive must find a way to perform the management role more efficiently.

The principal sources of data for this study are city executives themselves. A survey of 839 chief executives and principal assistants in the 418 United States cities having a 1980 population of 50,000 or greater was completed during the spring of 1985. As noted above, questionnaires were mailed to the city manager (or to the city manager equivalent in a given city—e.g., municipal manager, village manager) in council-manager cities and to one or more assistant city managers or persons of similar title (e.g., deputy city manager, assistant village manager, assistant to the city manager). In mayor-council and commission cities, questionnaires were mailed to the mayor and to the person identified as the chief appointed official or the mayor's principal assistant (e.g., chief administrative officer, city administrator, deputy mayor, assistant to the mayor). Although each official was encouraged to respond personally, the instructions acknowledged the likelihood that some questionnaires would be completed by aides and simply requested that such aides identify themselves in a space provided on the survey instrument. A second mailing was sent to those officials not responding to the first.

Responses were received from 559 officials (66.6%), but 32 were identified as having been completed by aides. The remaining 527 responses (62.8%), reportedly completed by officials personally, provide the data for the analyses reported throughout this book; the 32 responses from aides are excluded.

Although a time allocation study based upon self-reporting has some weaknesses in comparison to other techniques such as observation, it offers the major advantage of making a vastly expanded data base practical. The most apparent weaknesses of a questionnaire approach in contrast to direct observation of executive actions by a researcher are the vagaries and possible ambiguities in self-reporting. Such problems are not easily dismissed, and no attempt is made to do so here. However, even direct observation techniques are not spared the problem of ambiguity in the assignment of a given executive action to one category or another on a researcher's checklist. Moreover, the more expensive direct observation almost inevitably places undesirable, practical restrictions on sample size.

The survey approach taken for this book provides a rich source of data, with far greater breadth than would have been possible via direct observation. Input from 527 city executives, representing a mix of chief executives and principal assistants in differing forms of local government, provides a solid basis for perceptual findings. Because practical, as well as methodological, constraints limit the viability of alternate approaches for securing data, the question arises as to whether a better way really exists for gaining insight into the nature of executive roles and activities in city government than through the perceptions of the men and women who occupy those positions. The approach taken here provides such perceptions in great number.

What the Book is Not

Perhaps as important as clarifying the scope and purpose of this book and of the study on which it is based is a declaration of what the book is not. It is not a recitation or ranking of the myriad problems that challenge, befuddle, and sometimes overcome municipal officials. Such lists, subject to almost constant change with fluctuations in the economic, social, and political forces that shape the municipal environment, may be found elsewhere in the literature of municipal management.[14]

Nor does this book focus on the identification of requisite skills for coping with problems facing municipal leaders. The results of the study may be instructive in that regard, but the consideration of skills needed today or in the future is not a principal component.[15]

Finally, this work is not an attempt to develop a model to explain mayoral and managerial behavior under a variety of differing circumstances.[16] It is, instead, an exploration of municipal leadership roles, demands, foci, and work activities, using reported time allocations as the researchers' divining rod.

Organization of the Book

Following this introduction are seven other chapters. Chapter Two provides an overview of concepts pertinent to executive functions in general and leadership in particular. Special attention is drawn to factors that appear to distinguish managerial work and leadership roles in one setting from those in another, concentrating especially on differences between public and private sector management.

The focus in Chapter Three narrows to city government. The reader is oriented to the major structural changes introduced in city government organizations over the past 100 years, primarily in response to the widespread corruption in turn-of-the-century American cities and the reform movement it spawned. The ramifications that different forms of local government hold for executive roles and responsibilities are examined, including the seemingly perpetual debate over the supposed administrative domain of appointed executives and exclusively policy domain of elected officials—the so-called politics-administration dichotomy. Chapter Three will also provide a comparison of city executive role perceptions in 1985 with those of city managers surveyed by Deil Wright in 1965.[17]

Chapters Four, Five, and Six offer a detailed examination of the results of the survey of city officials. Data on executive working hours, demands on executive time, foci of managerial endeavors, specific work activities, and control of executive time are tabulated in Chapter Four and, where applicable, compared with the results of previous studies. Correlations across the various dimensions of executive work are explored in Chapter Five, noting, for example, the association between predominance of a particular category of work demand and emphasis of a particular work activity. In Chapter Six, an attempt is made to explain the variations in the work of local government executives, including as a component of that explanation the testing of five hypotheses offered by Mintzberg for explaining variations in the work of executives.[18]

Readers with an aversion to numbers are forewarned that they may find Chapter Five and perhaps Chapter Six a bit tedious. The various coefficients demanded by graduate scholars are reported faithfully, although the most number-ladened tables have been relegated to the book's appendix. In deference to nonstatisticians, each analytic technique used is explained briefly and in layman's terms, permitting comprehension without advanced statistical background. Moreover, the less methodical reader should find the narrative explanation of findings to be satisfactory. The impatient reader anxious to get to the results will no doubt discover the summary at the end of each chapter and find it to be a useful capsule of major findings even in these more difficult chapters.

Chapter Seven provides a review of the literature on time management, with special attention to the relevance of that literature to city executives, given the nature of their work. Suggestions, including cautions, are offered.

Finally, conclusions to the study are drawn in Chapter Eight.

Chapter Two

AN EXECUTIVE IS AN EXECUTIVE IS AN EXECUTIVE?

Leadership: What It's All About

If one took a HAC (haphazard/accidental/convenient) sample of citizens strolling along Main Street of Any City, USA, and asked each individual to name community leaders, some respondents might be stymied, some would name well-known business figures, and some undoubtedly would name public officials. If respondents were asked more explicitly whether they considered the mayor or city manager to be a leader, the answer would almost surely be "yes," even if the style or substance of their leadership were contrary to the preferences of the respondents or a matter of little interest to them. But what is a leader, and what do leaders do?

The empirical study reported subsequently in this book was undertaken with the intent of developing an improved understanding of the nature of executive roles and managerial work in city government through an examination of how municipal executives allocate their time and what work characteristics they display. The findings are examined in light of what is known about corporate executive time allocation and theories on leadership. After all, a study of executives—whatever their organizational base—is by definition a study of leadership since executives must accept that mantle as part of their responsibility. As corporate executive H. Ross Perot notes, "People cannot be managed. Inventories can be managed, but people must be led."[1] Successful executives are effective leaders. This empirical study thus examines what executives, as leaders, *do*.

This chapter provides an overview of theories about leadership preparatory to Chapter Three's more focused review of three distinct roles played by executives in exercising leadership in a municipal setting. Leadership, as a topic of inquiry, spans many disciplines and subdisciplines: organization theory and behavior, political science, public administration, business management, social and industrial psychology, sociology, history, and philosophy, to name a few. As a consequence, the literature is diffuse, with many focal points and at most only general agreement on findings and conclusions. A mere sampling of the literature is provided on the following pages.

What is a Leader?

Few writers approach the clarity of James McGregor Burns in depicting the leader as one who serves not only as the facilitator of organizational processes (what Burns calls "transactional leadership"—i.e., making sure that "things happen") but also as the promoter of organizational values, including new moral and ethical levels (what he labels "transformational leadership"—i.e., deciding what "things *should* happen").[2] Burns's explanation is particularly useful to a study of municipal executives, the focus of this book, for it helps to identify those city officials in whom executive leadership responsibility is vested, regardless of any apparent restrictions that may be implied by a particular title.

While the terms "executive" and "manager" are often used interchangeably by practitioners and the popular media with absolutely no harm, they have distinctly different meanings to some leadership theorists. Harold Gortner, Julianne Mahler, and Jeanne Nicholson, the authors of a recent text on organization theory, posit distinctive differences in the activities of three administrative levels: executives, managers, and supervisors. Executives are described as individuals having major responsibility for establishing organizational climate, goals and broad structure: what Burns calls "transforming." In contrast, the focus and responsibilities of managers and supervisors are perceived to be much narrower and more tightly constrained. Managers are seen as focusing on processes and specific structures, while supervisors are viewed as having the much more limited responsibility of accomplishing only specific objectives.[3] As readers consider the policy, political and managerial roles of executives that will be identified in Chapter Three, it may prove useful to keep these distinctions in mind. After all, city *managers* are really executives regardless of their title. They meet the Burns description of leadership as well as the

Gortner-Mahler-Nicholson description of executives. City managers, like mayors, must consider "the big picture"—goals, climate, environment—as well as internal processes.

In exploring the question of "what is a leader?," the "big picture" perspective and the value-setting responsibilities of leaders are concepts encountered repeatedly. In their best-selling examination of business organizations, *In Search of Excellence*,[4] Thomas Peters and Robert Waterman heavily emphasize Burns's transformational leadership notion. In case after case, they found the executives of "America's best-run companies" fulfilling their value-setting responsibilities and inculcating those values in others in the organization.

What Do Executives Do?

A successful individual at the top of an organization, be it public or private, provides leadership for that organization. Thus, a simple answer to the question of "what do executives do?" is that they lead. But leadership is a complex, multifaceted phenomenon, manifested in different executives in a variety of different shapes and forms. Leading is something executives do all right, but curiously it has sometimes been overlooked as one of their discrete functions.

Classical organization theory answered the question of "what do executives do?" by setting forth seven functions common to the work of all chief executives: planning, organizing, staffing, directing, coordinating, reporting, and budgeting (POSDCORB).[5] Classical theorists, whose period of preeminence lasted through the 1930s, focused on formal organization. The formal side of organization includes such concepts as: (1) hierarchy (the pyramidal structure common to most organizations, as typically depicted in organization charts, with the fewest people but greatest authority at the top); (2) line and staff relationships (the relationships between organizational units responsible for producing the product or delivering the service to the client and those units that serve in support roles, such as personnel and purchasing offices); and (3) chain of command (who reports to whom). Collectively, these concepts are termed "scalar and functional principles."[6] Each deals with formal relationships, establishing the vertical lines of authority and functional priorities in an organization.

The classicists emphasized formal organization to the point of ignoring the importance of the human element in organizational dynamics, an oversight that has generated considerable criticism from modern scholars. Yet their emphasis on structure has resurfaced numerous times, and the modern concept of task structuring, seen as one component of leadership, is conceptual heir to classic principles. Nevertheless, POSDCORB includes no "L" for leadership. Apparently for the classicists, leadership was a given, a quality presumed to be present in the planning, organizing, directing, and coordinating functions (PODCO of POSDCORB). Perhaps they simply assumed leadership to permeate each of the specified functions through some mysterious force of the effective manager's persona, if not through the formal authority of the executive's position in the hierarchy. At any rate, leadership was at best an implicit executive function in the most widely accepted listing of that era.

Thirty-five years later, Henry Mintzberg, whose concepts underlie a large portion of the empirical study of city executives reported in this book, ventured beyond POSDCORB, emphasizing in his study of executives the importance of people, of the environment, and of leadership.[7] In short, Mintzberg's depiction of executives includes multiple roles of greater variety and complexity than those enumerated by the classicists.

Mintzberg, for example, identifies 10 roles that a manager plays. Three—figurehead, leader, and liaison—are interpersonal; three—monitor, disseminator, and spokesman—are informational; and four—entrepreneur, disturbance handler, resource allocator, and negotiator—are decisional.[8] Although Mintzberg identifies leadership as a distinct role, his definition of the role is narrow: as leader the manager is "responsible for the motivation and activation of subordinates; responsible for staffing, training, and associated duties." In reality, however, manifestations of leadership are not confined to the "leader" role. Other roles cover aspects of leadership subsequently discussed in this chapter. For example, the entrepreneurial role encompasses strategic vision and action while the information roles include most boundary-spanning leadership activities.[9]

While Mintzberg's categorization of managerial roles hinges on the process invoked in a given behavior, other writers use a different perspective. For example, Michael Cohen and James March have identified eight roles assumed by a particular set of chief executives, college presidents, depending upon their view or "model" of their system. Those perceiving their system as a competitive market behave as an entrepreneur. A "collective bargaining metaphor" generates mediators; an "administration metaphor," managers; a "democracy metaphor," politicians; a "consensus metaphor," chairpersons; an "anarchy metaphor," catalysts; an "independent judiciary metaphor," judges; and a "plebiscitary autocracy metaphor" encourages presidents to act as philosopher-kings.[10]

Not all of the classicists' contemporaries had truncated notions of executive functions. Chester I. Barnard, a telephone company executive cum scholar, established a basis for much of the later theorizing about organizational behavior. He was a pioneer in setting forth such concepts as an interactive social system (each component part of the system—e.g., the environment of informal subgroups—affects the others), of relational authority (authority is meaningless if not accepted by subordinates), of exchanges (e.g., work in exchange for rewards), and of the communication process (how messages are sent and received).[11] Specifically in answer to the question, "what do executives do?," he saw leadership as a primary function. For Barnard, leadership existed on two planes: (1) a technical plane encompassing maintenance of the communication process, task management, and the formulation of goals and purposes, and (2) a higher plane encompassing executive responsibility, which "is that capacity of leaders by which, reflecting attitudes, ideals, hopes, derived largely from without themselves, they are compelled to bind the wills of men to the accomplishment of purposes beyond their immediate ends, beyond their times."[12] In other words, leaders are responsible not only for making the organization work in a technical sense but also for establishing the organization's culture and instilling a set of values in its people. Burns's thinking 40 years later mirrored that of Barnard in the former's comments about a dichotomy (levels) of leader responsibilities—the transactional and the transformational.[13]

Phillip Selznick identified administration with leadership. His views on leadership are somewhat similar to those of Barnard in that he also was concerned with the leader's role in the formulation of goals and purposes and with capacity building (task management). In addition, he expanded his list of leadership components by including executive responsibility for conflict resolution and for preserving the values and identity of the organization.[14] Selznick perceived the possibility of external threats to the organization and, thus, introduced the idea of environmental interaction and the importance of the context in which the executive operates. Although Selznick first published his broadened conceptualization of executive behavior in the 1950s, his emphasis on the environment fits well with contemporary thinking.

Especially for the public executive, most of whose actions are subject to scrutiny by citizens, (other) elected officials, and the press, the importance of the sociopolitical and economic context is considerable. " . . . executives are expected to pay close attention to the environment so that they can take advantage of opportunities that arise, protect the bureau when it is attacked or in danger, and generally represent it in the inevitable political frays."[15]

The volatile nature of the external environment requires the modern executive to be a strategic manager, that is, to recognize threats and opportunities and to respond to them in a creative manner, and to have a broad view of the workings of the organization.[16] In addition to "empowering others" and "creating structure" (concepts encountered frequently in the literature to denote mobilizing people, creating rules, and organizing tasks), "vision" is normally considered to be an important quality for the chief executive in city government and is frequently mentioned as an essential component of strategic management.[17]

In summary, what does the literature tell us about what an executive does? The answer, although less precise than would be ideal for the practitioner or the empiricist, is nevertheless instructive. First, the literature suggests that the executive, as leader, "welds diverse elements into a cooperative enterprise"[18] both by integrating individual and organizational goals and by exercising power. Functions associated with welding diverse elements include those enumerated in POSD-CORB and the interpersonal executive functions spelled out by Barnard and others. Second, the executive interacts with the organization's environment, developing the fundamental standards of the organization (moral and ethical precepts) and strategies for success.

In What Environment Do They Do It?

The most oft-cited shortcoming of the classical theorists is their failure to incorporate human relations into the principles of organization. However, for those who study public organizations, a shortcoming of equal seriousness is the early theorists' failure to analyze the external environment in the public sector and to account for its effect in their propositions and prescriptions. Disagreement exists regarding the nature and magnitude of differences in the environments of public and private organizations. Some writers contend that the environments are sharply differentiated;[19] some, that they are different but rapidly losing their [20] distinctions; and others, that they are not fundamentally different.[21] Our position is that the environment of the public organization can be differentiated, at least in degree, from that of the private organization. That difference has important ramifications for executives attempting to change sectors or merely attempting to apply the lessons of the other sector to their own.

Modern organizations are perceived as open systems characterized by permeable boundaries and numerous transactions and communications with other social systems;[22] much of the important action takes place at these boundaries. While there are internal boundaries and internal boundary disputes (e.g., "turf" battles, especially over functions spanning multiple departments), the external boundaries are often of greater concern to the public organization. Not only are jurisdictions sometimes overlapping or responsibilities unclear, but also the easily crossed boundaries invite attention from interested parties outside the organization.[23] External individuals, groups, and organizations often seek to dominate the internal goals of public organizations, frequently prompting the formation of coalitions between the public organization and external groups, both public and private, as a survival tactic.[24] Witness, for example, the adeptness with which some library directors marshal the skills and influence of the "Friends of the Library" when an ultraconservative group expresses an intent to purge the library of classic but controversial books. Sometimes, these support groups are used to gain internal political advantage, as is the case, for example, when the Animal Control superintendent enlists the aid of the local Humane Society to avoid a budget cut. Consequently, the public executive expends considerable energy in the dynamic, sometimes threatening world of dealing with outsiders, engaged in boundary-spanning (and sometimes boundary-protecting) behaviors. "The 'coin of the realm' in the public sector is *influence*. Influence is gained through the skillful playing of the game called 'politics,' and *power* is the reward received by the most skillful players."[25]

Francis Rourke summarizes the sources of bureaucratic power as support from elected officials, clientele groups, and the public; expertise and information; and leadership.[26] The executive, as well as lower-level bureaucrats, draws on the support of "interested others," knowledge, and skills in personal leadership and persuasion. Indeed, persuading other people of the soundness of one's position, based on the authority of office and the assumption of superior knowledge, often may be a large share of the game.[27]

The public organization is different from the private on a variety of dimensions with important behavioral ramifications conceivably reflected in time allocation patterns. The discovery of substantially greater amounts of time spent by the public sector executive in dealing with diverse outside interests and contending with external efforts to dominate organizational goals is a plausible expectation. The two sectors differ in other fundamental ways, as well. John Millett identifies four major distinctions between the public and private organization: (1) the limited scope of public agencies, especially the need to avoid conflict with the private sector; (2) the internal system of decisionmaking, including an emphasis on power and politics; (3) differences in funding, especially the reliance on taxation in the public sector rather than sales in the marketplace; and (4) the system of social responsibility that binds public agencies to the principle of equity.[28]

Louis Gawthrop, expanding on the notion of differences in internal decision processes, notes that government decisions are primarily "consolidative"—that is, decisionmakers avoid taking risks—while business decisions are more innovative. Gawthrop bases this conclusion on two factors: (1) the inherent conflict between efficiency (which he contends subordinates creativity) and innovation (which Gawthrop says requires a loosening of efficiency controls) and (2) people's basic consolidative, security-oriented nature.[29] Although Gawthrop's premise may be challenged by those who insist that the successful pursuit of efficiency often demands extraordinary creativity, his views lead him to perceive a greater capacity for innovation in the private sector.

Moreover, individuals who have held both public and private sector positions have found them to be different. Michael Blumenthal, for example, in comparing his experiences with Bendix and as Treasury Secretary, found the environment of the public agency to differ from that of the business corporation in such matters as influence, media exposure, the constraints of the civil service system, congressional turnover, shared power, and the complexity of the "rules of the game."[30] Donald Rumsfeld, comparing his corporate experience with his life in the public sector (he served first as a member of Congress and later on the White House staff), found a number of similarities but greater time demands in the public sector.[31]

Nevertheless, not all observers of both public and private organizations perceive them to be appreciably different; some have found a lack of empirical evidence to support contentions regarding substantial differences.[32] Public executives themselves may also be finding new similarities with private executives. One observer notes, "the modern governor has become a manager, more like a corporate chief executive officer than a traditional politician."[33] Our study of city executives' allocation of time is, in fact, an effort to help fill the gap in empirical evidence regarding presumed differences by affording a direct comparison with Mintzberg's findings about other types of organizations.

We conclude with Graham Allison that "public and private management are at least as different as they are similar, and that the differences are more important than the similarities."[34] The modern public executive who fails to comprehend that democratic morality is of concern, that government has primary responsibility for the promotion of social goals, and that efficiency without responsiveness is an incomplete approach to governance is also likely to have a short tenure in office. In fact, differences reported by executives with experience in both sectors focus less on internal management efficiency than on environmental constraints.

It is with regard to the importance of executive leadership in setting and articulating organization values and maintaining a broad perspective on concerns and goals of their organization that the distinction between the top-level executive—even when called city *manager*—and subordinate managers may be truly fundamental. Mid-level managers and supervisors whose focus is much more likely to be directed exclusively toward a single operation perhaps more nearly can concentrate on production efficiency, while the executive must share that concern and also worry about successful spanning of organizational boundaries, about values and strategies, and about the political climate in which the organization exists. A declaration that "leaders are people who do the right things, and managers are people who do things right"[35] is tempting for its simplicity, but the fact of the matter is that persons called "managers" who operate in highly responsible positions often exercise leadership and are concerned both with doing things right and with doing the right things.

Christopher Bellavita notes that the sharp distinctions made in theory between the visionary role of leaders and the "dirty" work of managing an organization's activities fade in actual practice. He cites John Kennedy's shrewd management skills in events surrounding the Cuban Missile Crisis and William Webster's vision as director of the FBI as evidence that leaders can be adept managers and managers can be effective leaders. According to Bellavita, leadership is an organizational process that consists of four elements that in most cases will be directed by more than one person—whatever their titles or reputations:

- a vision that provides meaning and direction to the organization's work;
- political support for the vision;

- people willing to work to achieve the vision; and
- the technical ability to carry out the vision.[36]

John W. Gardner, former secretary of Health, Education, and Welfare and president of the Carnegie Corporation, echoes the assertion that managers can be effective leaders:

> Many writers on leadership are at considerable pains to distinguish between leaders and managers. In the process leaders generally end up looking like a cross between Napoleon and the Pied Piper, and managers like unimaginative clods. This troubles me. I once heard it said of a man, "He's an utterly first-class manager but there isn't a trace of the leader in him." I am still looking for that man, and I am beginning to believe that he doesn't exist. Every time I encounter an utterly first-class manager he turns out to have quite a lot of the leader in him.[37]

On the other hand, Dianne Feinstein of San Francisco, recognized by one national panel as the country's best mayor in 1987, asserts the importance of the management function to effective public sector leadership.

> My belief is that the executive branch of governmental service, whether it be local, state, or national, should be managerial. The days of a hale fellow well-met, whether it be a mayor, governor, or president, are over. Nothing says that more eloquently than the national budget deficit.[38]

Good Genes and the "Right Stuff": Dimensions of Effectiveness

What makes an effective leader? Over the years, many answers have been offered. A few of the most notable are the following:

- the "great man" theory—i.e., "leaders are born and not made";
- the leadership traits theory—i.e., all leaders display common characteristics;
- the leadership styles theory—i.e., how leaders approach their leadership roles determines effectiveness;
- the contingency/situational theory—i.e., "it all depends on the situation."

Great Man Theory

Before there was scholarship on the concept of leadership, there were nevertheless theories about leaders. What made an Alexander, a Caesar, an Elizabeth I, or a George Washington great? Absent a systematic examination of leadership, the initial answer was that "leaders are not made; they are born," or "the great man theory." The born-leaders approach was the only available answer to the question of "what makes a good leader?" until the twentieth century. One either had "good genes" for leadership, or one did not.

A leading exponent of the great man theory was Thomas Carlyle, a nineteenth-century man of letters and critic, whose work on heroes gave rise to the label "great man." According to Carlyle, "the history of what man has accomplished in this world, is at the bottom the History of the Great Men who have worked here."[39] The "historical men" concept of Friedrich Nietzsche, a contemporary of Carlyle, is philosophically similar.[40]

While modern leadership literature cites the great man theory only as an historical artifact, it retains some popular credibility. Former Dallas mayor Jack Evans demonstrated that subscribers to the great man approach are not extinct when he summed up the keys to his success as an elected official and businessman by saying, "I really think I have natural leadership."[41]

Traits

Through the first half of the twentieth century, scholars began to seek a more thorough explanation than merely leadership by birthright. Accordingly, they began to examine the traits, both innate and acquired, exhibited by leaders who were acknowledged to be effective by their subordinates, their peers, and the public. If specific traits could be associated with acknowledged leaders, these scholars thought, then we would not only have a better understanding of the leadership phenomenon but we would also be able to identify potential leaders and, possibly, to develop desired traits in individuals who were candidates for leadership positions. The traitist approach, as it was refined in the 1900s, thus moved somewhat beyond "good genes" to incorporate the possibility of characteristics that could be acquired through training or development.

Age, sex, symbolic manipulation, cognitive skills, interpersonal skills, analytical skills, articulateness, and ambition are among the many examples of identified traits. Ralph Stogdill, however, examined the conclusions drawn from 124 articles on leadership traits published between 1904 and 1947 and found a lack of commonality in and lack of agreement on the traits associated with great leaders. These findings suggested to Stogdill the need for research that would allow a comparison of leaders' personalities with the characteristics of and situations in organizations.[42] Later scholars reached similar conclusions, namely that one-half century of traitist research had failed to yield a definitive list of traits that could be attributed consistently to leaders.[43]

Attempts to use the trait theory of leadership illustrate a major reason for the development of contingency/situational theory, discussed subsequently. For any given trait, one can always find contradictory evidence suggesting that it is or is not important in particular cases. For example, if age is an important trait, what is the optimal age for a leader? Is the answer the same for a church youth director as for the president of the local chapter of the American Association of Retired Persons? If analytical skills are necessary for a leader, what about the charismatic politician who is reelected again and again on the basis of stirring rhetoric that may have little basis in logic?

Increasingly, modern students of organization find the "trait" theory, as well as its progenitor, the "great man" theory, to be deficient. Still, interest in traits remains evident, both in the continued production of lists of desirable traits and in biographical studies of individual leaders. Such lists and studies are often fascinating and occasionally provocative. As topics of conversation or contemplation they are harmless enough. The insidious danger of leadership trait lists lies in their occasional use, consciously or subconsciously, as a measuring stick for determining whom to designate for a leadership role, or, worse, whom to "write off" as without possibilities regardless of the situation.

Modern Lists. Little controversy remains over the futility of attempting to produce a comprehensive and unimpeachable list of leadership traits. However, such lists appear periodically in popular publications ranging from newsletters of professional organizations to widely circulated magazines. The lists are rarely the same, but the presumption is constant. One recent list reduced everything to (1) "intelligence: past, present, and future" (meaning use of available information and experience, understanding the task at hand, and creativity); (2) flexibility; and (3) "guts" (the willingness to take risks).[44] Neat, simple, and undoubtedly deficient!

Studies of Individual Leaders. Authors of leadership "success stories" frequently cite characteristics that they think made the individuals being studied successful leaders. Although some common characteristics may be derived from a collection of such studies, even a cursory review—far short of the more systematic analysis conducted by Stogdill cited previously—reveals that no two authors ever produce identical lists. The variations among such lists may, in fact, be testimony to the value of the contingency/situational approach to be discussed later in this chapter. Nevertheless, a review of selected findings demonstrates the nature of that strain of leadership research.

The traits listed below, drawn from studies of public- and private-sector executives, are some of the attributes most frequently associated with effective leadership. They describe characteristics of successful public-sector executives at the helms of such diverse organizations as cities, federal agencies, hospitals, and school districts, and private-sector executives representing an array of industries ranging from high technology to manufacturing, from financial services to leisure services. The situations in which executives operate vary greatly. Moreover, some of the "traits" identified are actually matters of leadership or management style (e.g., numbers 8 and 10 below) rather than personal characteristics. Traits commonly associated with leadership effectiveness in individual case studies include the following:

1. willingness to take risks,[45]
2. flexibility,[46]
3. organizational loyalty/dedication,[47]
4. realistic goals,[48]
5. self-awareness,[49]
6. great vision,[50]
7. excitement/enthusiasm,[51]
8. communication/interpersonal skills,[52]
9. positive attitude,[53]
10. participative management style,[54] and
11. line experience.[55]

Leadership Style

Thus far, we have reviewed what a leader is, what executives do, the leadership environment, and two largely bereft theories of leadership—the great man and leadership traits approaches. The third theory, one which is still in vogue, is leadership style. Leadership style refers to *how* leaders behave, how they gain acceptance of their ideas and wield power to mold organization members into a coherent entity.[56] Style also connotes a predilection for a particular type of behavior from which the leader rarely, if ever, deviates.[57]

Every subordinate quickly develops a set of expectations about a given leader's behavior based in part upon perceived personality and in part upon evidence of that leader's style of operation. Aspects of one's personality, however, may be hidden from subordinates; under most circumstances, actions are more obvious. Style is important not only for the direct response—positive or negative—that it evokes, but also for the more subtle clues it provides to employees about the values and priorities of the "boss" and other leaders and clues about how they are likely to behave; in turn, these expected behaviors cue employees about how they should behave. President Ronald Reagan, while making what he considered to be a positive statement about his approach to managing the federal government, found himself caught in the irony of the Iran-Contra arms deal. In September 1986, he summarized his leadership style with the following statement: "Surround yourself with the best people you can find, delegate authority, and don't interfere."[58] His subordinates evidently read the behavioral clues to mean they could act unilaterally in making decisions of international consequence. In the controversy that ensued, criticisms of presidential detachment were common.

If analysis of traits alone does not explain enough about the leadership phenomenon, will an examination of how leaders behave tell us more about effectiveness? How does the use of authority relate to leadership style?[59] The following discussion draws on the words of some of the biggest names in the management literature—names such as McGregor, Lewin, Likert, Blake and Mouton, Ouchi, Bennis, Fiedler, Hersey and Blanchard, and Tannenbaum and Schmidt. The discussion makes no attempt to separate leader behavior from leadership style. Rather, they are seen as related concepts. Whatever their labels, the roles emphasized by a particular executive/manager and the manner in which the associated work activities are conducted comprise the leader's style.

Tasks and People. Two principal, interrelated concerns emerge consistently in the leadership style literature, virtually all of which focuses on the intraorganizational behavior of mid-level managers and front-line supervisors rather than top-level executives. Treatment of the two concerns is often intermingled, as most scholars address both halves of what we might call the leadership style equation. One half of that equation consists of the leader's concern for people in the organization—typically subordinates. The other half is the degree to which the leader focuses on tasks to be accomplished. These two halves constitute, respectively, relationship behavior and task behavior.[60]

The two concerns form the axis of what Robert Blake and Jane Mouton have termed the "Managerial Grid.®"[61] Every manager's style may be defined by placement on the Grid (Figure 2–1). The preferred

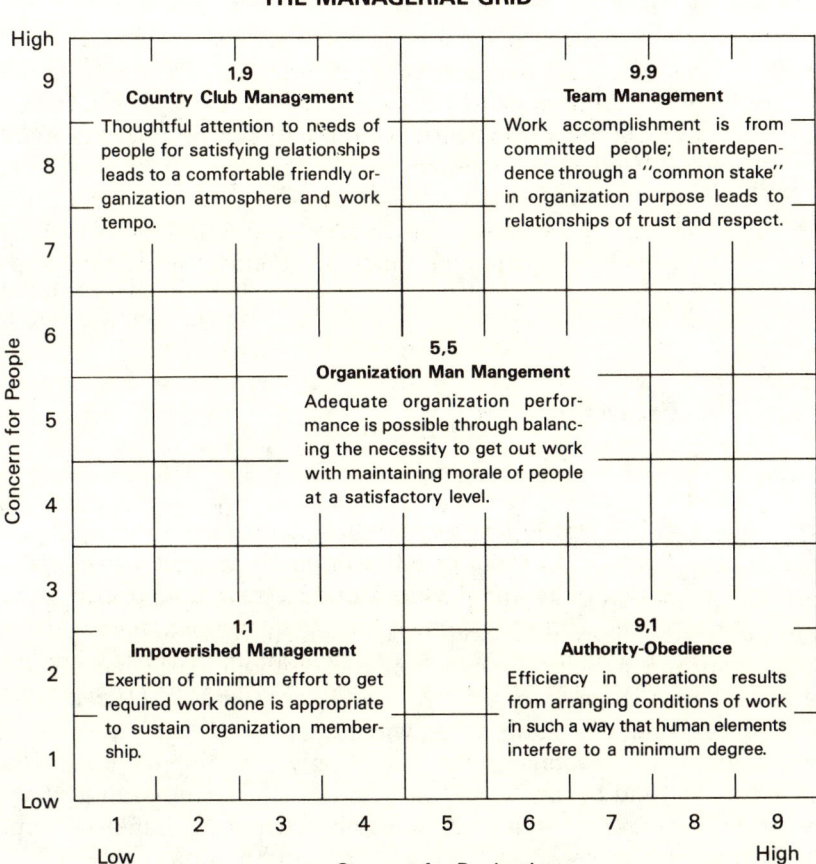

Figure 2-1
THE MANAGERIAL GRID®

Concern for People	Concern for Production
1,9 Country Club Management — Thoughtful attention to needs of people for satisfying relationships leads to a comfortable friendly organization atmosphere and work tempo.	**9,9 Team Management** — Work accomplishment is from committed people; interdependence through a "common stake" in organization purpose leads to relationships of trust and respect.
5,5 Organization Man Management — Adequate organization performance is possible through balancing the necessity to get out work with maintaining morale of people at a satisfactory level.	
1,1 Impoverished Management — Exertion of minimum effort to get required work done is appropriate to sustain organization membership.	**9,1 Authority-Obedience** — Efficiency in operations results from arranging conditions of work in such a way that human elements interfere to a minimum degree.

SOURCE: Robert R. Blake and Jane S. Mouton, *The Managerial Grid III* (Houston: Gulf Publishing Company, 1985), p. 12. Copyright © 1985. Reproduced by permission.

style, according to Blake and Mouton, is "team management," featuring high concern both for people and production.

While Douglas McGregor's explicit purpose was not the creation of a model of management styles, his well-known Theory X and Theory Y concepts raised questions about managerial effectiveness and were based on differing views of the individual and how individuals fit within organizations.[62] The tenets of Theory X include a negative view of human nature—including lack of initiative, resistance to change, and inability to identify with the organization's objectives—and the presumed need for close supervision of employees. Therefore, one may conclude that Theory X managers have little concern about relationship behavior. Theory Y tenets, on the other hand, embrace a more optimistic view of human nature—including a belief that under proper circumstances employees can enjoy their work, demonstrate initiative in contributing toward the achievement of organizational objectives, and respond favorably to a variety of nonmonetary as well as monetary incentives. A Theory Y manager is thus more likely to stress relationship behavior.

William Ouchi's Theory Z, popularly associated with "Japanese-style management," encompasses far more than style (for example, corporate philosophy and cultural context), but follows a similar vein to McGregor's Theory Y. One component of Theory Z is humane treatment of workers, and the theory is seen as a strategy for managerial effectiveness.[63]

Perhaps the most popular typology of leadership style is the continuum that labels managers as "authoritarian," "democratic," or "laissez-faire," according to their use of formal authority. These labels stem directly from Kurt Lewin's theoretical work and subsequent application of that theory to a study of the leadership in boys' clubs[64] The democratic style featured group participation under managerial control. The authoritarian style was characterized by a high task orientation and a heavy use of "orders" without participation. The laissez-faire style (subsequently named "free rein"[65]) offered wide discretion to subordinates (in Lewin's case, the boys in the club subjected to this leadership style) and only broad guidance by the leader. Lewin and his colleagues in the boys' clubs study found that a democratic leadership style was generally preferred by the boys and resulted in greater creativity, although the authoritarian style yielded the greatest task accomplishment. The laissez-faire style was neither preferred nor productive.

Rensis Likert's analytical scheme is similar to Lewin's in that he found four distinctive management systems—exploitive authoritative, benevolent authoritative, consultative, and participative—in his analysis of managers and supervisors. An exploitive authoritative manager is completely task-oriented, shows little confidence in subordinates, motivates by instilling fear in subordinates, emphasizes top-down communication and decisionmaking, and generally centralizes authority. The benevolent authoritative manager is condescending toward employees, also emphasizes top-down communication and decisionmaking, but does invite some comment on the establishment of organizational goals. The consultative manager displays confidence in employees, encourages two-way communication, delegates some control to subordinates, and generally seeks subordinates' opinions on issues affecting them. The participative manager heavily emphasizes relationship behavior, including positive motivation, open communication, substantial employee participation in decisionmaking, and the dispersal of the control function. Likert concludes that supportive supervisors (those who were employee-centered and who fell into the consultative or participative categories) are more effective than nonsupportive ones (those who were task- or job-centered and who were classified as exploitive or benevolent).[66]

More recently, Warren Bennis and Burt Nanus have concluded that leaders have a capacity for managing attention through vision (i.e., they develop specific agendas based upon vision credibly articulated), managing meaning through communication (i.e., they develop an organizational culture that provides a common perspective for interpreting events), managing trust based upon reliability and "mutuality of concern," and managing self (i.e., leaders understand their strengths and weaknesses, can accept advice, and can learn from their mistakes).[67] Curiously, in view of their use of the term "management" in describing leadership, Bennis and Nanus distinguish management from leadership, attributing crucial importance to each but noting that a capacity for both management and leadership does not always reside in the same individual.

It All Depends on the Situation

Is it possible for the manager/executive to identify the *one* most effective style? Kenneth Blanchard (of *One-Minute Manager* fame) says, "Absolutely not. Successful leaders must adapt themselves to the particular situation . . . . That depends on the developmental level of the follower in any particular case."[68] By "developmental level"

Blanchard refers to factors such as the technical sophistication and emotional maturity of subordinates. In short, the situation is the governing variable. This view, emphasizing the importance of the given situation, forms the basis of the final approach to examining leadership explored in this chapter: contingency theory.

Basically, contingency theorists—also called situation theorists—contend that factors crucial to leadership success may vary from situation to situation; in short, the answer to the question of what makes leaders effective is, "it all depends."[69] The leader's task is to determine what the relevant situational factors are, how to deal with them, and how to adapt to change. Herbert Kaufman sees the situation as so all-important that he contends that success in an organization is far more a product of chance and timing than of any traits or behavior of designated organizational leaders.[70] A frequently cited example of the difference the situation makes is the case of Sargent Shriver, who was rated "brilliant" as the first administrator of the Peace Corps but generally was regarded as a much less effective director of the Office of Economic Opportunity. Presumably, Shriver's management style did not change appreciably—the situation did. Similarly, when Mayor Harold Washington of Chicago died suddenly in 1987, the tributes to him included the following: "He was almost like a deity in the black community, like Jack Kennedy was in Catholic homes in the '60s."[71] Washington was thus perceived as highly effective in those roles of special ethnic significance—be they symbolic or substantive; but he had many detractors with regard to his performance of other mayoral roles. Few regarded him as ineffective in one "situation"; the judgment was much less uniformly favorable regarding his effectiveness in other situations.

One of the pioneers of contingency theory was Fred Fiedler, who developed a scale of situational control emphasizing three important dimensions that he contends determine leadership effectiveness: (1) the relationship between leaders and followers, ideally producing trust in and support for the leader; (2) the clarity with which the leader defines tasks and procedures; and (3) "position power," or the leader's formal authority to gain compliance with directives or desires.[72] Fiedler argues that effective leadership behavior depends on the appropriate mix of these three elements in a given situation.

Many of the writers who have developed task-people orientation models of managerial effectiveness have enhanced their models with additional situational variables. For example, Paul Hersey and Blanchard's matrix adds the variable of subordinate maturity as a factor in determining the most effective mix of concern for people and tasks.[73]

Their argument is similar to that of Chris Argyris, who posits that organizations often treat employees as children, thereby failing to achieve an optimum integration of the organization and the individual.[74]

William Reddin, also relying on a mix of task and people orientations, conceptualizes a three-dimensional model representing a mix of concern for people with concern for tasks, with effectiveness stemming from a "style's appropriateness to the situation in which it is used." Figure 2–2 shows the basic elements of Reddin's model. The core of the model consists of four basic styles or types of managerial behavior: integrated, separated, dedicated, and related. Integrated

Figure 2-2
THE 3-D STYLE MODEL

	Developer	Executive
	Bureaucrat	Benevolent autocrat

Related	Integrated
Separated	Dedicated

RO = Relationships Orientation
TO = Task Orientation
E = Effectiveness

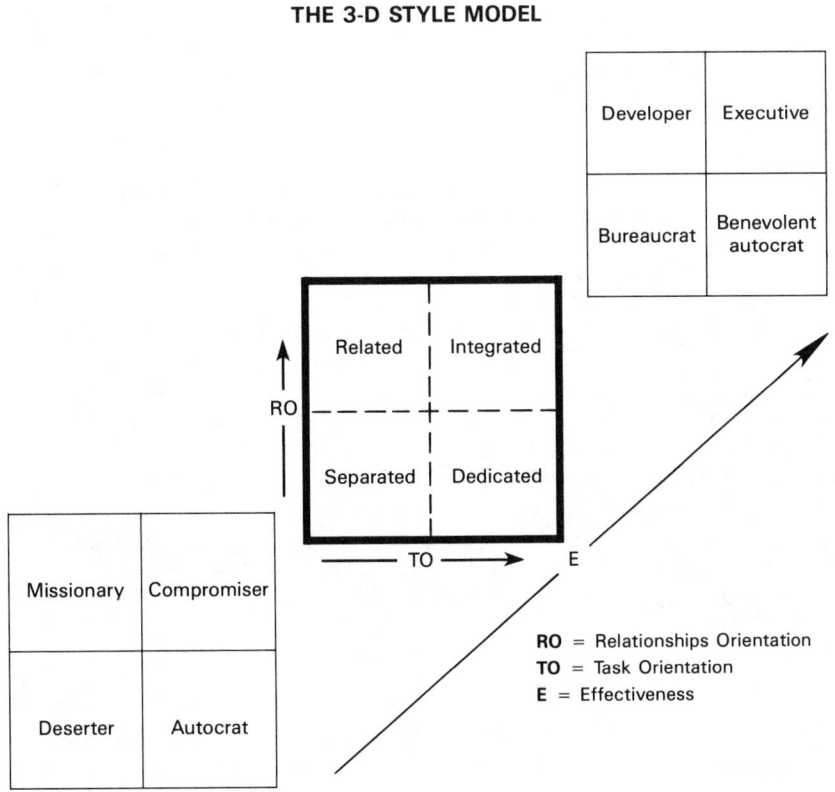

Missionary	Compromiser
Deserter	Autocrat

SOURCE: William J. Reddin, *Managerial Effectiveness* (New York: McGraw-Hill, 1970), p. 41. Copyright © (1970) by McGraw-Hill. Reprinted with permission.

refers to a high orientation toward both tasks and relationships; separated, to a low orientation to both tasks and relationships; dedicated, to a high-task/low-relationship orientation; and related, to a high-relationship/low-task orientation. Reddin further develops four specific pairs of managerial styles, with half of each pair representing an appropriate use of one of the basic behaviors and the other half, a less appropriate use. These pairs of management styles, with the less effective one listed first, are compromiser-executive (integrated style); deserter-bureaucrat (separated style); autocrat-benevolent autocrat (dedicated style); and missionary-developer (related style). The key to managerial success, according to Reddin, is the flexibility to adapt and to use behaviors appropriate to a situation.[75]

One of the best-known studies of leadership behavior is that of Robert Tannenbaum and Warren Schmidt,[76] who developed a sevenfold continuum of leadership behavior (Figure 2-3), ranging from a purely authoritarian management style to a purely laissez-faire style. The graphic depiction of their continuum is frequently reproduced as a

Figure 2-3
CONTINUUM OF LEADERSHIP BEHAVIOR

Boss-centered leadership ⟵⟶ Subordinate-centered leadership

Use of authority by the manager

Area of freedom for subordinates

| Manager makes decision and announces it. | Manager "sells" decision. | Manager presents ideas and invites questions. | Manager presents tentative decision subject to change. | Manager presents problem, gets suggestions, makes decision. | Manager defines limits; asks group to make decision. | Manager permits subordinates to function within limits defined by superior. |

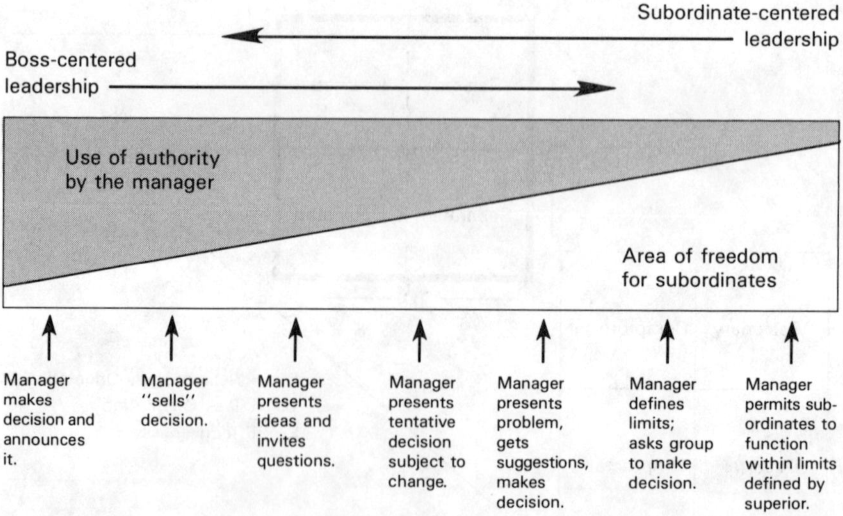

SOURCE: Robert Tannenbaum and Warren H. Schmidt, "How to Choose a Leadership Pattern," *Harvard Business Review*, 36 (March/April 1958), p. 96. Copyright © (1958) by the President and Fellows of Harvard College; all rights reserved.

conceptual aid, but the underlying premise must be placed in context, namely that three major sets of forces determine which types of behavior are *practical* and *desirable*. These forces include: (1) the manager (values, confidence in subordinates, leadership inclinations, security); (2) subordinates (needs for interdependence, readiness to assume responsibility, tolerance for ambiguity, interest in a given problem and a feeling that it is important, understanding of and identification with the goals of the organization, necessary knowledge and experience to deal with the problem, learned expectation to share in decisionmaking); and (3) situation (type of organization, group effectiveness, problem itself, pressure of time).[77] The variable mix of these three forces suggests which leadership behavior is most appropriate.

Gary Yukl has been critical of the relationship-task models of leadership behavior and, along with his colleagues, has sought to develop a leadership taxonomy that is better, although more complex, than the models previously cited. The Yukl taxonomy is based on the interaction of two key sets of variables: those that influence individual and group behavior and those that are situational. Table 2–1 provides a list of 23 managerial behaviors as defined in Yukl's taxonomy.[78]

A final variant of the situation approach is path-goal theory, which links motivation, leader behavior, and organizational performance. Its focus is on how leader behavior influences subordinate performance. Robert House and Terrance Mitchell describe four types of leader behavior—directive, supportive, achievement-oriented, and participative—and contend that the relative effectiveness of these behaviors is subject to the contingency factors of tasks ("work setting") and employee characteristics. The proper mix of behaviors and factors, according to House and Mitchell, leads to employee motivation, job satisfaction, and performance.[79]

Contingency theory combines useful findings from studies of leadership traits and behavior with other knowledge about organizational behavior. It represents the most sophisticated of the approaches to leadership described here.

Summary

This chapter has briefly explored the topic of leadership, beginning with an assumption that executives and managers must accept that mantle as a key role of their positions. The environment of the

Table 2-1

DEFINITION OF MANAGERIAL BEHAVIORS IN YUKL'S TAXONOMY

Performance emphasis: the extent to which a leader emphasizes the importance of subordinate performance and encourages subordinates to make a maximum effort.

Role clarification: the extent to which a leader informs subordinates about their duties and responsibilities, clarifies rules and policies, and lets subordinates know what is expected of them.

Training-coaching: the extent to which a leader provides any necessary training and coaching to subordinates, or arranges for others to provide it.

Goal setting: the extent to which a leader, either alone or jointly with a subordinate, sets specific, challenging, but realistic performance goals for each important aspect of the subordinate's job.

Planning: the extent to which a leader plans in advance how to efficiently organize, and schedule the work, coordinate workunit activities, accomplish task objectives, and avoid or cope with potential problems.

Innovating: the extent to which a leader looks for new opportunities for the work unit to exploit, proposes new activities to undertake, and offers innovative ideas for strengthening the work unit.

Problem solving: the extent to which a leader takes prompt and decisive action to deal with serious work-related problems and disturbances.

Work facilitation: the extent to which a leader provides subordinates with any supplies, equipment, support services, and other resources necessary to do their work effectively.

Monitoring operations: the extent to which a leader keeps informed about the activities within his/her work unit and checks on the performance of subordinates.

External monitoring: the extent to which a leader keeps informed about outside events that have important implications for his/her work unit.

Information dissemination: the extent to which a leader keeps subordinates informed about decisions, events, and developments that affect their work.

Discipline: the extent to which a leader take appropriate disciplinary action to deal with a subordinate who violates a rule, disobeys an order, or has consistently poor performance.

Representation: the extent to which a leader promotes and defends the interests of his/her work unit and takes appropriate action to obtain necessary resources and support for the work unit from superiors, peers, and outsiders.

Consideration: the extent to which a leader is friendly, supportive, and considerate in his/her behavior toward subordinates.

Career counseling and facilitation: the extent to which a leader offers helpful advice to subordinates on how to advance their careers, encourages them to develop their skills, and otherwise aids their professional development.

Inspiration: the extent to which a leader stimulates enthusiasm among subordinates for the work of the group, and says things to build their confidence in the group's ability to successfully attain its objectives.

Praise recognition: the extent to which a leader provides appropriate praise and recognition to subordinates with effective performance, and shows appreciation for special efforts and contributions made by subordinates.

Structuring reward contingencies: the extent to which a leader rewards effective subordinate performance with tangible benefits, such as a pay increase, promotion, better assignments, better work schedule, extra time off, etc.

Table 2-1--Continued

Decision participation: the extent to which a leader consults with subordinates before making work-related decisions, and otherwise allows subordinates to influence his/her decisions.

Autonomy delegation: the extent to which a leader delegates responsibility and authority to subordinates and allows them discretion in determining how to do their work.

Interaction facilitation: the extent to which a leader emphasizes teamwork and tries to promote cooperation, cohesiveness, and identification with the group.

Conflict management: the extent to which a leader discourages unnecessary fighting and bickering among subordinates, and helps them settle conflicts and disagreements in a constructive manner.

Constructive criticism: the extent to which a leader criticizes subordinate mistakes and poor performance in a constructive, calm, and helpful manner.

Source: G. Yukl, "Innovations in Research on Leader Behavior," paper presented at a meeting of the Eastern Academy of Management, Baltimore, May 14, 1982, cited in Kenneth N. Wexley and Gary A. Yukl, *Organizational Behavior and Personnel Psychology*, rev. ed. (Homewood, Ill.: Richard D. Irwin, 1984), pp. 172-173. © Richard D. Irwin, Inc., 1984. All rights reserved. Reprinted with permission.

organizational leader is dynamic and sometimes threatening and effective leaders must be adept at dealing with extraorganizational matters as well as those confined to the organization itself.

What makes an effective leader? Many answers have been offered over the years, including the great man theory, the importance of leadership attributes such traits or style, and the relevance of a particular situation. Modern studies of leadership focus mostly on leadership style or behavior and on situations. Two critical factors in leadership effectiveness are task management and relating to the people in the organization. The degree to which the factors are in balance or one is emphasized over the other says much about a particular executive's leadership or management style.

The third chapter turns to an examination of specific roles played by two types of municipal executives, mayors and city managers. These executives are acknowledged to be key leaders in local government.

Chapter Three

CONTEMPORARY VIEWS OF LOCAL GOVERNMENT EXECUTIVE ROLES

An understanding of the nuances that comprise contemporary views of local government executives first requires an examination of past views. The roles of the modern mayor and city manager are the products of a century of developments in local government theory and practice. Consequently, this chapter looks first at the reform movement in local government, including a brief review of forms of municipal government and a discussion of the once-popular belief that a clean separation could be made between policymaking and administration— i.e., the so-called politics-administration dichotomy. Next, we explore changing attitudes about postreform local government, emphasizing increasing awareness of the need for policy leadership from the chief executive and recognition of the political involvement of the city manager. Modern perceptions of the role of the city manager are summarized, and the creation of the hybrid known as the chief administrative officer form of local government is discussed as a proposed solution to the need for both political and managerial leadership. A comparison of city executive role perceptions in 1985 with those found in 1965 by Deil Wright concludes the chapter.

Reformism in American Government

The history of American government is one of point and counterpoint, with the emphasis of one era often leading first to excess and, then, to significant change in the next period. Thus, the excesses embodied in several Jacksonian concepts such as the notion that any public job could be mastered by a man of average intelligence led to a different emphasis on neutral competency. In turn, the excesses of neutral competency such as domination of policymaking by independent boards and commissions led to an emphasis on executive leadership.[1] Today, the excesses of executive leadership—seen particularly at the national level in what has come to be labeled the imperial presidency—have led to a new quest for representativeness through citizen and employee participation.

In the nation's cities, significant changes in the structure of government took place during the last quarter of the nineteenth century and the first decade of the twentieth. By then, Jacksonian democracy, with its emphasis on individual interests and the distribution of electoral spoils, had led to a pattern of partisanship, parochialism, and boss-centered corruption. Reformers wanted to "eliminate" politics (meaning bosses, corruption, and partisanship), make government more democratic, and ensure its efficient delivery of services. The manifestation of this desire for change had at least four dimensions: organization, information, participation, and evaluation.

First, reform-minded individuals created organizations as springboards for prescription and action. Citizen/taxpayer organizations (such as the Municipal Voters' League of Chicago, the National Municipal League, the National Short Ballot Organization, the Proportional Representation League, and the National Popular Government League) were prominent among these advocacy groups. Collectively, these organizations emphasized governmental effectiveness, reduced numbers of elected officials, nonpartisan elections, citizen participation, and direct democracy.

Second, reformers called for improved information and analysis in the hope they would lead to improvements in local government even if political changes were not forthcoming. Beginning with the Bureau of Municipal Research in New York in 1906, first privately financed local research organizations and later university research bureaus were created to provide information and, ultimately, training to local officials. For almost a century, these organizations have remained true to their ideal of reform government.

Third, the reform movement resulted in major changes in citizen participation, both in an expansion of the means of citizen involvement and in changes in electoral systems. The means of citizen involvement were broadened through the institution of "direct democracy"—the initiative, referendum, and recall—in many cities and some states. The initiative, through a petition process, allows citizens to force legislative consideration of issues; the referendum requires voter approval of specified issues before they become law; and the recall, also through a petition, gives citizens the power to force an election to determine whether an elected official should be removed from office. Electoral reforms included changing from partisan, ward elections held simultaneously with state and national elections to nonpartisan, at-large municipal elections held separately from state and national elections. No longer would party affiliations be important; no longer would officials owe their allegiance to the voters of one ward only; and no longer would local elections be won or lost on the coattails of national or state politicians. One of the most significant results was a movement away from the mayor-council form of government first to the commission form, then to the council-manager form. Some scholars, including Charles Adrian and Charles Press, contend that the reform movement "placed a misleading overemphasis upon forms and structures of government,"[2] expecting too much from a structural fix.

Fourth, a single criterion for evaluation of reformism emerged. Reformers assumed that local government was essentially apolitical, with efficiency the dominant standard for measuring success. The emphasis was on administration, not resolution of political issues. One of the most influential statements ever made in the literature of public administration was that of Woodrow Wilson, then of Princeton University, who stated in 1887 that:

> . . . administration lies outside the proper sphere of *politics*. Administrative questions are not political questions. Although politics sets the tasks for administration, it should not be suffered to manipulate its offices.[3]

Although Wilson's call for the separation of administration from politics was not original,[4] it became the classic statement of a concept that was accepted by the academic world for 50 years. Ironically, Wilson's purpose in writing this article was to advocate the goals of the National Short Ballot Organization, and he intentionally overstated his case, but that overstatement did not become clear until the lost preface to the article was discovered at the outset of World War II. How the concept of the politics-administration dichotomy affected administrative theory and practice in reform cities will be detailed subsequently.

The notion of administrative efficiency is incorporated into reform theory and practice. So important has been the desire to ensure business-like practices in the municipal corporation that the most prevalent reform government, council-manager, has often been compared to the business corporation. The city manager is hired by the city council and is responsible to it, much as the corporate president is responsible to the board of directors. Like the corporate president, the city manager is selected on the basis of training and expertise to handle the administrative affairs of the organization. However, rather than democratizing the municipality, reform government often solidified the control of the business community. Edward Banfield and James Q. Wilson contend that

> It was not against bosses and boodlers that the reform program got its logic . . . . It got that from the middle-class political ethos, and the logic would have been the same if bosses and boodlers had never existed. Indeed, it was in relatively small, middle-class cities, where indeed those persons had never existed, that reform measures were most popular. Many such cities adopted the Model City Charter in its entirety almost at once. Most of the large cities adopted some parts of it, but none ever adopted the program as a whole.[5]

In their classic comparison of reform and nonreform cities, Robert Lineberry and Edmund Fowler found little difference in the demographic characteristics of reform cities—those with nonpartisan, at-large election of council members and the council-manager form of government—and nonreform cities—those with partisan, ward elections and the mayor-council form of government. However, they found considerable differences in their behaviors, with a high degree of reformism leading to a propensity both to spend and tax less than nonreform cities and yielding a proportionately lower degree of responsiveness to citizen demands. They note that the centralization inherent in the council-manager form severely restricts the access points of citizens to their government.[6] Their conclusion complements the earlier observations of Banfield and Wilson in that both are saying that efficiency—a business-like approach—may be dysfunctional in the resolution of political conflicts and the addressing of particularized citizen interests.

Robert Boynton has summarized the characteristics of reform government more fully as follows: council-manager form, nonpartisan ballots, at-large elections, the separation of municipal elections from state and national elections, merit systems, and the initiative, referendum, and recall processes. In contrast, he sees the political (nonreform) model of government as maximizing the value of representativeness, including the representation of political interests especially as those interests might be organized geographically (i.e., in districts or wards); strong mayor-council government; political conflict and its resolution; and often partisanship.[7]

The empirical study incorporated into this book emphasizes differences in role perceptions and preferences in the mayor-council (nonreform) and council-manager (reform) forms of local government. The once-popular but unrealistic notion that politics and administration are distinguishable and separable in governmental activities—a notion that is in many respects responsible for the variety of local government forms in existence today—is a key factor underlying fundamental differences in role prescriptions and perceptions. A brief review of the prevailing forms of government in American municipalities provides a useful prelude to an explanation of the importance of the politics-administration dichotomy as the foundation of many of the notions relating to executive roles still associated with council-manager government and its proponents.

Forms of Government

United States cities were first organized along the lines of what today we would label the "weak mayor-council form." The role of the executive was deemphasized in favor of strong council powers in keeping with a fear of strong executives prevalent in Colonial America. The strong mayor-council form, which emphasizes executive leadership, began in the 1880s in Brooklyn and Boston.[8] The commission form emerged in the aftermath of a devastating hurricane that struck Galveston, Texas in 1900; Galveston gained approval by the Texas legislature in 1901 to implement a form of government that assigned each of five commissioners broad power to handle specific tasks related to recovering from the storm. Through the 1920s, the plan was widely adopted in cities undergoing political reform. The first widely recognized use of the council-manager plan came in Staunton, Virginia, when Charles E. Ashburner was appointed city manager in 1908. Staunton previously had an unwieldy bicameral council with 22 members and 30 legislative committees. One of those committees recommended the hiring of a municipal "director" to enable the city to function more effectively. How do these forms differ? The essential features of each are displayed in the hypothetical organization charts of Figure 3–1 and outlined below.

Weak Mayor-Council Form
1. A large council is elected by wards.
2. The mayor is elected at-large but has limited administrative

Figure 3-1
FOUR FORMS OF LOCAL GOVERNMENT: HYPOTHETICAL ORGANIZATION CHARTS

MAYOR–COUNCIL

Strong Mayor

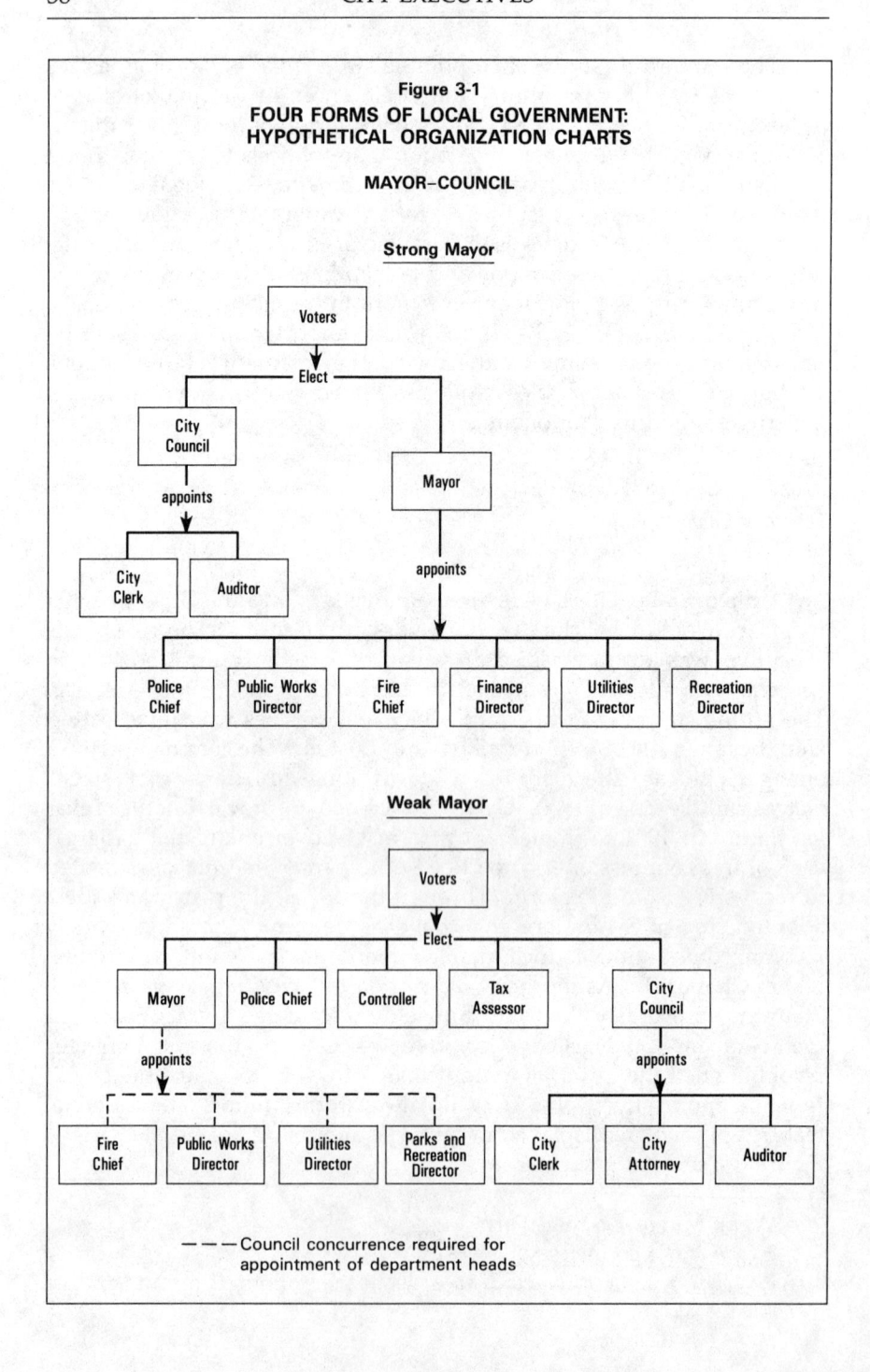

Weak Mayor

– – – Council concurrence required for appointment of department heads

Figure 3-1 (continued)
FOUR FORMS OF LOCAL GOVERNMENT:
HYPOTHETICAL ORGANIZATION CHARTS

COUNCIL-MANAGER

Voters
↓ elect
Mayor and Council
├── appoint → City Attorney, City Clerk
└── appoint ↓
City Manager
↓ appoints
Utilities Director | Fire Chief | Police Chief | Finance Director | Public Works Director | Recreation Director

COMMISSION

Voters
↓ elect
COMMISSION: Commissioner | Commissioner | Mayor | Commissioner | Commissioner
↓ Supervises (each)
Public Works | Public Safety | Finance & Administration | Utilities | Leisure Services

SOURCE: Carl Vinson Institute of Government, University of Georgia

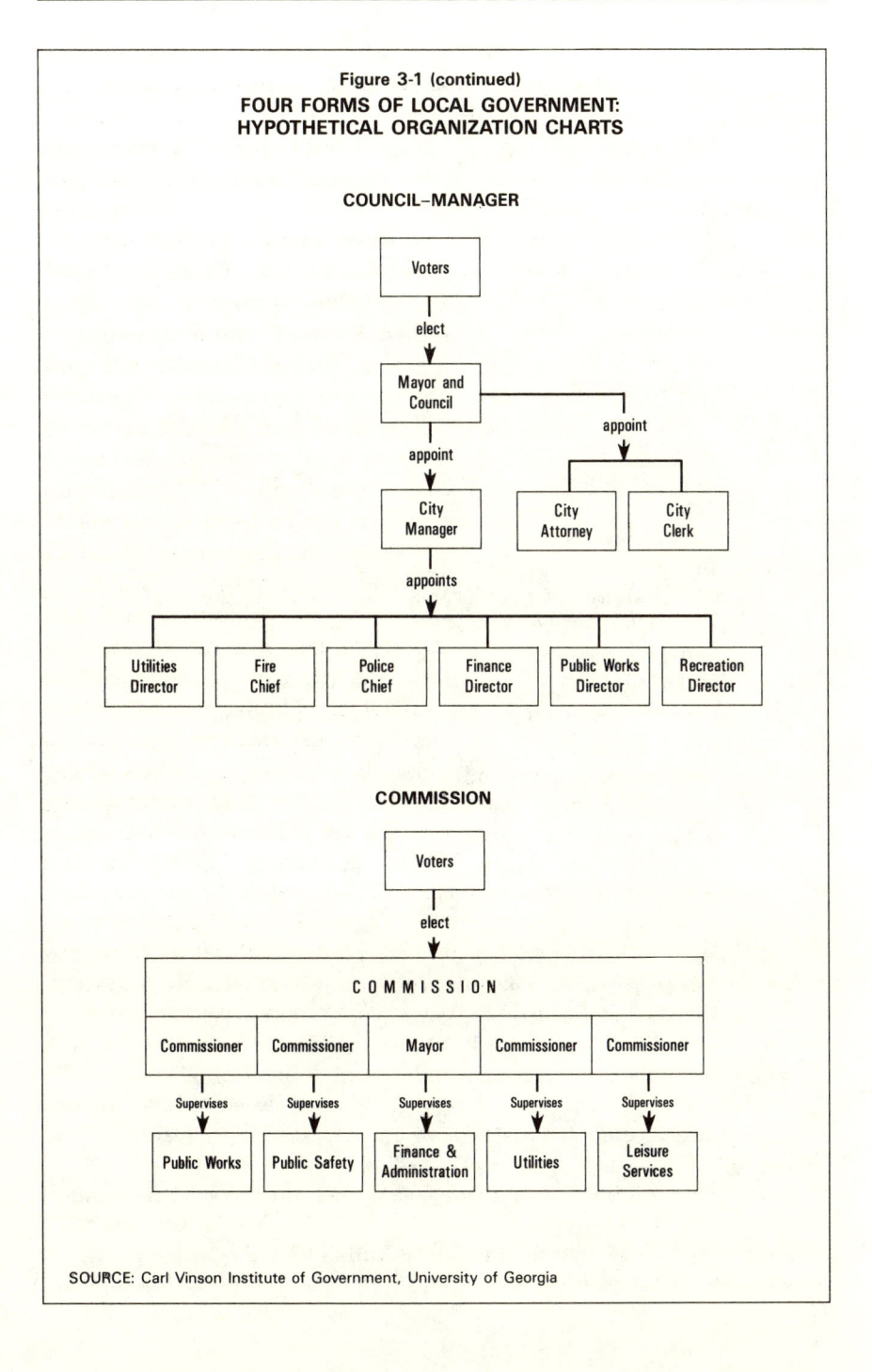

authority, in part due to a long ballot. Typically, the city attorney, treasurer, and several other officers are elected, as are administrative boards.
3. The mayor has veto power, but a veto typically can be easily overridden.

Strong Mayor-Council Form
1. The council is elected at-large or by wards.
2. The mayor is elected at-large and has appointment and removal power over city department heads.
3. The mayor is responsible for budget preparation.
4. The mayor has veto power.

Commission Form
1. A small commission is elected at-large to serve as the legislative body.
2. Each commissioner acts as head of an administrative department.

Council-Manager Form
1. A small council is elected at-large.
2. All legislative and policymaking functions are vested in the council.
3. The mayor is elected by the council from among its members or, in some cities, is simply the council member who was elected by the largest margin of popular votes.
4. The council employs a professionally trained city manager to oversee municipal administration, including appointment and removal of department heads. The manager is subject to dismissal by the council at any time.
5. The manager is responsible for budget preparation and presentation to the council.

The essential characteristics outlined above represent each of these forms of government as a "pure type." However, in actual practice, individual cities have developed variants. As examples, sometimes a council is called a commission, but the organizational structure is really a council-manager or mayor-council form. Increasingly, in larger council-manager cities, the mayor is elected at-large and council members are elected by districts or in a mixed district and at-large system.[9]

Both the commission and weak mayor-council forms have fallen into disfavor in recent years due to the lack of executive leadership inherent in both of them. Both forms diffuse leadership, making the presumed chief executive only *primus inter pares* (first among equals).

Politics-Administration Dichotomy

Council-manager government is a product of its political time. Conceived during an era of dual concerns over blatant political influence in government and the desire to find the one most efficient way to carry out the activities of government, council-manager government was at once the progeny and victim of the myth of the politics-administration dichotomy. The ramifications that different forms of government hold for executive roles and responsibilities have led to a seemingly perpetual debate over the supposed administrative domain of appointed executives and exclusively policy domain of elected officials.

The early writings on council-manager government both justify and set norms for this form of government along the lines of scientific management or "Taylorism."[10] Frederick Taylor, an engineer and early efficiency expert, emphasized the importance of structure to gain the utmost efficiency from an operation. He is remembered for his pursuit of the "one best way" to accomplish a given task. Taylor's fondness for efficiency was reiterated a generation later by Luther Gulick, who averred that "efficiency is thus axiom number one in the value scale of administration."[11] If efficiency is viewed as the primary administrative value, the logical leap to a separation of politics and administration is relatively easy.

Nowhere are the basic concepts of council-manager government so explicitly embodied as in the *Model City Charter*, originally published by the National Municipal League in 1915. In retrospect, writing 57 years after the first council-manager government form was implemented,[12] Richard Childs, the reformer who is considered the father of council-manager government, listed three major merits of the plan: better (more diversified, less political) city councils, better (more professional) administrations, and better political terrain (nonpartisan elections, the absence of machines).[13] He remained adamant that the council should be elected at-large and that the mayor should be selected by the council, matters of controversy in manager cities for more than two decades. Indeed, Child's unyielding concept of council-manager government led John Porter East to conclude that his vision was that of a closed system "because in its initial construction all factors are accounted for and no others are allowed subsequently to intervene. The result is a scheme that is impervious to change or alteration."[14] Yet, while eschewing politics in local government, Childs acknowledged that managers are heavily involved in proposing policy and even encouraged their publicly defending and promoting council positions.[15] Nevertheless, the emphasis of Childs and other early writers whom he influenced was on a separation of management and politics, the former conducted by the city manager and the latter by the council.

Clarence Ridley, a former city manager and long-time executive director of the International City Managers' Association (ICMA), was more pliable in his attitudes. Early in his theorizing, Ridley enthusiastically embraced Taylorism, with its one best way of doing things and its emphasis on structure, complete with an absence of politics, but his later writings showed a reversal. Ridley posited a set of guideposts that made it clear that city managers are a source of policy ideas and that they must be willing to explain and defend council policies; he did not see managers as "up front" community leaders, however.[16] Ridley's own evolution in thought somewhat parallels the increasing flexibility found in various versions of the ICMA Code of Ethics, which, in its 1938 edition, had embraced the tenets of Taylorism.

Acknowledgment of Politics

Born as a device to help cities rid themselves of political corruption during an era when no less a figure than the president of the United States preached on the theme of the "Double E Movement"—economy and efficiency in government—the council-manager form was the darling of the reformers, the apparent solution to their quest for the separation of politics and administration, and business-like efficiency. Nevertheless, early city management practitioners and scholars soon recognized that the manager was inextricably caught up in political issues and tactics. In his pioneer study of city managers, Leonard White observed:

> In general, the council-manager charters attempt to make a sharp division between these two major activities, policy and administration, assigning the duty of determining city policy to the council or commission, and the duty of carrying out the policy and attending to the routine of city business to the manager. It is, however, extremely important to inquire what has been the actual working relationship arising out of these charter provisions. For it is perfectly clear that the legal terms of city charters are often far from describing the patterns of behavior which actually develop.[17]

Such early observations of the cracks in the proverbial wall separating politics and administration established a conceptual foundation for later examinations of the behavior of local government executives and paved the way for modifications of the "pure" structure of council-manager government, especially with regard to the electoral system.

The Stone-Price-Stone study published in 1940 was another early acknowledgment of the political role of the city manager as well as a revelation that council-manager government did not operate in a universal one best way in all cities. Harold Stone, Don Price, and Kathryn Stone, who reviewed the first 25 years of council-manager government, concluded that the manager was, indeed, a community (political) leader who was "careful to give the general impression that his recommendations were always controlled by his expert knowledge and professional interest, never by selfish considerations or political friendships."[18] Mark Keane, in introducing Bill Gilbert's study of the long-time city manager of Kansas City and prototype of the professional manager, L. P. Cookingham, summarized Stone-Price-Stone as follows:

> Harold A. Stone, Don K. Price, and Kathryn H. Stone first took note of the policy leadership role of management. They observed in 1940 what most of us now know: that it is not possible "for the city manager to escape being a leader in matters of policy . . . . These men," they concluded, "have made great contributions in the technique of administration, but they have made even greater contributions as leaders of municipal policy."[19]

Keane's acknowledgement of the truth of the Stone-Price-Stone conclusions is especially relevant in that he served for many years as ICMA's executive director.

Stone, Price, and Stone also found numerous flaws in the theretofore common depiction of council-manager government as analogous to the corporate executive and board of directors. For example, they observed that the successful city manager must devote considerable energies to community relations, policy initiation, and even vote-getting, especially in support of local referenda. They did not see the corporate executive as having such profoundly political duties or having to determine constantly how far he could and should go in policy and political activities lest he create problems with the board of directors. Perhaps their most important finding for later studies of managerial roles was that the council-manager form of government was not a separation of powers, but, in their view, a more effective use of powers.[20]

Richard Stillman's 1974 history of the city management profession, the first comprehensive follow-up study to the Stone-Price-Stone history, describes the growth of council-manager government after World War II in the burgeoning suburban cities, which sought technical and administrative help to deal with new and more complex services, facilities, and intergovernmental relations.[21] These same issues held many policy implications and called for community leadership, thereby prompting a renewed concern over the appropriate roles for a city manager.

During the 1950s, a rich debate ensued over the policy and political roles of city managers (often seen as inseparable, if not synonymous), not so much as to the reality of their existence but as to their effectiveness and propriety. Dorothy Pealy, for example, argued that council-manager government created a fundamental problem: "weak policy-making and leadership by the elected officials in council-manager cities and the complementary entry of the manager into policy areas that should be reserved for those elected."[22] Karl Bosworth observed that risks are inherent in managerial policymaking, particularly if the manager represents narrow interests or if elected officials are not broadly representative of the community. Cautioning managers to be concerned about representing diverse interests, he noted, "city managers . . . must seek to be among the best politicians in town."[23]

The 1952 Code of Ethics tried to placate advocates of both the position that the manager should be a political leader and the position that policy implementation is distinct from policy making. Echoing Stone-Price-Stone, ICMA's 1958 "green book" (one of a series of books devoted to various city management topics, all bound in green covers) indicated the impossibility of separating "why" (policy) and "how" (management) judgments, drew distinctions between local government and the business corporation, provided a list of expectations that city managers and their councils have of each other, concluded that policy matters require a team approach, and hinted at a distinction between the political and policy roles, a distinction that later gained prominence.[24]

The 1962 Gladys Kammerer et al. study of tenure among Florida city managers noted ICMA's growing acknowledgment of the manager's political role, an acknowledgment that seemed to be coupled with a concern that the manager "should avoid as much as possible calling attention to the fact."[25] Otherwise, the high-profile manager might find his tenure to be short. "Managers tend to play major policy roles in the making of the principal decisions of the city, and, therefore, they tend to incur political hazards."[26]

As the thinking about the political dimensions of council-manager government evolved, Norton Long—in 1965, the same year that Childs provided a 50-year review of this form of government still couched in the tenets of orthodoxy—rued the inadequacy of the plan's rationale. He confirmed the Kammerer et al. conclusions about the fleeting nature of managerial tenure.

> The city manager is perhaps the most striking case of the public administrator whose role has outrun his profession's self-rationalization. The city manager today is an expert politician for hire, rather than a political expert. His professional mortality is more likely to arise from his political failings than any inadequacies in what was once supposed to be his appropriate expertise.[27]

By 1971, the ICMA green book had moved to a more explicit description of the manager's policy and political roles:

> [T]he urban administrator will increasingly find himself playing the role traditionally ascribed to the politician: a catalyst in the formulation of urban policy, 'brokering' or compromising and satisfying the multitudinous and conflicting demands made by special interest groups.[28]
>
> Realistically, an examination of decision making must not only deal with those who formally decide, but also those who influence. The fact that a council formally ratifies a matter does not mean an absence of other participants, such as managers.[29]

Knowledge of the actual dynamics of municipal decisionmaking muffled the debate in academic and professional circles over whether a manager should be a policy and/or political leader, with the principal prescription being the avoidance of overt partisanship. A major factor in the decline of the politics-administration debate in those arenas was the increasing complexity of intergovernmental politics, in which the manager was expected to play a significant role and to keep elected officials involved. Describing intergovernmental relations as a type of game, Frank and Fran Aleshire observed that "the new game is a 'team' effort and the city manager is not the only player."[30] The importance of this aspect of the manager's political dimension is attested to by the attention the notion receives in the 1983 successor to the 'green book' series.[31]

Nevertheless, it should be noted that not all actors in local government subscribe to the academic and professional view of reality. Most city charters that establish council-manager government call for a separation between the policy role of the council and the administrative role of the manager. Many council members guard their prescribed domain zealously, as do many city managers theirs—although perhaps less zealously, given the nature of the council-manager relationship.

City Manager Role Perceptions

Ruing the piecemeal approach to local government research in the late 1950s, Lawrence Herson referred to the field as a "lost world."[32] One tack for introducing more system into the study of local government has been through the application of role theory. Neal Gross, Ward Mason, and Alexander McEachern state that "A role is a set of expectations . . . a set of evaluative standards applied to an incumbent of a particular position."[33] The scholarly work employing the concept of roles is the theoretical underpinning for the empirical study reported in part later in this chapter. Role theory has mainly been coupled with survey research data and detailed case studies. Its utility has been especially high when constructing typologies from large amounts of information. Role theory is implied, as well, in commentaries by practicing managers describing their own experiences and what was expected of them.

Conceptually, role theory and the politics-of-administration literature are both grounded in the realities of managerial behavior rather than the idealism of Childs. Both bodies of literature encompass studies of how managers depart from the orthodox view of a separation of politics and administration, and both regard efficiency as only one, not necessarily the paramount, value of local government. Many of the studies using role as the orienting concept, in fact, place special emphasis on the policy or policy/political behavior of city managers.

Charles Adrian, in his study of three council-manager cities in Michigan, explicitly examined the roles of the manager, the mayor, and the council members. He found that the manager "played the social role expected of him by his professional organizations . . . [and] avoided taking a public role of policy innovator, except at the specific request of the council or in cases involving matters on which he could be considered a technical expert."[34]

Two other early studies that used role theory were conducted by Jeptha Carrell (1962) and John Buechner (1965). Both were limited by small sample size, but both afforded some comparison of manager and council perceptions.[35] Neither study included contextual variables such as city size or community belief patterns in the design. In examining six cities in Kansas, Illinois, and Missouri, Carrell emphasized the manager's position as professional head of the city administration rather than the individual roles comprising the position of city manager. His conclusions provide useful insights into six areas of potential conflict between appointed and elected officials: power prerogatives, personality clashes, the political setting, policy expediency differences, managerial inflexibility and rectitude, and communication and cognition difficulties. Buechner's study was an expansion of Carrell's, as he examined 36 home-rule, council-manager cities in Colorado. Specifically, he hypothesized the existence of systemic differences in the role perceptions of city managers and city council members, and found agreement on professional-administrative roles but not on policy-political ones.

The Kammerer et al. study, cited previously in describing the relationship between managerial tenure and political climate, was another relatively early examination of managerial roles. Two of the study's assumptions concerned the political nature of city manager behavior; the authors note that "there is no sharp distinction between politics and administration despite the polemical literature to the contrary" and that "the city manager is . . . a political participant in the policy process."[36] Important as a comparative analysis, the Kammerer et al. book is also noteworthy because it attempts to determine factors that influence city manager role expectations such as how the mayor is selected and whether the community is in the midst of high population growth. As was true of the Adrian, Carrell, and Buechner studies, the Florida report was based on a small sample size (10).

Deil Wright identified three functional roles of city managers—management, policy, and political—and found a strong orientation toward the management role in the city managers' time allocation patterns.[37] His study included responses from 45 managers in cities with populations of 100,000 or greater. Wright concluded that the successful manager amalgamates all roles. Because the Wright findings are used for comparative purposes later in this chapter, more will be said about Wright's work subsequently. However, one important facet of his work in the context of the development of managerial role studies is his separation of the policy and political roles, with the policy role seen as encompassing council relations and the political role as encompassing relationships with intergovernmental and nongovernmental groups and organizations. The management role was seen in terms of traditional administrative activities.

Testimony to the salience of the city manager function and managerial roles as issues of importance to public administration is the dedication of a 1971 issue of the field's leading journal, *Public Administration Review*, to a symposium on those topics. Contributions to that symposium differed from other role studies in that the analysis tended toward the qualitative rather than the quantitative, although not exclusively so.[38] (Indeed, the Wright data are the basis of one of the pieces.) Nevertheless, especially because of the number of practitioners represented among the authors, the perspectives on managerial roles in the early 1970s are helpful. Keith Mulrooney, a city manager who subsequently served as executive director of the American Society for Public Administration (ASPA), for example, stressed the need for flexibility, for social awareness and capability to address social problems, and for council-manager government to overcome its historic narrow ties to the middle-class business community in order to tackle the needs of ethnic minorities and the poor.[39]

Two years later, another practitioner, William Donaldson (who served as city manager of three cities, including Cincinnati) contended that "managers live their lives in the world of politics, and their success as managers is based on their ability to deal with this world."[40] To master the position of city manager (i.e., to learn the roles comprising the position), he not only prescribed gaining firsthand experience in the street-level tasks of municipal service delivery but also gaining political experience (by such means as involvement in a school board or legislative election).[41]

Ronald Loveridge's fourfold typology of managerial policy orientations has been an influential contribution to the literature on city managers' role behavior.[42] The four categories he identifies are Political Leader (most political), Political Executive, Administrative Director, and Administrative Technician (least political). Political leaders epitomize the broadest policy role for managers and serve as change agents in their municipal organizations and beyond. Political Executives have a similar orientation, but approach policymaking more conservatively either because of community values or personal deference to the authority or power of the city council—a deference perhaps gained through painful experience. Administrative Directors operate under the belief that the city manager should be involved in the policy process, but they eschew innovation and allow the perceived limitations on their policy role to inhibit action in that arena. Administrative Technicians hold the narrowest view of the policy role, seeing themselves as conservators of existing policy and perceiving their role as circumscribed in a manner approximating the orthodoxy of a politics-administration dichotomy.

The Loveridge study has been used frequently as a basis for subsequent role-oriented studies of council-manager government. Three features have made it particularly attractive in that regard. First, it focused on the policy role—as separate from the management or political roles—and offered a comparison of the role orientations of managers and council members. Second, the fourfold typology provided a useful analytical tool for other scholars. Third, the sample size—435 council members and 58 city managers in the San Francisco Bay Area—was larger than for any previous study of a similar nature.

As the Loveridge typology was applied to city managers and council members in less homogeneous cities than those of the Bay Area, other scholars found, with Loveridge, that council members tend to perceive the role of the city manager as more narrowly managerial than did city managers themselves. However, they failed to find Loveridge's roughly equal distribution of managers across the four categories of the typology. For example, role perceptions of Texas city managers were found to be concentrated in two of Loveridge's four categories— Political Executive and Administrative Director.[43] The preponderance of role perceptions of Washington, Oregon, and Idaho city managers also fell into only two of the Loveridge categories, namely the Administrative Director and Administrative Technician categories.[44] A large national study of 1,616 city managers resulted in the conclusion that Loveridge's fourfold typology was too compact and should be expanded into a sevenfold typology. Almost half of the role behaviors reported by survey respondents fell into two of the seven categories, the Traditional/Cooperative type (equivalent to Loveridge's Political Executive) and the Team/Moderate, a category having no direct equivalent in the Loveridge typology.[45]

Thus, studies conducted at different times among varying survey populations failed to yield concurring results. One possible explanation offered by Timothy Almy is that the Bay Area city managers in the Loveridge study may be more cosmopolitan than managers as a whole.[46] The concept of cosmopolitans and locals is one associated with Alvin Gouldner, who distinguished among organizational members according to their attachment and loyalty to the organization and community. Locals display a high degree of identification with the organization and the community while cosmopolitans are more attuned to broader national professional norms.[47]

In addition to the concept of role typology, another important idea in the study of city manager roles is role dissonance. Role dissonance refers to conflicts and ambiguities among the functions managers perceive that they are expected to perform. Discord among roles is directly related to the old politics-administration dichotomy in that many managers receive conflicting signals about the behavior expected of them. On the one hand, managers believe that council members expect them to place administrative tasks first and to exercise little, if any, political leadership.[48] On the other hand, "administrators must exercise power to implement, defend, and improve controversial programs,"[49] and must increasingly develop their leadership in the areas of policy recommendations and public opinion formation.[50] Consequently, city managers view five political and policy-related factors as being among the seven greatest sources of professional frustration.[51]

Following his 1987 appointment as city manager of Dallas, Richard Knight received mixed signals in the published comments of council members regarding his early performance and their expectations for the future. Some, such as Councilman Jerry Rucker, believed that Knight's predecessor Charles Anderson had attempted to take on overt leadership roles inappropriate for the city manager and that Knight's arena should be more narrowly circumscribed: "Chuck was more prone to take the role of visionary and spokesman, and make speeches that I thought elected officials ought to make. Richard understands more what a city manager is supposed to do."[52]

Others contended that Knight's success as the city manager would hinge on his ability to move beyond his image as a highly skilled "Mr. Fix-It," whose proficiency in internal administration was highly regarded, to providing broader and more assertive leadership. Councilman Dean Vanderbilt (a former assistant city manager in Dallas) remarked, "What I've really been looking for is a little more definition of what we're doing. He at least has to point out the directions we have to go in and lay out the choices."[53]

Political advisers to Dallas Mayor Annette Strauss and to two of her predecessors in that office also believe that the city manager has a leadership role to play. Dan Weiser was quoted as saying, "There always has to be someone looking out for the longer-term vision of the city. That's in his job description. We've given that power over to the manager."[54]

Similarly, John Weekley, political adviser to former Dallas mayors A. Starke Taylor and Jack Evans, commented, "The city manager has to be more than a technician. He does in fact make policy by what he presents to the council."[55]

In a recent ICMA book, Wayne Anderson, Chester Newland, and

Richard Stillman comment on the increasing ambiguity in roles played by the modern city manager. They observe:

> The vast and increasing responsibilities of the current and future manager are not susceptible to easy blueprinting or precise definition. The job calls for a blend of interpersonal, professional, and technical skills. To say that the managerial function is primarily to administer the council's policies is to neglect a large number of activities that make up a typical day on the manager's calendar. It would be more appropriate to describe the 'managerial function' as the shorthand term for everything the local manager is expected to do.[56]

In another ICMA publication, the Committee on Future Horizons describes the nature of the city manager's job in the future, focusing upon the importance of compromise, leadership by being led, intergovernmental relations, shared power, less reliance on legal parameters, more career capriciousness, the emergence of specialists in internal management, and a quest for humanity.[57]

Donald A. Blubaugh, city manager of Hayward, California, contends that a dramatic shift in managerial emphasis and time allocation has occurred:

> Now, approximately 70 percent of an urban manager's time is spent developing local policy, encouraging cooperation among policymakers, and coordinating efforts with other governmental jurisdictions in order to provide the best possible services given the limited financial resources available.
>
> This is new turf for those of us in the professional urban management business. Although many of us have said for years that we are not politicians, we increasingly find ourselves fashioning compromises in order to make things work. I am not suggesting that such activity is unethical, nor am I suggesting that one needs to be the leader and out front in the strongest political sense, but we must diligently work behind the scenes to bring together the diverse interests that confront us on virtually every public meeting agenda.[58]

The national survey data reported subsequently indicates that his is only a moderate overstatement of the time allocation experience of most city managers.

The modern literature acknowledges the involvement of city managers in policy and political issues, and, indeed, much of it focuses on policy and political role orientations, perceptions, and conflicts. Why then does interest in the extent of this involvement and its propriety continue? James Svara directs us to a useful answer by positing that there is both a separation and sharing of responsibility in local government. Politics and administration may be viewed as points on a continuum that encompasses mission, policy, administration, and management, with elected officials alone dominating mission determination and managers dominating pure management. "What is shared is responsibility for middle-range policy and administration."[59]

Political Leadership

The focus on the policy and political roles as actual and proper functions of the city manager has dual stimuli. One stimulus is the desire among scholars to use empirical evidence to mount a convincing refutation of the Childs orthodoxy that separated politics as a function of the mayor and council from administration as a function of the city manager. The other stimulus is a practical concern for effective political leadership in city government—a desire, in effect, to remove long-standing blinders and assess the actual sources of leadership and the efficacy of those sources, and to limit artificial barriers that restrict the full expression of leadership talent.

The Job of the Mayor

While more attention has been paid in the literature to the roles played by city managers than to the roles of other city executives, continuing interest has also been shown in the job of the mayor, both as the political leader in council-manager cities and as the political and administrative executive in mayor-council cities. However, studies of mayors have tended to be case studies of individual mayors rather than systematic, comparative studies using data from many cities or studies focusing on mayoral roles.

In examining mayors in council-manager cities, scholars have concentrated on resolving the question of whether it is the elected mayor or the appointed city manager who actually is the dominant political official. Concern about the dominance of the city manager led Pealy to a relatively early call to fortify the mayor's role in council-manager cities. She wanted to remove the city manager from the spotlight, provide better staffing for the mayor, and even institute partisan elections.[60] The value of partisan elections as a means of enhancing mayoral leadership, however, may be overrated by Pealy and others who have advocated this solution for improving political leadership in municipalities. Adrian, for example, in examining in detail three cities with different electoral systems, could not ascertain whether the method of electing the mayor was instrumental in determining the mayoral policy role.[61] Probably a more realistic commentary on the perennial issue of local political leadership is that there is room for both the elected mayor and the appointed city manager to share political leadership. Nelson Wikstrom points out that city managers welcome the assistance of activist mayors who "adopt an aggressive policy leadership position, rather than a more retiring and, hence, less involved role."[62]

The debate over the political role of managers is paralleled by concern over performance of the managerial function by elected executives. Stated simply, a politician's expertise in wooing voters offers few assurances of similar expertise as an administrator once in office. Assessing the performance of Fiorella La Guardia in New York, Rexford Tugwell noted that Mayor La Guardia was so much the consummate politician that he regarded the winning of elections as his objective and failed to provide leadership on some long-term issues affecting the administrative vitality of the city.[63]

The analysis of La Guardia's mayorship illustrates the importance of multidimensional local leadership. Just as city managers must juxtapose management, policy, and political roles, so also must mayors in mayor-council cities play all three roles. The strong mayor bereft of administrative talent is akin to the city manager bereft of political skills. Neither can successfully perform all of the roles assigned to the position.

Although administrative and political skills are both needed by city executives, Banfield and Wilson observed an advantage for those whose skill mix is weighted toward the administrative side, even in mayor-council cities, because of the types of issues facing U. S. cities. They summarized this observation by noting that it is probably easier for the professional administrator to develop political skills than for the politician to develop administrative ones.[64] Their view is buttressed by Mayor Ed Elbert of Overland Park, Kansas, a council-manager city, who expressed his fears both about a perceived trend toward strong-mayor systems and about the tendency to move from part-time to full-time mayors even in council-manager governments: "The down side to having a full-time mayor is that he or she is liable to screw up . . . . To be elected to public office requires no qualifications. A full-time mayor might assume he's running the city and rely less on professional staff."[65]

Banfield's subsequent study of nine major mayor-council cities reached two general conclusions. First, structure does make a difference. Comparisons of weak and strong mayor-council cities, with their variations in the formal powers of the chief executive (e.g., Detroit and Seattle) revealed a greater ability for strong mayors to achieve their objectives. Second, contextual variables are important. The history, ethnicity, economy, and political tradition of a community affect the functioning of local government. El Paso, for example, was portrayed as a city of two cultures (Hispanic and Anglo), a factor that governed policies and elections. The passivity of Boston blacks in the 1960s contrasted sharply with the activism of Atlanta blacks during the same period, influencing the initiatives and successes of the respective mayors of those cities.[66]

The importance of structure was also stressed by Robert Boynton and Deil Wright, who found seven patterns of leadership interaction in their examination of 45 council-manager cities with populations of 100,000 or greater. Detected patterns ranged from that of a strong mayor-administrator, with an elected mayor who is the dominant executive despite city charter prescriptions to the contrary, to a manager "boss," with an appointed city manager whose actual power far exceeds charter authorizations. Focusing on policy-initiating and policymaking teams, they found that differences between strong mayor-council government and council-manager government diminish when the latter incorporated "nonreform" elements such as direct election of the mayor and ward and/or partisan elections. With a highly politicized mayor and council, fewer expectations for community leadership were placed on the city manager.[67]

A persistent question in much of the literature on mayor-manager relationships is whether council-manager cities can successfully address the problems of minority constituents and major social issues that divide many cities. Many analysts think that an affirmative response is contingent on expansion of the mayoral leadership role. Thomas Fletcher was city manager of San Jose, California, when he wrote:

> We must now recognize that the directly elected mayor must assume a much stronger role in our city governments. The leadership of our community must be placed in the hands of our elected political leaders; and the manager must subject himself willingly and enthusiastically to encouraging that shift in responsibility.[68]

The ability of mayors in council-manager cities to respond to the problems of minority constituents and to other pressing socioeconomic and political problems in their communities may depend upon alteration of the staffing patterns as well as attitudes in those cities. Cortus Koehler's study of information and communication in council-manager cities notes the dependence of the mayor and council on professional staff information.[69] A shift to stronger mayoral leadership, as advocated by Fletcher, would require substantial revision of the information channels and filtration processes in place in most council-manager cities. David Morgan reinforces this idea, indicating that a prerequisite of mayoral leadership is adequate staff and financial resources.[70]

A major systematic study of mayors is that of John Kotter and Paul Lawrence.[71] Noting a history of idiosyncratic approaches to the study of mayors, they identified ten models—six behavioral and four contextual—from the literature. Although finding none of the ten workable when applied to multiple cases, Kotter and Lawrence drew on selected elements to fashion their own model involving three key processes and four contextual variables.[72] With the assistance of an expert panel, they selected for analysis 20 mayors who had held office for more than four years in large cities. Included were mayors from weak and strong mayor-council cities and council-manager cities. Finding that the successful mayors were those who were able to coalign the processes (i.e., agenda setting, network building, and task accomplishment) and the context (i.e., the mayor's own personality, the formal structure of the city government, the distribution of power in the community, and the city itself), Kotter and Lawrence label their concept the "coalignment model."[73]

Kotter and Lawrence discovered five "approaches" to the job of mayor that resemble roles commonly associated with city managers, as described earlier in this chapter, and leadership styles described in Chapter Two. These include: Ceremonial, Caretaker, Personality/Individualist, Executive, and Program Entrepreneur. The Ceremonial mayor adopts a style that is low-key and individualistic, and has a minimal direct effect on the city. The Caretaker mayor relies on the city bureaucracy to accomplish a rather limited agenda. The Personality/Individualist mayor focuses on annual and multiyear objectives, lacks formal power, but aggressively seeks to accomplish his agenda through force of personality. The Executive mayor also has long-range objectives, uses a variety of network-building techniques, and masters the bureaucratic process. The Program Entrepreneur mayor has a complex, sometimes reform-oriented agenda and uses networking and bureaucratic resources to accomplish objectives. Kotter and Lawrence note that the mayors see themselves in a more simplistic way: they take a political approach if they are professional politicians, and a "one best way" management approach if their background is business.[74]

Douglas Yates took a somewhat different tack. In looking broadly at urban politics, he examined mayoral strategies or styles—a variant of the "approaches" cited by Kotter and Lawrence. Yates identifies the Crusader, the Entrepreneur, the Boss, and the Broker, based on a mixture of the mayor's political power base and his degree of activism or innovation in office.[75] The Crusader has a weak power base but strong interest in innovation. The Entrepreneur has a strong power base and is prone to activism. The Boss has a strong power base but limited enthusiasm for innovation. The Broker has a weak power base and little interest in innovation.[76]

Perhaps because theirs is the proper style, strategy, or approach, the effective mayor, as columnist James Brady writes, becomes one with the city.

> Great mayors, and 'greatness' admits of flaws and error, literally become their cities. Mayor Richard Daley of Chicago, a man most liberals of my age despised, was a great mayor of Chicago. Under Daley, the city worked. He wasn't just the mayor, he *was* Chicago . . . . You ever ride in a New York cab? [Mayor Edward] Koch is the city's quintessential cabbie, wisecracking and kvetching and arguing and occasionally getting lost and assuring you all the time he knows precisely what he's doing and where he's going.[77]

The Chief Administrative Officer Form

The debate over the extent to which a city manager *should* be a political and policy leader is based not only on democratic theory but also on practicalities. Cities require the leadership of a chief executive who can present issues to the community and rally public support. In a council-manager city, the city manager commands the resources of information and the city staff and is a full-time employee while the mayor may have few, if any, staff resources and is usually part-time. As a consequence, the city manager can relatively easily assume the role of community leader, although it is the mayor, not the manager, who is an elected official. In fact, the mayor and other council members often expect such leadership from the city manager. Yet the city manager who either chooses to be the principal community spokesperson and either performs the role poorly or conflicts sharply with dominant political forces, or the manager who is expected to play the role and fails to live up to expectations, is not likely to find longevity in office. In analyzing the short tenure of Austin city manager Nick Meiszer, Janet Wilson found an eventually fatal unwillingness to depart from the apolitical role prescribed in the classic council-manager plan:

> But it was his political naivete that played a major role in the eventual loss of job. Meiszer's philosophy on the manager-council form of government dictated that the manager leave political considerations to the elected officials. Therefore, he was never able to understand the importance of politics, the need for elected officials to work on a timetable suited to their re-election plans and to cater to their political supporters. In most cases, Meiszer did not know who was supporting whom, until some of those powerful supporters came into conflict with his staff.[78]

Some city managers restrict their own overt political leadership while simultaneously allowing (although often grudgingly) blatant incursions of council members into their administrative domain. Research suggests that this tendency, in its most passive form, may be a function of community size and region. Edward Lewis found that while Southern managers in smaller cities " . . . avoid intruding into public and political arenas, they are more inclined than those of any other region not to discourage council intrusion in day-to-day administrative matters."[79]

John Martin, in analyzing the advent and setbacks of reform government in Peoria, Illinois, quotes a city staff member as saying, "We experts have a tendency to take ourselves too seriously, to think that 'papa knows best,' to just go ahead and do things. In administrative government you forget that politics underlies everything in a democracy."[80] That statement is a succinct way of summarizing the ongoing struggle between experts and elected officials for control of urban decisions. The issue is no longer whether the manager, as chief expert (or perhaps expert chief), does engage in policy and political activities; rather, it is whether the manager *should* be a major political leader in a community and, if so, what measures would enhance the effectiveness of that leadership.

One option advanced as a possible solution to this ongoing issue by those who advocate a limited role for city managers proposes a series of electoral reforms including those called for by Pealy in the late 1950s to expand the influence of elected officials and enhance the politicization of city government.[81] Direct election of the mayor and district/ward election of council members in manager cities have shifted the political spotlight back to elected officials. Svara concludes that coupling district elections with nonpartisan voting will have a number of salutary effects for local politics, including greater and more democratic participation.[82]

Another proposed solution to the quest for simultaneous political leadership and administrative skill in city government is a hybrid form of government known as the chief administrative officer (CAO) form. The professional manager, rather than reporting to the council as a whole, reports to the mayor. The result is a combination of selected elements of the strong mayor-council form with some of the characteristics of the council-manager form. San Francisco adopted this system in 1931, and other major cities such as Philadelphia, New Orleans, and New York City followed suit.[83] The CAO form is also sometimes called "mayor-manager" or "general management government."[84] This form has been summarized by Banfield in describing the government of Los Angeles, which may be atypical in the sharing of power between the mayor and the council: "A city administrator stands between the mayor and the council and is an adviser to both. He is appointed by the mayor with the consent of the council; the council itself, however, may remove him by a two-thirds vote."[85]

During the heyday of debate over whether the city manager should be a politician, an article written by Wallace Sayre became the classic statement advocating the CAO form as a device for providing political leadership while presumably leaving the manager free to concentrate on management tasks. While leery of the ability of council-manager government to provide essential political leadership in larger cities, Sayre found the CAO form to provide both the administrative advantages (professional control over departments and daily operations) of council-manager government and the political advantages (elected executive leadership) of mayor-council government.[86]

Sayre's enthusiasm for the plan was shared by Adrian, who nevertheless noted possible weaknesses if the mayor and administrative staff did not have a clear conceptualization of the CAO's role.[87] John Bebout, responding to Sayre's article one year later, disputed the virtues of the CAO form in favor of the proven advantages of traditional council-manager government.[88]

James Hogan, the chronicler of the CAO plan in the vein of White's, Stone-Price-Stone's, and Stillman's studies of city managers, noted that many variations exist among the cities that have adopted CAO government. "The role of the CAO," he found, "can vary all the way from errand boy to competent administrator performing functions similar to those of city manager."[89]

The Los Angeles version has produced a chief administrative officer so similar in duties to a city manager that CAO Keith Comrie was selected by a panel of experts as the all-pro "city manager" for 1987 in one national publication.[90] "He's hard working and very, very knowledgeable about government operations. He has to run the city, then come and sit in front of the council and be bombarded with questions from 15 different directions. He handles management well," according to John Ferraro, president of the Los Angeles city council, in comments remarkably similar to utterances in praise of renowned city managers.[91]

City Executive Roles in the Mid-1980s[92]

As noted in Chapter One, the empirical study that is the central focus of this book concentrates on time allocation not only as evidence of conflicting demands and responsibilities but also as an indication of managerial emphases. How city managers *actually* spend their time, how they *ought* to spend their time, and how they *prefer* to spend their time have been issues of both controversy and curiosity in public administration. That we remain interested in such issues is not surprising because they emerge from the fundamental nature of council-manager government and reflect the evolution of reform government in the United States.

The council-manager form of government was introduced in part to secure expert administration through the appointment of a chief executive with requisite managerial skills. The assumption at the outset was that the city manager would devote his attention to a purely management function, devoid of policy or political involvement. Although these early notions have been modified, if not discarded, the matter of executive roles remains salient because an executive's time is limited. The manner in which that time is divided tells us much about the directions in which local executives exert leadership.

The relevance of issues pertaining to the role perceptions of executives themselves and role expectations held by other local government actors, constituents, and scholars suggests a series of research questions about changes in managerial perceptions as council-manager government has evolved over the years and about contrasts between the perceptions of municipal administrators who are not city managers and those who are. What role dominates the time of city managers? What role do they see as most important? What role do they prefer to play? How do the roles and preferences of assistant city managers, mayors who serve as administrators of nonmanager cities, and the chief assistants to those mayors differ from those of city managers? Answers to these questions were sought by studying how urban administrators allocate their time. Responses to these questions lead to two general observations: (1) managerial role perceptions have changed markedly over time, and (2) the four sets of actors noted above do vary in their perceptions about role performance, role importance, and role preference.

Academic views regarding normative and actual executive roles have changed substantially over time toward recognition of the importance of the city manager in the policymaking process. Evidence of similar changes among practitioner views would corroborate a dramatic shift from a narrow management science focus to a focus appearing in many cases to embrace unabashedly policy analysis, policy advocacy, and in some, even political leadership. A study offering a particularly useful benchmark for documenting the extent of shifting role perceptions is Wright's examination of municipal executive roles.[93] That study has been replicated in part and expanded for this chapter. Because the data for this chapter were collected in 1985 and Wright's data were collected in 1965, the two studies allow a comparison after 20 years.

As Chapter One noted, 527 usable responses—excluding survey instruments completed by an aide rather than by the official being queried—were received. Approximately 43% were from officials in cities with populations of 100,000 or more; 20% from officials in cities with populations between 75,000 and 100,000; and 36% from cities with populations between 50,000 and 74,999 people. A more precise profile of the respondents is provided in Table A–1 (appendix).

A series of three questions that examine the role categories introduced by Wright in his study were posed. In those questions, respondents were asked to indicate the approximate percentage of time devoted to the management role, to the policy role, and to the political role; the approximate percentage of time they would *prefer* to devote to each of the three roles; and which of the three roles they believe to be most important to the successful performance of their job. In order to parallel the Wright study, the management role was associated parenthetically on the questionnaire with administrative activities; the policy role was clarified to include council relations; and the political role was associated with community leadership.

Wright's perception of the management role includes such functions as staffing, budgeting, and supervision, including reporting relationships. The policy role includes control over the council agenda and policy initiation and formulation, while the political role includes relationships with nongovernmental groups and individuals within the city and intergovernmental relations.

Although some ambiguity exists in the role distinctions suggested by Wright, the ambiguity is modest compared to the degree of apparent consensus on the principal components of the three roles. Popular perceptions regarding the management role normally include such activities as staffing, directing, evaluating, counseling, coordinating, preparing budgets, and executing policy. The policy role is typically thought to include the development of proposals for future city policy, contacts and individual meetings with the mayor or members of the city council, council meetings, responding to special requests of council members, the orchestrating of controversial issues on council agendas, and managerial defense of or opposition to ticklish budgetary items. Perceptions of the political role normally include all actions taken to enhance influence with officials of state, federal, and other local governments; nongovernmental groups; and individuals, as well as public relations encompassing meetings, speeches, and ceremonies.

Analysis of the 1985 data has three focal points: time allocation differences among city managers, assistant city managers, mayors, and mayoral assistants; identification of explanatory variables of relevance to differing allocations of managerial time; and a comparison of the 1985 data with Wright's 1965 findings.

Differences among Municipal Executives and Assistants

City government chief executives and their principal assistants work much more than the standard 40-hour week. Mayors and their assistants in mayor-council and commission cities report average workweeks of 66.4 and 59 hours, respectively. City managers and their assistants report average workweeks of 56.5 and 52.7 hours, respectively. Analysis of the patterns of reported work hours for each of the groups strongly suggests that the differences are systematic rather than coincidental (i.e., in statistical terms, the means differ from one another significantly at the $p<.05$ level). Mayors and their assistants in noncouncil-manager cities tend to spend more hours per week performing their functions than do city managers and their assistants, perhaps because the former must both manage and provide overt political leadership. Generally, but not uniformly, the number of hours worked increases as city size increases. For example, mayors serving cities of 50,000 to 74,999 people reported an average workweek of 65 hours, compared to 68 hours for mayors in cities of 75,000 to 100,000 and 67 hours in those with populations greater than 100,000. For city managers, the reported average workweeks were 56 hours in the smaller cities, 55 hours in those of intermediate size, and 58 hours in the most populous cities.

All four groups of city officials tend to devote a more substantial portion of their time to the management role than to the policy role or the political role (Table 3-1). Only mayors as a group spend less than

Table 3-1

MEAN PERCENTAGE OF TIME DEVOTED TO THE "MANAGEMENT," "POLICY," AND "POLITICAL" ROLES BY PERSONS IN VARIOUS EXECUTIVE POSITIONS IN CITY GOVERNMENT

	\multicolumn{5}{c}{Percentage of Time Devoted to Specified Roles}
	Mayors	Mayoral Assistants	City Managers	Assistant City Mgrs.	Mean
	% (N)	% (N)	% (N)	% (N)	% (N)
Management Role	44.2* (71)	55.3* (100)	50.8* (142)	60.7* (198)	54.6 (511)
Policy Role	25.6 (71)	27.0 (100)	32.2* (142)	25.9 (198)	27.8 (511)
Political Role	30.2* (71)	17.6 (100)	17.0 (142)	13.4* (198)	17.5 (511)

*Denotes that mean comparisons (t-tests) for time devoted to a specified role differs significantly (p < .05) from time devoted to the same role by other categories of city officials.

half of their time on the management role—although at 44.2% that role still commands the lion's share of mayoral time. Mayoral and managerial assistants report greater percentage time allocations to the management role than do their bosses, suggesting municipal evidence of a dyadic relationship reported in the private sector literature "in which the chief executive concentrates on the external roles (figurehead, liaison, spokesman, negotiator), leaving much of the responsibility for the internal roles (leader, disseminator, resource allocator, disturbance handler) to his second in command."[94]

Comparison of the two types of chief executives reveals that city managers spend significantly more of their time on both the management role (50.8%) and the policy role (32.2%) than do the mayors (44.2% and 25.6%, respectively), who spend almost twice as much of their time on the political role (30.2% compared to 17% for the city managers). Given the historic rationale for mayor-council government in larger cities, namely that it provides strong political leadership, this difference in allocation of time is not surprising insofar as the management and political roles are concerned. The extensive involvement of city managers in policy matters, however, clearly contradicts an early assumption of that form of government.

Many factors could combine to explain why a particular city executive devotes more or fewer hours than others do to the job or why a higher or lower percentage of time is devoted to one role or another. Those inclined to think that such variations are purely matters of personal characteristics and idiosyncrasies would be surprised to learn that one-fourth of the variance in working hours per week and more than one-fifth of the variance in percentage of time devoted to the political role may be explained by two factors that are at best only indirectly linked to personal characteristics: official position (i.e., mayor, city manager, mayoral assistant, or assistant city manager) and jurisdiction size. Expressed in statistical terms, the municipal official's position and the population of the jurisdiction served explain 25.8% of the variance in working hours per week among the respondents and 22.4% of the variance in percentage of time devoted to the political role (general linear models $F = 15.90$ and 13.06, respectively; $p = .000$). Those variables, however, account for only 15.1% of the variance in percentage of time devoted to the management role ($F = 8.07$; $p = .000$) and 8% of the variance in percentage of time devoted to the policy role ($F = 3.97$; $p = .000$) (see Table A–2 in appendix).

Most officials appear to be generally satisfied with their allocation of time to the three roles. Even if given the opportunity to shift time from one role to another, few major reallocations would occur.

Differences in mean responses by position to the questions of actual time allocation and preferred time allocation were modest—especially for city managers. On average, city managers report devoting 50.8% of their workweek to the management role, 32.2% to the policy role, and 17% to the political role. Their average preferred time allocations are 50.7%, 32.1%, and 17.2%, respectively. For mayors, the actual time allocation for the political role is precisely the preferred allocation average (30.2%), but they would prefer to reduce their management role allocation by 3.8 percentage points and apply that time to their policy role. Mayoral assistants and assistant city managers would also prefer to reduce their management role time allocations. Mayoral assistants would apply the 4.7 percentage points saved primarily to their policy role (+3.7 percentage points) and secondarily, to their political role (+1 percentage point). Similarly, assistant city managers would increase the time allocation to their policy role (+2 percentage points) a little more than they would their political role (+1.2 percentage points).

Examination of Explanatory Variables

Responses of chief executives—mayors and city managers—were examined in greater detail in an attempt to identify potential explanatory variables of relevance to differences in working hours and percentages of time devoted to the management, policy, and political roles. Eight variables were examined for their relevance to executive working hours through the step-wise regression technique: (1) population of the jurisdiction served, (2) age of the chief executive, (3) whether the chief executive was a mayor or a city manager, (4) whether the executive held a master of public administration (MPA) degree, (5) number of years the executive had been employed in the current position, (6) percentage of time allocated to the management role, (7) percentage of time allocated to the policy role, and (8) percentage of time allocated to the political role (for details see Table A-3 in appendix). Only the position and age of the official were found to be significant at the .05 level, explaining 20.6% of the variance in working hours per week. The likelihood of longer working hours increased if the official served as mayor rather than city manager and decreased as the age of the official increased.

A similar process was used to explore possible explanatory variables for percentage of time devoted to each of the three executive roles. Six potential explanatory variables were examined: (1) population of the jurisdiction, (2) age of the chief executive, (3) whether the executive was a mayor or city manager, (4) whether the executive held an MPA degree, (5) working hours per week, and (6) years employed in the current position. Four significant variables combined to explain 13.3% of the variance in percentage of time devoted to the management role. Not surprisingly, city managers were more likely than mayors to devote greater percentages of their time to the management role. Older executives and those serving smaller populations were also more likely to devote greater portions of their time to administrative activities. Furthermore, officials holding MPA degrees tended to devote lower percentages of their time to the management role than did those without such training. Such a finding is surprising if one considers the MPA to be a professional management degree narrowly construed, but much less surprising when one considers the vehemence with which many modern public administration scholars have refuted the notion of public executives as mere technicians.[95]

Three significant variables were found to explain 13.9% of the variance in percentage of time devoted to the policy role among mayors and city managers. City managers, younger officials, and those serving larger populations were more likely to devote greater percentages of their time to the policy role.

Two significant explanatory variables accounted for 25.8% of the variance in percentage of time devoted to the political role among chief executive respondents. Mayors and officials holding MPA degrees were more likely than their counterparts to devote greater percentages of their time to the political role.

Comparison with Wright's 1965 Findings

Wright found that 37% of the respondents in his 1965 survey of city managers perceived the management role as being most important to job success. The political role was identified as most important by 33% of his respondents and the policy role by 22%. Wright's findings are compared in Table 3–2 with the responses of the four groups of city officials included in this study. Because Wright's data were drawn only from officials serving cities with populations greater than 100,000, the responses of officials serving smaller jurisdictions in 1985 were omitted from the tabulation.

Table 3-2

MUNICIPAL OFFICIALS' 1985 DESIGNATION OF MOST IMPORTANT ROLE COMPARED WITH WRIGHT'S 1965 FINDINGS (POPULATIONS GREATER THAN 100,000)

	Wright's Study of City Managers 1965[ad]	City Mgrs. 1985[a]	Mayors 1985[b]	Assts. in Council-Mgr. Cities 1985[a]	Mayoral Assts. 1985[b]
Role perceived as most important to job success					
Management Role (administrative activities)	37%	38.5%	23.1%	75.0%	75.5%
Policy Role (and council relations)	22%	55.8%	34.6%	25.0%	18.4%
Political Role (community leadership)	33%	5.8%	42.3%	0.0%	6.1%
N	45	52[c]	26[c]	80[c]	49[c]

[a] Council-manager form of government.
[b] Mayor-council or commission form of government.
[c] Missing data and ties are omitted from computations.
[d] Deil S. Wright, "The City Manager as a Development Administrator," Chapter 6 in *Comparative Urban Research: The Administration and Politics of Cities*, ed. Robert T. Daland (Beverly Hills, Calif.: Sage Publications, 1969), p. 236. Although this chapter appeared in 1969, the data were gathered in 1965. The Wright column does not add to 100%.

The percentage of city managers in 1985 perceiving the management role as most important is remarkably similar to the 1965 response—38.5% in 1985 compared to 37% in 1965.[96] In contrast, only 23% of the mayors perceived the management role to be most important to job success, while 75% of the managerial and mayoral assistants perceived it to be their most important role.

The most striking contrast between Wright's 1965 findings and the 1985 responses is the dramatic increase in the proportion of city managers perceiving the policy role to be most important and a correspondingly dramatic drop in the percentage perceiving the political role as most important. While 22% of Wright's respondents deemed the policy role most important and 33% the political role, 55.8% of the 1985 city managers regarded the policy role as most important and only 5.8% so designated the political role. Among these respondents, only the mayors accorded the degree of preeminence to the political role granted by Wright's city managers.

Conclusions about the 1985 Study

The classical theorists of council-manager government were correct in their assumption that form does make a difference. Although scholars may debate the degree to which form influences policy and service, form of government does influence the activities and role emphases of key officials. City managers and mayors, both of whom serve as chief executives, clearly differ as to how they allocate their time, how they prefer to allocate it, and which role they see as most important to job success. Furthermore, level of executive responsibility—as well as form of government—prescribes differences between the emphases of chief executives and their assistants. Most assistants are appointed primarily to assist with managerial functions, and their responses so indicate.

Perhaps more important than distinctions deriving from different positions and forms of government are perceptual changes among persons filling a particular executive post—changes made evident among city managers in this case by Wright's 1965 baseline data. The job of the city manager has evolved over time, with fewer managers perceiving community leadership as their key role and more according policy initiation and council relations that priority. One may speculate that these differences have been propelled, at least in part, by the trend beginning in the 1970s for council-manager cities to amend their city charters to provide for direct election of the mayor and council elections by districts. Direct mayoral election more clearly established an official with a mandate to fill the high-profile community leadership role and to perform public relations duties, while district election of council members simultaneously created a greater need for, but more difficulty in gaining, consensus for public policy. Thus, it is no wonder that the modern city manager emphasizes the policy and council relations role. Richard Childs and other early advocates of separation of politics and administration could at least be pleased with the nominal deemphasis by city managers of the overtly political role.

The findings presented in this chapter suggest that researchers hoping to account for major portions of the variance in time allocation to the various executive roles in local government probably will be challenged greatly. The variety of factors impinging on the executive post and its incumbent defy simple explanation. Henry Mintzberg, a noted authority on executive roles and time allocation in the private sector, posits a contingency theory of managerial work that holds that an executive's actions are influenced by four complex variables: the environment, the job, the personality and style of the incumbent, and the situation.[97] Surely, the determinants of municipal executive work are no less complex. Considered in this light, models such as those presented here that account for 26%, 21%, or even 13% of the variance in executive time allocation using only two, three, or four executive and community characteristics are less remarkable for how little they explain than for how much.

Summary

This chapter has reviewed a variety of perspectives on the roles of local government executives and provided a foundation for understanding role differences attributable to distinctive forms of local government. The reform movement, with its apolitical bias, resulted not only in the creation of the commission and council-manager forms of government but also left council-manager government with a dubious legacy, namely the politics-administration dichotomy. Although both scholars and practitioners acknowledge the necessary blending of the two, the legacy nevertheless underlies the continuing quest to determine the extent to which city managers are policy and community leaders and, more importantly, the extent to which city managers should and must assume these ostensibly nonmanagement roles. As city managers attempt to resolve this issue for themselves, they must grapple with the practical realities that make the contingency/situational theories of leadership described in the previous chapter so compelling: the answer varies with time and circumstance. Mayors face a similar dilemma in determining how to balance policy and political roles against management functions, particularly given the complexity of modern municipal government and the resulting need for an integrated leadership style.

The dynamic nature of local government is illustrated by the greater emphasis given to the policy role and the corresponding deemphasis of the political role by city managers in large cities across the 20-year time span covering Wright's 1965 survey and the authors' 1985 research. The implication, perhaps, is that elected officials in large cities, especially the popularly elected mayor, may provide much of the community leadership in the 1980s but look to the city manager for guidance on policy issues.

The next three chapters provide greater details on the findings of the 1985 survey.

Chapter Four

NOT ENOUGH HOURS IN A DAY

The literature on executives alternately portrays the top manager as the master or the marionette. Some perceive the executive as a string puller, directing the actions of an army of subordinates. To others, it is the executive's strings that appear constantly vulnerable to the whims of an array of puppeteers. Almost invariably, however, the executive is depicted as a busy, sometimes harried figure with workaholic tendencies and little time for personal pleasures. For many executives, the depiction is accurate; for some, perhaps, it is even an understatement of reality.

Long Hours

Complexities abound in the occasional efforts of biographers and other researchers to determine the number of hours that executives work in a typical week. Should only hours at the office be counted? What about work-related social engagements, or time at home reflecting on a problem encountered in the office that afternoon, or reflecting on the organizational ramifications of actions being contemplated by the state legislature as reported by an evening news analyst? Despite such ambiguity, it is clear that most executives exceed the 40-hour-week standard by a wide margin.

When the top managers of four intermediate-sized private sector organizations were each observed for one week, researchers concluded that they worked on average of 44 hours per week.[1] A 1980 survey of local government managers conducted by the International City Management Association (ICMA) indicated an average 53-hour workweek, with an even higher average for managers in large, central cities.[2]

Civilian managers in the U. S. Navy reported average workweeks of 52 hours, with an additional eight hours per week at home spent on job-related activities.[3]

Some municipal executives report enormously high work hours—almost incredibly so, in a few cases. Reports of city managers starting work early in the morning and toiling late into the night, working weekends and holidays, devoting 10 to 14 hours per day or 60 hours per week to the job are not uncommon.[4] The same is true of mayors. Dianne Feinstein, former mayor of San Francisco, reportedly worked "from 8:00 or 9:00 each morning until 10:00 or later most nights."[5] Mayor Henry Cisneros of San Antonio is said to work "sixteen- to eighteen-hour days seven days a week."[6] Even prior to his election as Philadelphia's mayor, W. Wilson Goode, serving then as the city's top appointed administrator, reportedly "dazzled" business leaders with his "no-nonsense work pattern—15 hours each weekday, 12 hours on Saturday, 8 hours on Sunday."[7] Mayor William H. Hudnut III of Indianapolis is said to consider 16 hours to be a slow workday.[8]

A tale that perhaps epitomizes the apparent devotion to duty among many of the leading municipal executives is told about Baltimore's former mayor and now Maryland's governor, William Donald Schaefer, by an assistant who had been forced by a 1979 snowstorm to walk miles to get to work. Rather than praise for his perseverance when he arrived at 8:27 a.m., the assistant was singed by the mayor's "Where in the hell have you been?" Schaefer, it turned out, had spent the night at City Hall.[9]

Time Allocation

With a few notable exceptions, time allocation of managers—that is, the manner in which managers spend their time—has received relatively little attention. Despite widespread popular and academic interest in management as a field of study and the importance of an awareness of managerial time allocation to a genuine understanding of management functions and demands, systematic research is rather sparse.

Among the earliest efforts to examine managerial time allocation was a study by Sune Carlson, published in 1951, in which the chief executives of 10 Swedish firms carefully recorded their daily activities.[10] Carlson's was a pioneering effort in the diary method of studying time allocation and was followed by studies by Burns; Copeman, Luijk, and Hanika; Dubin and Spray; Brewer and Tomlinson; Hinrichs; Horne and Lupton; Stewart; Lawler, Porter, and Tennenbaum; and a few others, all of which relied on some form of self-reporting by the manager.[11]

Other researchers have examined managerial time allocation by observational methods. Researchers such as Guest, Ponder, Kelly, Choran, and Kurke and Aldrich have observed supervisors or managers in great detail, typically for a day or a week each.[12] The best-known of the observational studies was conducted by Henry Mintzberg in the late 1960s.[13] Mintzberg observed five chief executives for one week each. His findings have influenced virtually all subsequent research and writing on the subject of time allocation and managerial roles. Mintzberg concluded that "job pressures drive the manager to be superficial in his actions—to overload himself with work, encourage interruption, respond quickly to every stimulus, seek the tangible and avoid the abstract, make decisions in small increments, and do everything abruptly."[14]

Time allocation studies generally have characterized the manager's job as filled with fragmented activities with multiple interruptions, a heavy reliance on verbal communications, and little time for reflective thinking. The research designs used in those studies represent methodological trade-offs. Some have relied on diaries; some on researcher observation; and some on modified forms of the diary or direct observation methods—e.g., sampling rather than constant observation or time allocation questionnaires rather than diary keeping by the subject. Observational studies and rigorous diary studies are less susceptible to the problems of definitional ambiguity and reporting imprecision than are various forms of after-the-fact self-reporting. Yet, the more precise observational and diary studies typically have been limited to extremely small samples—many attempting to reach conclusions based upon samples of five, four, or even three managers. Many of the self-reports, although less precise than Carlson's diary method from which they evolved or the various observational studies, provide a much more substantial sample from which to generalize findings.

More recent studies have sometimes attempted to combine methods[15] or to apply questionnaire methods to samples selected for particular managerial characteristics—e.g., a group of managers noted for their effectiveness or ineffectiveness—in hopes of associating particular time allocation strategies or tendencies with the presence or absence of those characteristics.[16]

In his seminal study, Mintzberg portrays the manager engaging in his activities at a relentless pace. On a typical day, the executives in his study handled 36 pieces of mail, five telephone calls, and eight meetings. "A true break seldom occurred. Coffee was taken during meetings, and lunchtime was almost always devoted to formal or informal meetings. When free time appeared, ever-present subordinates quickly usurped it."[17]

Mintzberg describes five kinds of days, as follows:

1. 'Catch-up' days, generally following trips or extremely heavy schedules, find the manager spending much time at his desk catching up on the mail, returning telephone calls, scheduling appointments, and making himself available informally to subordinates who have been looking for him.
2. 'Crisis days' find the manager delaying all that can be delayed so that he can concentrate on a major disturbance that has suddenly developed.
3. A 'free day' sees few scheduled meetings; instead, old mail is processed, tours may be taken, and subordinates, who abhor an activity vacuum, are received. (One such day was the busiest of the 25, when one chief executive had only three scheduled meetings, but 14 desk work sessions, 17 unscheduled meetings, and five tours.)
4. 'Heavily scheduled days' find the manager in scheduled meetings most of the day, wedging in only important telephone calls and urgent mail.
5. 'Normal days' bring the usual heavy load of mail, callers, and meetings (scheduled and unscheduled).[18]

How does this pattern of executive activities differ from that of the chief executive in municipal government—the mayor or city manager? There is considerable anecdotal evidence suggesting that the difference is not great. A former mayor of New Orleans described his typical day as follows:

> My driver would come by at a specified time depending upon my appointments. We'd probably stop on the way downtown and have a cup of coffee, and then go to my first appointment. Occasionally there were openings of new businesses, new stores, etcetera, and they invited the mayor to cut the ribbon.
>
> So I'd go to my office after having made a couple of stops, and I'd have an agenda of appointments prepared in advance. I never closed

my door to the public, regardless of who they were. I always kept my name in the telephone book.

On the way downtown I'd notice the streets. Some streets may have been beginning to fold up a little or there may have been too many leaves on some lots, or trash on the streets. All of these things . . . . You've got to keep your eyes open because you're the only mayor. There is nobody you can pass the buck to.

Then during the day I'd have appointments and usually every lunchtime there was some sort of thing like the United Fund or the Heart Drive. Someone would write a speech, and I would give it.

I'd go back to City Hall and meet with some more people. I'd have committee meetings to deal with the street problem or the crime problem, or whatever had come up.[19]

The typical day of Henry Maier, mayor of Milwaukee for 28 years before retiring in 1988, provides an even stronger depiction of the fragmented activities and hurried pace of the municipal executive:

MORNING

- Soon after he arrives, his personal secretary enters his office . . . . She presents him with the early morning papers that he must sign and a picture he has been asked to autograph.
- He looks at his list of incoming calls left over from late the previous afternoon, and asks about the call from the building inspector. The inspector wants to see him as soon as possible. The Mayor says that he'll see him immediately.
- [After] the inspector has left . . . the Mayor spends the next hour reviewing some reports on his desk. These concern his operational plans, the priorities for action that he has established, and involve a number of decisions. He tells his secretary that he wants to see the planning coordinator and the economic development director in the late afternoon.
- Coming through the door . . . is a secretary who will be in and out of the Mayor's office several times during the day. He is the combination press secretary, troubleshooter, appointments secretary, political secretary, and operational subchief of staff. The secretary mentions a number of people whom the Mayor ought to see. The secretary informs him that the evening paper is doing a story on organized labor's influence in local government and wants to interview him on his labor appointees. He informs the Mayor that a reporter wants to know if he will answer the governor's apparent criticism of the city. He says that up until now the communications media have not shown much interest in the Mayor's charter message, but it is still early. He recommends acceptance of

several civic invitations. The Mayor discusses all items with him, accepts or rejects his suggestions, then with a grin tells him to get busy and turn out some work.
- Later, taking a breather, the Mayor walks around the outer offices. He exchanges pleasantries . . . . He winds up discussing some of the latest endeavors of the division of economic development and then returns to his office.
- At noon he enjoys a luncheon with some members of the Common Council. He seeks out their reactions to various proposals and, where differences exist, tries to find a common ground.

AFTERNOON

- Back in his office after lunch, the Mayor answers some of the telephone calls that have piled up since late morning. He meets briefly with the civil defense director. While a television camera looks on, he takes part in the ceremonial signing of a proclamation in his office.
- After a while he leans back in his chair to relax for a moment, but his secretary flashes him on the intercom. "There is a gentleman here who insists on seeing you," she says, and gives him a name. "Send him in," he answers. The door opens and a citizen walks in. He wishes to talk about a problem of much concern to him and his neighbors. "A number of people in our neighborhood want to meet with you to discuss trucking on our street," the citizen says. "All right, we'll hold the meeting," the Mayor says, "but all of the reports from our departments indicate that nothing can be done until the expressways are completed." He schedules the meeting, even though the local alderman has already informed the Mayor of the problem, regretfully remarking that there is no way to satisfy the citizenry immediately.
- To his office now come his chief aide, the director of economic development, and the planning coordinator. Their discussion concerns all of the Mayor's immediate dreams for the city, here in the form of 26 top-priority projects listed on the cards that lie before him on a table. The list includes matters as forward-looking as a long-range fiscal plan for the city, as prosaic as a proposed new system for combining the collection of garbage and refuse, as colorful as a potential world festival.
- When the meeting is over, the Mayor turns to the material he is preparing for a major policy speech. He calls two staff members for projections of estimated revenue needs for the next ten years.
- Exit staff men. Enter the reporters assigned to the city hall beat.
- When the reporters leave his office, he continues to think about a variety of things touched on during their visit. Where can he gather support to put across his state tax distribution program? How can urban renewal be speeded up? Delays resulting from the paperwork necessary between the local and federal governments seem to be causing much concern in areas slated for demolition. He wonders at what points he can

compromise on his reorganization plan without giving too much away.
- The typewriters are covered in the outer office and most people have gone home for the day. The Mayor is once again discussing a number of problems with his chief aide. He promptly decides some questions which require an immediate answer. They agree that several areas need further exploration before a decision can be made, and assignments are made for those who are to gather the facts.
- Later, an old personal friend and wise political advisor drifts in, and the remaining time turns into a congenial discussion of politics.

EVENING

- Finally, his security officer reminds him that he has a dinner engagement soon.
- At the convivial evening banquet, the Mayor is applauded by the audience. Afterwards, of course, there are those who stop him to lecture or advise. "Why don't you . . .?" "Why haven't you . . .?"
- At home, his wife asks, "How did it go today?" "Oh, so-so," he answers. He makes a few telephone checks on various items, and then he finally relaxes. His day is over.[20]

The hectic schedule of another big-city mayor is summarized in the following observation about Houston Mayor Kathy Whitmire:

> She's at her desk early in the morning and late into the evening. She regularly schedules 7:30 a.m. working breakfasts and sets meetings for as late as 7:30 p.m. Outside of the required ceremonial events she must attend and the two to five speeches she delivers every week, Whitmire spends most of her time in her spacious but functional office. "She's a mayor all the time. It's what she bought into," says a close aide.[21]

City managers, too, have extensive work-related evening engagements. In a 1980 survey, local government managers reported an average of more than seven hours of evening and weekend work per week, consisting primarily of meetings with city council and community groups, social events, and paperwork.[22] Wayne Anderson, Chester Newland, and Richard Stillman offer the following as a hypothetically typical day in the life of a local public manager:

> 8:00 a.m.   Arrives at work to polish off leftover paperwork/dictation from yesterday.
>
> 9:15 a.m.   Meets with mayor to review next week's council agenda prior to its publication.

10:00 a.m. Local business group offers ideas on newly proposed industrial park on east side.

10:45 a.m. City engineer and city treasurer join group to brief them on construction/financial details of site development.

11:30 a.m. Police chief and personnel officer review a pending grievance against the department by a member of the city employees' union.

12:15 p.m. Leaves ten minutes late for luncheon speech at League of Women Voters' monthly meeting to urge their help with the water bond campaign.

1:30 p.m. Back again for more discussion with the police chief on the same topic discussed in the morning.

2:15 p.m. Rides with public works director to inspect north side residents' complaints of "smells" from nearby city dump—mentally drafts responses to their council members and neighborhood group on return to office.

3:15 p.m. Returns stacked-up phone calls at office.

3:45 p.m. Talks with local newspaper reporter about the importance to the city of next month's special water bond vote.

4:10 p.m. Free time that was scheduled to review several pending budget items is interrupted by visit from two council members.

5:20 p.m. Goes home for dinner.

7:10 p.m. Leaves to attend meeting of south side citizen association, a predominately poor black group that the manager wants to involve more closely in community public housing planning.

11:00 p.m. Home to bed at last![23]

Varied Roles and Fragmented Activities

The fragmented activities that characterize the workday of most executives in both the private and public sectors are easily understood when consideration is given to the variety of roles that executives fill. In his study of executives, Mintzberg identifies 10 roles that he clusters into three groups (Figure 4–1). The roles of figurehead, liaison, and leader are grouped together as interpersonal roles. Each is derived from the manager's formal authority and status, giving the manager responsibility for representing his organization, interacting with people outside the organization, and motivating subordinates. The monitor, disseminator, and spokesman roles are clustered as informational roles, focusing upon the manager's responsibilities for receiving information and transmitting information both within and outside the organization. Mintzberg labels the final cluster as the decisional roles, including the

Figure 4-1
THE MANAGER'S ROLES

```
Formal Authority
   and Status
        │
        ▼
┌──────────────────┐
│ Interpersonal Roles │
│   Figurehead     │
│   Leader         │
│   Liaison        │
└──────────────────┘
        │
        ▼
┌──────────────────┐
│ Informational Roles │
│   Monitor        │
│   Disseminator   │
│   Spokesman      │
└──────────────────┘
        │
        ▼
┌──────────────────┐
│  Decisional Roles │
│   Entrepreneur   │
│   Disturbance handler │
│   Resource allocator │
│   Negotiator     │
└──────────────────┘
```

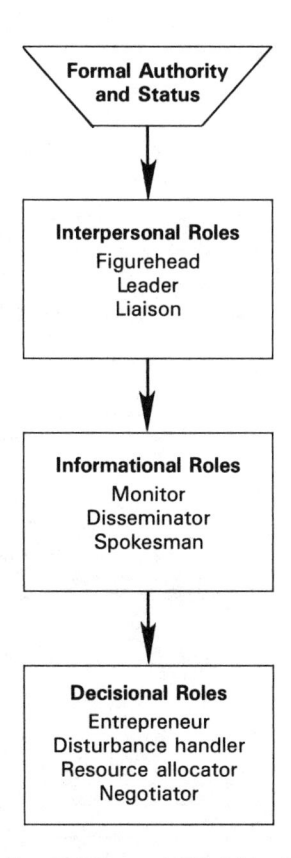

SOURCE: Henry Mintzberg, *The Nature of Managerial Work* (New York: Harper & Row, 1973), p. 59. Copyright © 1973 by Henry Mintzberg. Reprinted by permission of Harper & Row, Publishers, Inc.

manager's roles as entrepreneur, disturbance handler, resource allocator, and negotiator. These roles emphasize the manager's responsibilities for initiating change, coping with organizational threats, deciding upon resource commitments, and negotiating on behalf of the organization.[24]

Mintzberg identified what he perceives to be the key roles associated with eight managerial job types (Table 4–1). Of particular interest in this study is the "political manager," a job type for which the key roles are presumed to be those of spokesman and negotiator.[25]

Mintzberg notes that the political manager "must spend a good part of his time in formal activities, meeting regularly with directors or the boss, receiving and negotiating with pressure groups, and explaining the actions of his organization to special interest parties."[26] The priority given to the spokesman and negotiator roles are presumed by Mintzberg to be "typical of managers at the top of most governments and institutions, including hospitals and universities, where the political pressures from below are as great as those from outside."[27]

Is this an accurate reflection of the work of local government chief

Table 4-1

EIGHT MANAGERIAL JOB TYPES

Managerial Job Type	Key Roles
Contact man	Liaison, figurehead
Political manager	Spokesman, negotiator
Entrepreneur	Entrepreneur, negotiator
Insider	Resource allocator
Real-time manager	Disturbance handler
Team manager	Leader
Expert manager	Monitor, spokesman
New manager	Liaison, monitor

SOURCE: Henry Mintzberg, *The Nature of Managerial Work* (New York: Harper & Row, 1973), p. 127. Copyright © 1973 by Henry Mintzberg. Reprinted by permission of Harper & Row, Publishers, Inc.

executives? Mayors seemingly fit this mold with ease, and even city managers are adapting to it. ICMA's Committee on Future Horizons has projected a future in which "the prime skill of management will be brokering and negotiation."[28]

Normally, the responsibilities and, presumably, the roles of local government chief executives are spelled out in city charters. Prescribed roles and actual roles, however, may differ. A study by John Kotter and Paul Lawrence reveals fairly wide role variation across different forms of local government.[29] Although mayors in cities with council-manager charters tend to have smaller formal domains—or areas of responsibility—than mayors operating in mayor-council cities, substantial variations from prescribed authority exist, sometimes producing mayoral power of surprisingly little or surprisingly great magnitude. Kotter and Lawrence, for example, found the mayor of Dallas to have a larger domain than the mayor of New Orleans, despite the fact that New Orleans has a mayor-council city charter and Dallas, a council-manager charter. Such patterns defy charter-based explanations. Still, a few charter-related patterns do emerge in their study. Among 20 mayors examined in detail, Kotter and Lawrence found only four they would categorize as "ceremonial mayors," having only short-run agendas of very limited scope. All four were mayors in council-manager cities. All five of the mayors they categorized as "caretaker mayors" were from strong mayor cities. Caretakers were so characterized for their short-run agendas with fairly large scope.

"Personality/individualist mayors," with short-run and mid-range agendas of moderate scope, tended to represent council-manager cities, while "executive mayors," with short-run and mid-range agendas of fairly broad scope, most often served strong mayor cities. Only the fifth mayoral behavioral pattern, which Kotter and Lawrence call "program entrepreneur" for its short-, medium-, and long-range agendas of very large scope, exhibited no clear pattern of representation by one form of government or another.

In essence, formal roles prescribed in charters, while important, are not absolute determinants of executive roles. Consider the words of the ICMA Committee on Future Horizons:

> Managers will rely much less on fixed legal parameters—much more on political realities and on strategic thinking and persuasiveness [in the future]. Many reasons exists for the shift in emphasis. One is that a consensus already exists on the roles of both the manager and council in many places, a consensus that supersedes any written documents.[30]

Where consensus conflicts with written documents, in other words, put your money on consensus. Robert Boynton and Deil Wright have expressed in colorful style the difference between chief executive job descriptions and realities in many cities:

> The images of the offices of the American mayor and the city manager found in the literature of public administration and political science are related to the realities of those offices in much the same way as Smokey the Bear is related to the grizzly bear of the Northwest. The literary figures are benign, simplified caricatures of complex and not completely tamable realities.[31]

Kotter and Lawrence identify three key mayoral duties: agenda setting, establishing and maintaining important relationships, and actually undertaking specific tasks.[32] Most of the 20 mayors they studied tended to lie nearer the "muddling through" end of the planning continuum than to the "rational planning" end; they focused primarily upon short-run, reactive agendas. Mayors were less uniform in their network building techniques, using a variety of different processes. Approaches to task accomplishment tended to be what Kotter and Lawrence describe as bureaucratic (relying on formal organization channels) or individualistic (tied primarily to the executive's own personal skills), rather than entrepreneurial (hustling and promoting in an effort to secure the help of others).

The city manager's role would seem tightly prescribed by city council expectations, if not by the formal language of the city charter. David Welborn notes a fairly lengthy set of such expectations, which in reality is only an abbreviated list:

The council expects the manager to:

1. Be the chief administrative officer of the city and be responsible to the city council for the proper administration of all affairs of the city.

2. Appoint and, when necessary, suspend or remove officers and employees of the city except as otherwise provided by the city charter or law, and to direct and supervise their work.

3. Prepare the budget annually, and submit it to the council annually, together with a message describing its important features, and be responsible for its administration after adoption.

4. Prepare and submit to the council as of the end of the fiscal year a complete report on the finances and administrative activities of the city for the preceding year.

5. Keep the council advised of the financial condition and future needs of the city and make such recommendations as he may deem desirable.

6. Recommend to the governing body a standard schedule of pay for each appointed office and position in the city service, including minimum, intermediate, and maximum rates.

7. Recommend to the governing body (from time to time) adoption of such policies as he may deem necessary or expedient for the health, safety, or welfare of the community, or for the improvement of the administrative services.

8. Consolidate or combine offices, positions, or departments, or units under his jurisdiction, with the approval of the city council.

9. Attend all meetings of the city council unless excused therefrom and take part in the discussion of all matters coming before the council.

10. Supervise the purchase of materials, supplies, and equipment for which funds are provided in the budget.

11. See that all laws and ordinances are properly enforced.

12. Investigate the activities of the city or of any department or division. Investigate all complaints in regard to matters concerning the administration of the government of the city and in regard to service maintained by the public utilities in the city, and see that all franchises, permits, and privileges granted by the city are faithfully observed.

13. Devote his entire time to the discharge of his official duties.

14. Perform such other duties as may be required by council.[33]

Despite the impression fostered by a list of managerial duties dominated by matters of internal administration, city managers tend to focus less on "housekeeping and the nuts and bolts of day-to-day administration" and more on broader issues, priority setting, and representing the interests of their communities with persons and groups outside their organization or city.[34] Not surprisingly, such a disparity can cause confusion regarding the manager's role and potentially generate difficult "turf" struggles between managers and city councils.

Role ambiguity is not an insignificant problem. Charter prescriptions of managerial responsibility, managerial interpretations of those prescriptions, and council expectations regarding managerial activities and domain may diverge substantially. A National League of Cities

(NLC) survey of city managers, key staff members, and elected officials provides evidence either of performance expectation gaps or, perhaps more fundamentally, of role dissonance (Table 4–2).

Role ambiguity, no doubt, is heightened by the considerable variety of roles undertaken by mayors and city managers—and virtually all executives for that matter. Many mayors, in fact, serve in roles of

Table 4-2

CONCURRENCE RANKINGS: ADMINISTRATOR VERSUS GOVERNING BODY ROLE PERCEPTIONS

	Governing body (%) Agree	Disagree	Administrators (%) Agree	Disagree
The governing body and manager have a good working relationship.	60	40	40	55
The governing body deals with too many administrative matters and not enough policy issues.	40	40	75	20
The manager understands his or her role in the administration.	100	0	70	20
The governing body understands its role in the administration.	100	0	35	65
The governing body effectively draws on the expertise of the professional staff.	80	20	15	80
The manager provides the governing body with sufficient alternatives for making policy decisions.	0	100	80	15

SOURCE: National League of Cities, *Local Policy Leadership* (Wichita, Kans.: Wichita State University, Center for Urban Studies, 1978), as cited in Wayne F. Anderson, Chester A. Newland, and Richard J. Stillman, II, *The Effective Local Government Manager* (Washington, D.C.: International City Management Association, 1983), p. 65.

significance well beyond their cities' boundaries. Some, such as Edward I. Koch of New York City, are national political figures in their own right. Others, such as Feinstein of San Francisco, Cisneros of San Antonio, and Tom Bradley of Los Angeles, to name only a few, are projected as future stars on the national political horizon. Still others, such as Mayor Andrew Young of Atlanta, have pursued a variety of social and political agendas of national and even international scale during the course of their careers. Young, perhaps best known for his association with Martin Luther King, Jr., and the civil rights movement and later for his stint as U. N. Ambassador, refused to define his role as mayor in narrow terms, even when interaction with foreign political leaders—including several prominent leftists—in apparent hope of promoting Atlanta as a center of international trade created consternation among some constituents. One local supporter, concerned about fellow Atlantans "fussing about Andy having all these socialists and communists in here," captured the essence of role ambiguity when he told some of Young's critics, "You've got to draw a line right down the middle of Andy's head . . . . Keep the humanitarian, the preacher, the internationalist on the left side, and keep Andy Young, the mayor who's going after jobs and doing the hard-nosed business type things, on the right side."[35] Even that view of Mayor Young may be shortsighted, however, in that it fails to acknowledge the importance of his "evangelical zeal" in contending successfully with some of the more difficult aspects of the city's "business."[36]

Not only do roles vary within a single job, but the activities associated with that job typically are fragmented.[37] In separate studies of executive time allocation, Mintzberg found 49% of all executive activities lasting fewer than nine minutes and Kurke and Aldrich found 63% of executive activities consuming fewer than nine minutes. Only 10% of the activities of Mintzberg's sample of executives lasted more than an hour, compared to only 5% of the activities in Kurke and Aldrich's sample.[38]

Demands, Foci, and Activities in Executive Work

The executive workday may be examined from many perspectives. Three such perspectives involve the sources of demand placed on managerial time, the general foci of managerial efforts, and the specific tasks or activities in which executives are engaged. Each is examined in this chapter as it applies to chief executives in local government—mayors and city managers.

Demands

Persons in any work setting respond to a variety of demands that in many respects define the nature of their work. A person's boss, of course, potentially is a major source of demands that could control the dimensions of a particular job almost entirely. The "boss" of a chief executive is often less precisely identifiable than the boss of most other employees. Rarely is the boss a single person; more commonly, it is a board of directors and, indirectly, the body of shareholders or their analogue in local government, the citizens.

The mayor in a mayor-council form of government normally is elected directly by the voters and is answerable to the citizenry. The mayor is not an employee of the city council and is responsible to that body only in the sense that the council represents the citizens. The requests of the citizenry and, to a degree, those of the city council represent for the mayor as chief executive officer the closest thing to boss-assigned tasks. Not so for a city manager, whose status as an employee of the city council may be dramatized at the drop of a 4–3 dismissal vote.

Two types of demands that commonly fall on local government chief executives in addition to those imposed by "bosses" are intergovernmental demands and emergencies. Intergovernmental demands include the requests and requirements of other levels and units of government. Mayoral and managerial reputations have been won or lost by an executive's adeptness or ineptitude in dealing with Washington and the state capital, an adroitness often measured in grant dollars. Frank Rizzo, former mayor of Philadelphia, could be pugnacious in his statements and actions, even in his dealings with the federal government. One observer notes that Rizzo's unsuccessful fight against the Whitman Park housing development—an effort to keep blacks from moving into a poor white neighborhood—cost Philadelphia millions of dollars, as the Carter Administration cut off all Urban Development Corporation grants to the city in retaliation.[39]

Emergencies, of course, are the unanticipated crises that strike all organizations, perhaps merely challenging the patience or initiative of its individual or collective members, but perhaps, more significantly, jeopardizing their ability to achieve important objectives or even threatening their reputation and status. Severe organizational crises may come in a variety of forms including employee strikes, major financial shortages, natural disasters, the discovery of official misconduct or corruption, and any number of other headline grabbing events. Any such occurrence takes an enormous toll on executive time and attention.[40]

Municipal crises may focus on the local government organization itself, on the community it serves, or on something that the community holds dear. A threat to one of the community's prized possessions, for example, prompted Mayor Goode's exhausting, successful efforts to keep the National Football League's Eagles in Philadelphia and Mayor Schaefer's exhausting, unsuccessful efforts to keep the Colts in Baltimore.[41] Crises may be intensely personal, as in Mayor Feinstein's overwhelming victory in a recall election she found to be "deeply humiliating."[42] In some cases, the crises are matters of life and death. Mayor Goode faced such a crisis in his administration's dealing with a Philadelphia-centered cult called MOVE in 1985.

MOVE, a group whose name apparently had no special meaning, had been a problem to previous Philadelphia administrations and, increasingly, to the neighborhoods that group members occupied. MOVE advocated anarchy and practiced confrontation—and it made confrontation practically inevitable as its members blocked alleys, threw garbage in their yards, threatened neighbors, broadcast obscenities over public address systems, and brandished weapons. An earlier, 1978 confrontation had left a police officer dead. Now, Goode had authorized the Philadelphia police to remove the threat imposed by a fortified MOVE stronghold on Osage Avenue. The initial effort, high-pressure water jets, failed to dislodge a steel-reinforced bunker on the roof of the MOVE house, generating instead a 90-minute shoot-out. A second thrust, this one designed to penetrate a cellar wall, was also ineffectual. The third thrust led to destruction of huge proportions.

Two sticks of a nonincendiary blasting agent were dropped by helicopter onto the rooftop bunker. Within 20 minutes, the MOVE house was engulfed in flames that eventually would destroy two city blocks comprised of 61 homes. The blaze left 11 persons dead, including four children, and 250 homeless.

Goode was criticized sharply for his actions. One prominent columnist wrote that the mayor had "gone crazy" for a day[43] and a state senator lamented, "You just don't drop bombs on a row house in Philadelphia."[44] One neighborhood resident was quoted in a national newsmagazine as saying, "MOVE in its wildest day never perpetrated anything on our block like what Wilson Goode did."[45] Yet, Goode survived the devastating day with astonishingly little political damage.

The mayor made no attempt to deflect blame, accepting "full and total responsibility." His forthrightness, plus the solid reputation he had built over several years of service to the city, apparently caused the citizens to view his actions with empathy. According to one journalist, even those persons displaced by the fire were "more stunned than angry . . . . Those who did have harsh words for the mayor blamed him more for waiting too long than for the disaster that left them homeless."[46] Fortunately, crises of potentially devastating proportions are not daily occurrences in city government; but they do happen, and they can have dramatic effects on the careers of the executives who attempt to contend with them.

Aside from the demands imposed by superiors and outside or uncontrollable fores are the self-selected assignments of the executive. Self-selected tasks may include those mundane activities that the executive believes "go with the territory" or major initiatives that mark a progressive administration or, in the case of the mayor, may represent major directional changes promised during an election campaign.

Mayors and city managers report spending about one-third of their workweek on tasks selected by citizens, council, or in the case of city managers, mayors (Table 4–3). A somewhat larger block of time, although less than one-half of their workweek, reportedly is directed toward self-selected tasks. Intergovernmental demands and emergencies reportedly consume almost one-third of the average mayor's workweek and about one-fourth of the average city manager's.

Focus of Work

More substantial divergence between mayors and city managers becomes evident in reported allocations of time among work foci categorized in a fashion different from the previously reported work demands. Asked to indicate the percentage of time devoted to city council relations, intergovernmental relations, public relations, policy development, and internal administrative activities, mayors and city managers diverged rather sharply in average allocation in two areas: city council relations and public relations (Table 4–4).

Both sets of respondents indicated that they devote approximately one-third of their time to internal administrative activities not included among the four other foci, about one-tenth of their time to

Table 4-3

PERCENTAGE OF MANAGERIAL WORKWEEK CLAIMED BY VARIOUS DEMANDS

Demands	Mayors (N=70)	City Managers (N=149)
Citizen-, Mayor-, or Council-Selected Tasks	31.6[a]	33.0
Intergovernmental Demands	20.8	14.3
Emergencies	10.4	10.1
Self-Selected Tasks	37.2	42.7
Total	100.0	100.1[b]

[a]Includes only citizen- and council-selected tasks in the case of mayors.
[b]Column does not add to 100.0 due to rounding.

intergovernmental relations, and about one-sixth to policy development including the development of proposals for future city policy. Insofar as the two remaining foci were concerned, mayors were found to emphasize public relations over city council relations, with city managers reporting an emphasis of just the reverse. City council relations—defined on the survey instrument as all contacts with the city council and mayor either individually or in formal meetings, time spent responding to special requests of council members, preparation of agendas, budget review sessions, and other related activities—claimed on average more than one-fourth of the city manager's time but less than one-sixth of the mayor's time. Public relations—defined to include meetings, speeches, ceremonies, listening to citizen complaints, and all other contacts with nongovernmental groups and individuals—reportedly consumed an average of one-fourth of the mayoral time but only about one-eighth of the time of the city managers.

The relative emphasis of city council relations by city managers and public relations by mayors reflects a clear recognition of the obligation of the former to the city council and the latter to the citizenry in general for the positions they hold. The lesser emphasis of public relations by the city manager further reflects the fact that in council-manager

Table 4-4

FOCUS OF MANAGERIAL WORK IN CITY GOVERNMENT, BY POSITIONS— PERCENTAGE OF TIME DEVOTED TO VARIOUS FOCI

Foci of Work	Mayors (N=72)	City Managers (N=150)
City Council Relations	15.4	26.6
Intergovernmental Relations	11.6	9.0
Public Relations	25.5	13.1
Policy Development	17.7	17.5
Internal Administration...	[30.0]	[33.9]
...as manager	17.1	20.3
...as mentor	7.1	8.2
...as specialist/technologist	5.7	5.4
Total[a]	100.1	100.1

[a]Columns do not add to 100.0 due to rounding.

government other officials—i.e., the mayor and city council members—are expected to carry much of the public relations load, if not dominate in that capacity. Several cases may help to illustrate these points.

L. P. Cookingham is known as the "dean of city managers" for his illustrious career in Kansas City and elsewhere as well as for his enduring legacy to his profession in the many prominent city managers who received their starts under his tutelage. Cookingham demonstrated adeptness again and again in dealings with politicians and difficult political problems, but he preached an administrative line. "I don't think good government necessarily means reforming anything. What you are doing is applying good business practices to the business of government in a professional, nonpolitical manner."[47]

Yet, those who watched Cookingham work or have studied his

record marvel at his ability to read the temperament of a city council and act accordingly, his composure under pressure, and his remarkable sense of timing. One such observer wrote:

> Cookingham was really several different kinds of city manager during his nineteen-year tenure in Kansas City, depending upon the nature of the elected leadership and the political climate. He instinctively knew when to be out front and when to retreat to the background, when to push and when to lie low, when the mayor and council were willing and/or able to exert leadership and when they wanted him to, or when he could safely fill the leadership vacuum they created. And, of course, he had the political and administrative skills to successfully carry it all off.[48]

Three former subordinates who went on to distinguished management careers provided the following comments:

> He was the consummate half-a-loaf guy. He would always go after the whole loaf, but he wouldn't hesitate to grab half a loaf or three-quarters of a loaf. I can remember those pre-council sessions where we'd get knocked down to half a loaf of something by some council member and he'd go along with it and then, after the last councilman had left and we'd taken our last drink, he'd say, 'All right, let's get back on this and we'll get the rest of it pretty quick. We'll do it this way, or that way.'
>
> He never fought and he never argued with the council. He'd be tenacious sometimes, but his demeanor always and in every way reflected his basic tenet that he was the council's employee. *They* were boss.
>
> His sense of timing was unerring. He knew the time to push and the time to back off, the time to switch, the time to do all the things you have to do . . . . So many people are willing to pile themselves up on the shoals of frustration, being right and righteous and traumatic about what they're in favor of. They never accomplish anything . . . Of all the people I know who practice this business, he had the pragmatic approach . . . . He wasn't holier-than-thou. But he had a sense of what was good for that town and, without embellishment and without emotion, he just kept right after what he thought needed to be done.[49]

A managerial orientation, whether that of Cookingham or some variation unique to a particular individual, is operationalized in the style and substance of an administration. Enveloping such variation, however, is a strong consensus on the special importance of internal administration and city council relations. City managers address these foci through a fragmented work schedule in which they find time for each. Witness, for example, the "typical day" of Richard Helwig, city manager of Dayton, Ohio:

> Helwig . . . is a 'morning person.' A typical day has him in the office between 7 and 7:30 a.m.
>
> He spends the morning going through mail and meeting with key division heads, community leaders, and the mayor . . . .
>
> At noon, it could be a business lunch with a developer or someone else interested in doing business with the city or simply a sandwich alone in his office.
>
> 'I often prefer a quiet lunch in the office, to get my mind off the pace of things,' Helwig said. 'I can read and sign documents then.'
>
> Afternoons are much the same. Thursday afternoons, however, are devoted to meetings of the policy review committee, a small group of key assistants who review with the city manager both long-term policy and upcoming issues . . . .
>
> Helwig . . . . tries to meet with each commissioner at least once a month to brief them on issues before the city and answer any questions they might have.
>
> If he's lucky, his day ends between 5 and 5:30 p.m. when he leaves for home . . . where he'll spend an hour jogging . . . . Then a quiet evening helping his two sons with homework or doing some office paperwork . . . .
>
> [H]is family understands the 10- to 14-hour days and a briefcase full of papers to work on over the weekend, Helwig said. 'This is not a 40-hour-a-week kind of job.'[50]

The decidedly greater orientation of mayors toward public relations is readily apparent in case after case. It is through the public relations focus that most mayors craft their image—for better or worse—and most are willing to devote substantial time to that endeavor.

One of the best at public relations is San Antonio's Cisneros. Although not the mayor of a city with the mayor-council or commission form of government, in many respects Cisneros has more in common with the mayors who are the subject of this study than with his counterparts in council-manager cities, given their largely ceremonial roles and normally more limited spheres of influence. In naming an "all-pro city management team," in fact, a panel of more than 100 judges selected Cisneros over a field of "strong" mayors.[51] His peers elected him to a term as president of the National League of Cities. For reasons such as these, his experience is instructive.

> In the course of a day, Cisneros meets with dozens of his constituents, usually in groups of two or three. They sit informally on his sofa and are permitted to share his vision of San Antonio's future, to suggest goals and agendas on how to achieve them. 'Goals,' 'agendas' and 'programs' are words the mayor uses constantly. Nearly always, lurking in the background, there's the press. Reporters know they'll get their stories and film footage, that somehow Cisneros will work a press briefing into his crowded schedule. Often there is a visiting dignitary to share the limelight: the Japanese ambassador or the chairman of a major corporation announcing plans to open a plant in San Antonio.[52]
>
> For Cisneros, the workday that begins early invariably lasts until late, frequently until midnight . . . . 'He seems to work best under exhausting circumstances,' says Shirl Thomas, the mayor's administrative assistant.
>
> . . .In Cisneros' workday, the schedule is a tyrant. His staff fields the hundreds of daily requests for his time, as well as hundreds of phone calls and letters. The difficulty of getting in to see Cisneros is legendary.
>
> 'My schedule is demanding, but I just have to live with it,' Cisneros says. 'It becomes a part of my life, like breathing.'
>
> 'If anything, I'd like from time to time to get off the track. I could enjoy going to Big Bend [National Park], time to climb a mountain or raft down the river. If I was not mayor, I could do that. But I really don't believe I can take the time away. I rarely get away from San Antonio more than three days at a time.'
>
> 'What I do is noticed. I can't drive my own car anymore. I can't just go out to the movies,' says Cisneros . . . . ' I can't imagine living my life more in a fishbowl than it is.'[53]

Atlanta's Young credits Martin Luther King, Jr., for Young's successes in influencing public opinion. "Instead of being thermometers, taking political temperatures," he says, "politicians should be thermostats—setting the political temperature."[54] Taking such an activist role through direct interaction with the public and the press is not easy for all mayors, as noted by Houston's Whitmire. But a mayor can scarcely afford to ignore public relations.

> It took me a long time to realize that my success depends on how well I communicate to the press, the public, not just on what I do. I now understand that public relations has to be the number one priority of this administration. It is crucial to getting anything done. For a long time, I was horrified and miserable by all the personal attention, the TV cameras glaring me in the face.[55]

Not all mayors have been successful in creating an image of compassion, refinement, and brilliance. Whether through public relations ineptness or careful design, their images, and hence their political fortunes, often have suffered despite enthusiastic backing from a core of staunch supporters. Rizzo of Philadelphia and Emory Folmar of Montgomery, Alabama, for example, have suffered generally harsh media judgments. Both men built reputations as law-and-order mayors. Folmar, a former Army paratrooper, kept a police scanner in his office and wore a .38 Special in his belt through much of his first two terms as mayor. Eventually, his administration was criticized for being "warlike," and local editorials claimed, "By now most Montgomerians suspect that Mayor Folmar would defend almost any official excess—especially against blacks, whose votes he never sought anyway."[56]

Mayors like Folmar and Rizzo tend to draw large media audiences. In Rizzo's case, it has been argued, what transpired at interviews and press conferences was more often "bear-baiting than journalism. Reporters ask questions to incite outrageous answers rather than to elicit information, and their efforts have been rewarded with such statements as 'I'm going to make Attila the Hun look like a faggot'."[57]

Public relations is more than cutting ribbons, kissing babies, and addressing the press. It is also dealing with the public, individually and in groups, responding to requests for services and favors—both reasonable and unreasonable, simple and difficult—even when the response must often be "no." Some mayors excel in this difficult arena, deftly turning potential losses into major wins. Witness Baltimore's Schaefer:

> When the civil rights leaders showed up in their dashikis to shake down the new regime, Schaefer let them stew in the big outer office on the stiff, fussy, gilded chairs . . . . Then Schaefer entered and parked his squat frame at the elaborate desk.
>
> 'What are you going to do?' they demanded.

'Wait a minute. What are *you* going to do?'

'What do you mean? *We're* not supposed to do it.'

Schaefer's [double] chins tucked, and his eyes started shining. 'You want a playground?'

'Our people are *entitled* to playgrounds.'

'You gonna maintain it?'

'*We* can't maintain it.'

'Then piss on it. We're not gonna build it.'

Pretty soon he started demanding that the neighborhood group buy the swings or the jungle gym. 'It'll cost you $1,000, ' he'd say. 'I don't care if you gotta sell cookies—just get it.' If there was no neighborhood group, they had to make one. Then hold the bake sales. Then buy the swings.

And pretty soon, in a couple of neighborhoods, then a half dozen, then a few more, people stopped him to show him their playgrounds. They showed him how they'd changed the city's plans to make it more like they wanted it. And they showed where they wanted to put a recreation center for the older kids. Could the city kick in part of the money?[58]

A greater time allocation to public relations distinguishes mayors from city managers, but that difference normally is not made up primarily by shorting the time mayors allot to internal administration. As a whole, mayors report devoting only a little less of their time to internal administration than do the city managers. Those tempted to cut back in that area are well advised to recall the experience of former counterparts whose perceived administrative shortcomings contributed to political defeats. Two notable examples are Mayor Michael A. Bilandic of Chicago, who could not recover from his city's inability to clear the streets of deep February snows, and Philadelphia's Rizzo, whose numerous excesses included appointing his wife's hairdresser to an administrative job and camouflaging a budget deficit by claiming as forthcoming revenue taxes from a bankrupt railroad.[59] A third, more recent example is Richard Hatcher, longtime mayor of Gary, Indiana, who was defeated in 1987 by an opponent who accused him of ignoring Gary's problems while pursuing a national agenda.[60]

Activities

Mintzberg identifies five major categories of executive activities:

desk work, telephone calls, scheduled meetings, unscheduled meetings, and tours.[61] His findings regarding the allocation of time to those categories by private sector executives provide a useful benchmark for subsequent time allocation studies, including this study of municipal executives (Table 4–5).

The average time allocations to desk work found in four separate studies reported in Table 4–5 differ very little. Mintzberg's executives and those of Lance Kurke and Howard Aldrich, all of whom were studied through direct observation techniques, devoted an average of 22% and 26%, respectively, to desk work.[62] Alan Lau, Arthur Newman, and Laurie Broedling's study of civilian executives in the U. S. Navy, conducted primarily by means of questionnaires, indicated an average time allocation of 24% for desk work.[63] Mayors and city managers reported an average time allocation of 26% to desk work.

At 26%, the local government executives' time allocation for desk work fits within the 22% to 26% range established by the other three studies. Similarly, local government executives' reported allocation of 14% of their time to unscheduled meetings fits within the 10% to 17% range for the other executive studies.

In contrast, local government executives report spending twice as much of their time on telephone calls as their counterparts in any of the previous studies, substantially more on tours, and substantially less on scheduled meetings. Mayors and managers report spending 16% of their time on telephone calls, 34% on scheduled meetings, and 10% on tours.

The managerial value of tours or inspections, popularized in recent years as "management by walking around" (MBWA),[64] accrues from the direct exposure and personal interaction that come with a "hands-on" approach—a value thought to be important both to the manager and to the subordinates. Mayors and city managers, as a whole, report spending less time on this activity (an average of only 10% of their time) than on any of the other four activities listed. Even at 10%, however, the time allocated to MBWA is substantially more than that allotted by private-sector executives.

Not all local government executives practice MBWA. B. Gale Wilson reportedly "has little direct contact with the city staff of 350 employees" in Fairfield, California.[65] Yet, his record of accomplishments and his tenure of more than 30 years as city manager of Fairfield underscore a successful managerial style. More common, however, are accounts of extensive "walking around" by successful municipal executives.

Table 4-5
PERCENTAGE OF EXECUTIVE TIME DEVOTED TO VARIOUS ACTIVITIES—COMPARISON WITH PREVIOUS MANAGERIAL TIME ALLOCATION STUDIES

Category	Mintzberg Composite[a]	Kurke & Aldrich Composite[b]	Lau et al U.S. Naval Executive Composite[c]	Ammons & Newell CEO Composite[d]	Hospital Administrator	School Supt.	Kurke & Aldrich[b] Plant Mgr.	Bank Pres.	Mayor	Ammons & Newell[d] City Mgr.
Desk Work	22%	26%	24%	26%	28%	22%	25%	31%	25%	27%
Telephone Calls	6%	8%	7%	16%	16%	3%	8%	8%	17%	15%
Scheduled Meetings	59%	50%	45%	34%	37%	69%	57%	32%	32%	34%
Unscheduled Meetings	10%	12%	17%	14%	18%	5%	5%	22%	14%	14%
Tours	3%	3%	7%	10%	1%	0%	5%	6%	11%	10%

[a] Mintzberg data are based on observation of five chief executives for one week each. Henry Mintzberg, *The Nature of Managerial Work* (Englewood Cliffs, N.J.: Prentice-Hall, 1980).
[b] Kurke and Aldrich data are based on observation of four managers for one week each. Lance B. Kurke and Howard E. Aldrich, "Mintzberg Was Right!: A Replication and Extension of 'The Nature of Managerial Work'," *Management Science*, 29 (August 1983), pp. 975-984.
[c] Lau et al data are based upon questionnaire responses from 210 civilian executives in the U.S. Navy. Alan W. Lau, Arthur R. Newman, and Laurie A. Broedling, "The Nature of Managerial Work in the Public Sector," *Public Administration Review*, 40 (September/October 1980), p. 519.
[d] Ammons and Newell data are based upon questionnaire responses; N=222 for CEO composite (mayors and city managers).

In Kansas City, Cookingham adopted the practice of taking an extra half hour at lunch to visit a city work crew on his way back to the office.[66] As Philadelphia's managing director, Goode even rode a garbage truck for a day.[67]

Many mayors and city managers make a practice of noting litter, potholes, burned out street lights, and other problems as they drive around their cities. Typically, those notes become memos to appropriate department heads upon their return to City Hall. Probably few, however, punctuate their messages—whether written or oral—in quite the same fashion as did Schaefer as mayor of Baltimore:

> Sometimes he'd decide the problem was [that his subordinates] just couldn't . . . *see*. He'd be riding around like he does on weekends, with his driver and a cop riding shotgun, and *he'd* see the potholes, and broken streetlights, caved-in trash cans, dirty parks, housing violations, abandoned cars, crooked traffic signs, dead trees, a missing bus stop, trash at the curb. 'What are the bastards doing with the money?' he'd mutter aloud in the Buick. Then he'd get out his pen and his Mayor's Action Memos and tear into the thing:
>
> *Get the g————m trash off East Lombard Street . . . .*
>
> *Broken pavement at 1700 Carey for TWO MONTHS . . . .*
>
> *Abandoned car at 2900 Remington. Why?*
>
> Then the memos would be on their desks Monday morning, and the trash, the pothole, the abandoned car had better be gone when he drove by again. How'd it get there in the first place?
>
> One time he popped them an Action Memo: 'There is an abandoned car . . . . but I'm not telling you where it is.' City crews ran around like hungry gerbils for a week. Must have towed five hundred cars.
>
> That was NOT . . . GOOD . . . ENOUGH: Schaefer called in his cabinet, the best municipal government in America. The mayor held two fingers up, and he poked them at his own glittery eyes.
>
> 'Do you know what these are? *Do* you? These are *eyes*.' The mayor was jabbing at his face now. They thought he might hurt himself.
>
> 'I GOT TWO. AND YOU GOT TWO.'
>
> Then he grabbed a cabinet member and started menacing him with the fingers in the eyes. The cabinet guy's head was burrowing between his shoulders.

'So how come my eyes can see and a smart young fella like you can't see a damn thing, huh? HOW COME?'[68]

Schaefer's style differed from that advocated by organizational humanists, but he, too, was recognized by his peers and his constituents as an effective municipal executive. He was reelected as Baltimore's mayor in 1983, with 94% of the vote.[69]

The difference in time allocation between local government executives and other public and private sector executives may be interpreted in at least two sharply differing ways—one flattering and the other not. The time allocation by local government executives appears to reflect a greater tendency than among their federal and private-sector counterparts to handle matters through informal contact—whether by necessity or preference. Telephone calls and tours or inspections of municipal activities conceivably afford the local government executive the means of dealing with problems immediately as the need arises without resorting to rounds of formal meetings. That is the flattering view. On the other hand, the distribution could reflect a "brush fire" environment and "fire-fighting" mentality of local government executives in contrast to their managerial counterparts who devote more of their time to the kind of scheduled meetings at which problems looming on the horizon may be identified and addressed on a more coordinated basis.

Control over Time

The multidimensional demands, foci, and activities that characterize executive work lead many observers to abandon the notion of the executive as the conductor of the orchestra, the master of events, the one in control of his time. Consider, for example, the separate conclusions of Sune Carlson, cited previously in the introductory chapter, and Peter Drucker:

> Before we made the study, I always thought of a chief executive as the conductor of an orchestra, standing aloof on his platform. Now I am in some respects inclined to see him as the puppet in the puppet show with hundreds of people pulling the strings and forcing him to act in one way or another.[70]

Any analysis of executive contributions comes up with an embarrassing richness of important tasks; any analysis of executives' time discloses an embarrassing scarcity of time available for work that really contributes. No matter how well an executive manages his time, the greater part of it will not be his own.[71]

A study examining perceptual differences between public- and private-sector managers found that governmental managers thought themselves to have less control than did their industrial counterparts over how they allocate their time.[72] Another study concluded that mayors often value loyalty over other qualifications in the selection of a staff primarily because the mayor, who is "reminded daily of the frustrations caused by not having complete control over situations that affect his agenda items," desires at least the stability and perhaps even security of an intensely loyal staff.[73]

Mayors and city managers, however, seem less beleaguered by the sense that they lack control than previous writings would indicate. As a group, mayors estimated 63% of their workweek to be under their control, with the remaining 37% controlled by others. City managers estimated that they control 59% of their workweek and that others control 41%. On average, both groups perceive well over one-half of their time to be under their own control. Still, more than one-third of the time of the average mayor and city manager is thought to be under the control of others.

Mintzberg contends that an executive's attitude toward obligations is an important factor in how that executive both perceives and exercises managerial control. All executives face a daily barrage of demands from their "bosses," from other forces beyond their absolute control, and even from subordinates. But they can influence those demands and they can make the most of resulting obligations, turning duties into opportunities. In the words of Mintzberg:

> The unsuccessful manager tends to blame failure on his obligations. If not for the crises, the callers, and the ceremonial duties, he would have done better. But, what is an obligation to one is an opportunity to another. In fact, every obligation presents the shrewd manager with a chance to accomplish his own purposes. A crisis may simply be solved, or its resulting chaos may present an opportunity to make some desirable changes. A ceremonial duty may be a waste of time, or it may be an opportunity to lobby for a cause. The need to meet someone in a figurehead capacity may present the chance to tap a new source of information. The obligation to be present at a briefing session may give the manager a chance to exert some leadership. In everything he does the manager has a chance to extract information;

every time he interacts with a subordinate he has a chance to influence him as his leader. Whether or not he turns obligation to advantage determines in large part whether or not he will succeed.[74]

Summary

Local government chief executives, like their counterparts in the private sector, work long hours. Anecdotal evidence suggests that eight-hour workdays are extremely rare.

City charters prescribe roles and duties of mayors and city managers, but those documents reveal less about the fundamental nature of the positions than does a more detailed examination of the work being performed by the men and women holding those posts. A national survey of mayors and city managers indicates that about one-third of their time is directed toward tasks prompted by citizens or city councils. Roughly 40% is spent on self-selected tasks, while about 10% goes to addressing emergencies. Mayors report spending about one-fifth of their time on intergovernmental demands, and city managers, only a little less. Examining the work of local government executives from a different perspective—work focus rather than sources of demand—reveals a markedly greater focus on city council relations by city managers and a greater mayoral focus on public relations.

Time allocations of local government executives to particular work activities are in some ways similar and in other respects dissimilar to those found for private-sector executives in previous studies. Time allocations for desk work and unscheduled meetings are comparable across sectors. For three other activities, however, differences are substantial. Mayors and city managers report spending considerably greater percentages of their time on telephone calls and tours or inspections than do their private sector counterparts and less on scheduled meetings.

Although local government executives perceive a substantial portion of their workweek to be under the control of others, as a group they still perceive about 60% to be under their own control. Such a split provides little support for the notion of the mayor or city manager as the conductor of the "municipal orchestra," but, more encouragingly, it contrasts rather sharply with the imagery of the executive as marionette.

Chapter Five

ANALYSIS OF TIME ALLOCATION PATTERNS

How does the amount of time consumed by one type of demand on a local government executive affect the amount of time devoted to addressing other demands? Does response to one demand necessarily reduce the time devoted to *all* others, or do some demands go hand-in-hand—high percentage allocations for one tending to accompany high percentage allocations for the other? Furthermore, does a local government executive experiencing greater-than-average demands of a particular type tend to have a different focus of work or engage in different work activities than do other executives? These and other relationships in the time allocations of mayors, city managers, mayoral assistants, and assistant city managers are examined in this chapter.

Correlation

Stated simply, a correlation is the relationship between two variables. For example, if those variables are age and height in a sample of elementary school children and we find that height tends to be greater for older children, then our two variables are correlated positively. If, on the other hand, one variable tends to decrease as the other increases, then we have a negative correlation.

Pearson's product-moment correlation produces a coefficient ranging from 1.0 to -1.0 to indicate the degree of positive or negative correlation existing between two sets of variables. A correlation coefficient of 0.0 indicates no correlation—i.e., fluctuations in one of the variables does not accompany fluctuations in the other in any patterned manner.

Responses of local government executives participating in the time allocation survey have been correlated to determine the degree to which variation in a particular demand, focus, or activity is accompanied by similar or opposing variation in a different demand, focus, or activity. In some cases, the level of correlation is modest—so modest, in fact, that the reader should be cautious about drawing any conclusions about the nature of the relationship between the two variables. After all, not all city executives responded to the survey, and those who did not participate might have swung a weak relationship the other way had they reported their experience. While researchers normally are confident in projecting some sample responses as representative of the population as a whole (i.e., municipal chief executives and their assistants, in this case), they usually refrain from doing so in close calls or where the relationship is especially weak. A particularly small, positive coefficient may, in fact, be a valid indicator of a weak, positive relationship between two variables. On the other hand, it may be misleading to an insufficiently cautious analyst. While the relationship may be modestly positive for the sample of respondents, it *could* be negative for the "universe" of all city executives if the input of nonrespondents could somehow be added to the calculation. In other words, it is possible that the apparent relationship is attributable to a mere chance occurrence owing to peculiarities of the sample—in this instance, those who chose to respond to the survey as opposed to those who did not. In other cases, however, the level of correlation is so remarkable that there is less than a 5% likelihood that it would occur by mere chance. By convention, such correlations are said to be statistically significant ($p<.05$), and we can be much more confident in asserting that the relationship exists for more than just the sample of respondents—that it exists for municipal chief executives and their assistants in cities with populations greater than 50,000, as a whole. The relationship between the variables involved in such cases often is noteworthy.

Demands

The clearest image of the local government executive presented by correlating the various demands on managerial time is that of an executive whose own time allocation preferences (i.e., self-selected tasks) are extremely vulnerable to the demands of "bosses" and intergovernmental requirements. Tasks imposed by citizens, mayors (for the other three categories of executives), and city councils are obvious "boss" demands. The correlation of the time allocations to those demands with the time allocations to self-selected tasks yields a statistically significant, negative coefficient ($r = -.493$), meaning that as one of the two goes up, there is a strong tendency for the other to go down. The negative correlation of time for self-selected tasks and time devoted to intergovernmental demands is only a little smaller ($r = -.319$). Citizen-, mayor-, or council-selected tasks, however, appear to limit most greatly executive pursuit of self-selected tasks, under the presumably safe assumption that greater demands from the former result in reduced time allocation for the latter, and not vice versa. (For the full correlation matrix, see Table A–4 in the appendix.)

In no cases were the correlations of intergovernmental demands, emergencies, and citizen-, mayor-, or council-selected tasks of statistical significance. As a whole, greater-than-average intergovernmental demands were not associated significantly with greater-than-average or less-than-average time allocations to emergencies or boss-selected tasks. Nor were emergencies found to influence or be influenced by time apportioned to boss-selected tasks.

Foci of Work

The work of municipal executives may be subdivided into at least five, fairly distinct areas for attention that we have labeled foci. Three of those five foci (internal administration, policy development, and intergovernmental relations) command similar amounts of time from mayors and city managers; however, the time allocation practices of mayors differ from those of city managers regarding the other two foci (city council relations and public relations). Both groups report devoting about one-third of their workweek to internal administration, about one-sixth to policy development, and about one-tenth to intergovernmental relations. They differ, however, in the amount of time devoted to city council relations and public relations, with city managers emphasizing the former and mayors emphasizing the latter. This allocation of time conforms to the perceptions of city managers and mayors regarding the relative importance of different roles, as reported in Chapter Three; specifically, city managers believe the policy role to be more important to job success than the political role, whereas mayors tend to have the opposite orientation.

Examining the relationships between these foci for mayors, city managers, and their assistants reveals, above all else, that internal administrative activities are correlated negatively with each of the other four foci. (For the full correlation matrix, see Table A–5 in the appendix.) That is, executives with greater-than-average time allocations for internal administrative activities tend to have less-than-average time allocations for city council relations (r = −.497), intergovernmental relations (r = −.424), public relations (r = −.485), and policy development (r = −.396), and vice versa. None of the relationships between other executive foci (e.g., policy development versus city council relations or public relations versus policy development) produces a correlation coefficient as great as 0.2, positive or negative.

Subgroup Relationships

Although a fairly clear pattern of relationships is apparent for city executives as a whole, an individual, position-by-position examination is especially important in the case of relationships among the various foci of municipal executive work. A few important departures from overall tendencies become evident upon investigation of responses by a particular position.

A generally strong pattern of statistically significant negative correlations between time devoted to internal administrative activities and time devoted to all four of the other foci prevails across all positions. Greater variation by position is apparent for some of the other relationships. For example, only mayors exhibit a statistically significant positive correlation (r = .243) between time devoted to city council relations and time devoted to intergovernmental relations. Presumably, mayors operating in the highly politicized environment of mayor-council government are either inclined to work with other politicians—their local counterparts *and* politicians at other levels or units of government—or they are inclined to eschew such dealings to the extent possible. Mayors, it would seem, are in a better position than are their counterparts to conform to such predilections. Survey responses of mayors tended to be associated in such a pattern: either substantial time allocation to both city council relations and intergovernmental relations, or minimal time allocation to both. Rarely was minimal allocation to one accompanied by substantial allocation to the other.

Politics-Administration Dichotomy: Dead or Alive?

The allocation of time by city managers to city council relations is associated negatively with time allocations for public relations (r = −.208) and policy development (r = −.280). One may speculate that this relationship reflects philosophical views of city managers as much as the limited availability of time; that is, managers who see themselves purely and simply as the hired hand of the city council may be more inclined to leave public relations and policy development to the council while investing greater portions of their time in dealing with that body, in direct contrast to the time allocation priorities of a more activist city manager.

As noted in Chapter Three, council-manager government developed as a reform measure, designed to eradicate corruption through a structure embodying the then-prevailing sentiment favoring a separation of administration from politics. Although modern scholars scoff at the practicality or desirability of a politics-administration dichotomy, the notion remains intact in most city charters that specify the council-manager form of government. The enumerated responsibilities of the city council and the city manager, respectively, are not regarded as quaint historical artifacts to be disregarded at will in favor of more modern scholarship. Concern over "turf" and the overstepping of proper bounds is evident in common public pronouncements by city council members and backstage grumbling by staff when one party feels that its prerogative has been preempted by the other. But dichotomy or not, the shrewd city manager is wise to avoid irritating, upstaging, or even remotely appearing to upstage a city council member.

Often the easiest way for a city manager to avoid interpersonal problems with city council members, which because of the superordinate-subordinate relationship involved automatically become serious professional problems for the manager, is to avoid overt incursions into whatever a particular council considers its domain and to maintain a low profile—always a low profile.

Several city managers offer their advice:

> Technical stuff doesn't do you in—loss of trust with the council does.
>
> The more the manager gets involved in policy, the more the manager becomes an advocate for specific groups and issues.
>
> That manager manages best who speaks not at all.
>
> To help assure an effective relationship with the governing body, don't play favorites, don't spring surprises, and don't be a self-promoter.[1]

Public administration scholars Wayne Anderson, Chester Newland, and Richard Stillman identify four "types" of city managers: the chief executive, the administrative innovator, the administrative caretaker, and the community leader.[2] Each is perceived to be an appropriate type, if matched with the right community. Only the community leader, however, is inclined to plunge headlong into "the fast-moving hardball of local political life."[3] Prevailing wisdom, drawn from extensive anecdotal evidence, suggests that such managers are rarely long-tenured officials.

More common in reports of highly regarded city managers are reputations for exceptional interpersonal skills, technical competence, quiet devotion to duty, respect for the role and egos of the city council, and composure under pressure. Acknowledgement of "good leadership from the city council"[4] is expected from the prototypal city manager, whether deserved or not, and generally so is a "modest public profile and willingness to remain in the background when the plaudits are handed out."[5]

Marvin Andrews, city manager of Phoenix, Arizona, was identified by a national panel of more than 100 judges as the country's top city manager in 1986.[6] Cited for innovative management, Andrews is admired for his style as well as for his accomplishments. "He's somewhat low key," says a Phoenix councilman, "but he is firm. You don't push him around. I give him high marks as an excellent, efficient city manager."[7] Adds a former mayor, "He's an extremely modest man, but an extremely remarkable man, so conscientious."[8]

Even persons outside the city of Phoenix note some of the same characteristics in Andrews. A New York-based investment banker remarks, "My assumption is that there must be extraordinary pressure, but he's calm about it. The other thing that makes him special is that he's not a political type."[9]

Assistants' Responses

The responses of assistant city managers exhibited no statistically significant relationships among the various foci other than those involving internal administrative activities as one of the variables. In contrast, the responses of mayoral assistants yielded statistically significant negative correlations between time allocated for policy development and that allocated to city council relations ($r = -.223$) and public relations ($r = -.221$). Those with more time allotted to policy analysis tended to devote less time than most of their counterparts to city council relations and public relations, and vice versa. Such a relationship suggests a degree of specialization among mayoral assistants greater than that present among assistant city managers. It is conceivable that many mayoral assistants are selected either for their policy development skills or for their personality, depending on the needs of a particular administration. The niche filled by such assistants may allow them, more than their managerial counterparts, to concentrate on applying their particular strengths. Even so, it should be recalled that the "management role" is reported to be the dominant role for both sets of assistants, including the mayoral assistants.

Internal Administration

Each of the respondents to the 1985 survey was asked to subdivide the time allocated to "internal administration" into a trio of roles identified by Philip Marvin: the managerial role, the mentor role, and the specialist/technologist role.[10] In conformance with Marvin's definitions, the managerial role was described on the survey instrument as identifying things to do, developing plans for doing those things, organizing resources, staffing, assigning authority for the exercise of initiative, fixing accountability for achievement, and reviewing operations. The mentor role was to include showing others how to do things, helping them solve problems, sharing experiences, and evaluating the performance of persons under the manager's tutelage. The specialist/technologist role was defined to include those instances in which the manager's own time was devoted to specific applications or technologies, with the executive actually performing operational tasks rather than managing the work of others.

All four groups of city executives report spending a little more than one-half of their internal administrative time on the managerial role, ranging from 50.1% for mayoral assistants to 59.8% for city managers. When adjusted to take into account the percentage of the workweek devoted to matters other than internal administrative duties, these managerial role percentages represent roughly one-fifth of the executives' workweek (see Table 4–4). For mayors and mayoral assistants the managerial role represents 17.1% and 19.7% of their workweeks, respectively, and for city managers and assistant city managers, the percentages are 20.3% and 22.8%, respectively.

The four groups are remarkably consistent in reporting an average of about one-fourth of their internal administrative time devoted to the mentor role. Greater variation is evident in time devoted to the specialist/technologist role, with assistants spending more of their time on that role than do chief executives. City managers devote the least time among the four groups to the specialist/technologist role (15.9% of internal administrative time or 5.4% of the workweek as a whole), but only slightly less than mayors. Assistant city managers spend the most (26.1% of internal administrative time or 11.6% of the workweek as a whole), but only slightly more than mayoral assistants.

Negative correlations exist between the percentages of internal administrative time devoted to the three respective roles by city executives as a whole, indicating that as one role is emphasized the other two tend to be deemphasized. City managers, mayoral assistants, and assistant city managers all conform to this pattern when examined as separate groups, while a modestly positive, though statistically insignificant, correlation (r = .126) exists between mayoral time allocations to the mentor and specialist/technologist roles.

Work Activities

As reported in Chapter Four, responding chief executives in city government—mayors and city managers, as a whole—indicate that scheduled meetings consume 34% of their workweek; desk work, 26%; telephone calls, 16%; unscheduled meetings, 14%; and tours, 10% (see Table 4–5). Although time devoted to any particular category of activity denies that time to another category, it nevertheless is conceivable that some activities could be positively correlated, indicating preferences or managerial styles in which executives adopt a mode of operation emphasizing a particular combination of activities and deemphasizing others. No such pattern, however, was detected.

Correlations between the reported time allocations for the various executive work activities are almost uniformly negative and statistically significant. (For the full correlation matrix, see Table A–6 in the appendix.) The single exception for municipal executives taken as a whole is the virtual absence of correlation between time reportedly spent in unscheduled meetings and that devoted to inspections of municipal activities.

Relatively little variation in the overall pattern exists for individual positions although some relationships that are statistically significant for the group as a whole fail to achieve statistical significance for particular executive positions (e.g., telephone calls and inspections for mayors, scheduled meetings and unscheduled meetings for mayoral assistants and assistant city managers). Of greatest apparent noteworthiness is the degree to which meetings (scheduled or unscheduled) and desk work, as well as scheduled meetings and all other activities, appear to be incompatible with each other. The most remarkable incompatibility exists between desk work and scheduled meetings (r = −.617).

Relationships across Work Dimensions

Although an executive's personal characteristics, skills, and preferences are likely to influence the mix of work activities undertaken, work demands and foci are also likely to affect the type of activities and amount of time devoted to those activities by a given executive. Pearson correlation coefficients were calculated for the relationships between percentages of time reportedly allocated to each work focus or claimed by each demand and the percentage time allocation reported for each of five standard work activities (Table A-7 in appendix).

Several relationships between foci or demands and specific work activities are noteworthy for their magnitude; others are noteworthy for the apparent absence of any relationship. For example, the degree to which municipal executives focus upon city council relations appears to have virtually no effect on time distribution among the various work activities. All of the correlation coefficients for city council relations and individual work activities are extremely small. Virtually the same can be said for intergovernmental relations, although two modest correlations—with desk work (r = −.090) and with telephone calls (r = .091)—are statistically significant at the .05 level.

A focus on public relations is associated with a relative emphasis on telephone usage (r = .303) and a general deemphasis of desk work (r = −.166). Policy development and a focus on internal administrative activities, on the other hand, are associated with a deemphasis on telephone usage (r = −.111 and −.185, respectively) and have opposite patterns in their relationships with desk work and scheduled meetings. A focus on policy development is negatively associated with desk work (r = −.150) and positively associated with scheduled meetings (r = .183), while internal administrative activities are positively associated by the respondents as whole with desk work (r = .219) and negatively associated with scheduled meetings (r = −.113).

Relative emphasis of any of three particular work foci (public relations, policy development and internal administration) tends to have a fairly distinct effect on work activities. Executives who emphasize public relations tend to use the telephone a great deal and leave desk work to others. Those who emphasize policy development rely on scheduled meetings to a greater degree than do their counterparts. Those who emphasize internal administration are more likely to devote greater percentages of their time to desk work. In contrast, relative emphasis of a fourth foci, intergovernmental relations, has a very modest influence on work activities and relative emphasis of a fifth, city council relations, has virtually no effect at all.

Influence of Demands on Work Activities

Three sources of demands on executive time—citizen-, mayor- or council-selected tasks; intergovernmental demands; and emergencies—are positively associated by the respondents as a whole with telephoning as a work activity. A negative correlation between self-selected tasks and time devoted to telephone calls (r = −.196) suggests that telephoning, however, is not a favorite activity.

Particularly unsavory, no doubt, are the telephone calls that rouse a mayor or city manager from a night's sleep. Although hardly typical of the majority of calls received by those executives, the call from a disgruntled citizen in the wee hours is not as uncommon as might be supposed. The story line, plot, and conclusion of such episodes, as told by various executives, often have a remarkably similar ring. For example, Mayor Jack Harvard of Plano, Texas, tells of the 5 a.m. call from a man complaining of the noise of a cement truck in the street in front of his house. Because the noise disturbed his sleep, the caller decided to disturb the sleep of the mayor, as well. Later that day Mayor Harvard contacted the cement company and received assurances that the truck would not be returning. But the episode did not end there. At 5 a.m. the next morning, the mayor gave the man a call.

> 'He said, no, the truck wasn't coming any more, but what was I doing calling him at 5 a.m?' Harvard said.'
>
> 'I told him I just wanted to make sure the truck wasn't

bothering him, and if he'd like, I'd call him back every morning, just to check in.'[11]

Virtually the same story was told by L. P. Cookingham of his days as city manager of Kansas City—only the problem was a car stuck in the mud and the calls, both of them, took place at about 4 a.m.[12]

Not surprisingly, respondents reporting relatively greater percentages of time devoted to emergencies reported relatively less time with desk work ($r = -.204$) and relatively more time on unscheduled meetings ($r = .201$). City manager-selected tasks and scheduled meetings were positively correlated ($r = .144$) in the responses of assistant city managers.

Subgroup Analysis

Position-by-position analysis of correlation coefficients reveals relatively few deviations of substantial magnitude from the overall findings. There are, however, some exceptions.

The degree to which mayors focus upon public relations appears to have a major influence on mayoral work activities. In addition to a tendency for public relations emphasis to be associated with reduced desk work ($r = -.318$) and increased telephone usage ($r = .204$) (associations generally characteristic of the other executive groups, as well), a public relations emphasis is also strongly correlated with scheduled meetings for mayors ($r = .314$).

City managers exhibit a stronger negative correlation between time spent on boss-selected tasks and time for inspections of municipal activities ($r = -.227$) than do city executives as a whole, and a stronger positive correlation between self-selected tasks and such inspections ($r = .200$). The evidence suggests rather clearly that demands from city councils, mayors, and citizens impose time constraints on the city managers' ability to tour city operations and interact with lower level subordinates, restricting that activity to a much greater extent than does any personal disinclination among most city mangers.

Interestingly, positive correlations between time spent on internal administrative activities and time for desk work are stronger for mayors ($r = .347$) and mayoral assistants ($r = .225$) than for city managers ($r = .083$) and assistant city managers ($r = .119$). Perhaps executives in reformed governments have a broader conception of what constitutes internal administrative activities.

Relationships with Other Variables

Examining the relationships between the various work dimensions and population, work hours of the executives, and the perceived extent to which the executives' workweek is controlled by the executive or by others reveals mostly modest, although sometimes statistically significant, correlations (Table A–8 in appendix). Municipal executives serving large cities are more likely to devote greater time to a policy development focus, more time to scheduled meetings, and less time to desk work than are their counterparts from smaller jurisdictions. They are, of course, more likely to have a larger staff of assistants to whom to assign some of the desk work.

Municipal executives placing greater time emphasis on intergovernmental relations, public relations, and policy development and deemphasizing internal administrative activities insofar as percentage time allocation is concerned are likely to work longer hours than their counterparts. Similarly, a greater relative emphasis on scheduled meetings and a relative deemphasis of desk work are associated with longer executive work hours, as are relative time emphases on addressing the demands of citizen-, mayor-, or council-selected tasks, intergovernmental demands, and emergencies.

Perceptions of control over the workweek appear to be virtually unrelated to differences in work focus and only mildly related to different activity mixes. Executives who devote more time to desk work tend to perceive greater personal control, while those engaged more frequently in telephone conversations perceive less, though neither correlation is especially strong ($r=.112$ and $r=-.102$, respectively).

Substantially stronger associations exist between reported time allocations for responding to various sources of demand and perceived control. Not surprisingly, greater personal control is associated with more time spent on self-selected tasks ($r=.363$) and associated inversely with citizen-, mayor-, or council-selected tasks ($r=-.144$) and emergencies ($r=-.234$).

Position-by-position examination of correlations reveals several significant population relationships that distinguish one position category from the others. For example, the population variable has a statistically significant, positive correlation with emphasis on city council relations by city managers ($r=.241$) and assistant city managers ($r=.242$), a pattern absent among mayors ($r=-.113$) and mayoral assistants ($r=-.084$). Population had a significant, negative correlation with percentage of time devoted to internal administrative activities for mayors (r = −.271) and city managers (r = −.267), but not for mayoral assistants or assistant city managers. Population had a greater, statistically significant effect on mayoral assistants with regard to their policy development focus (r = .214) and for assistant city managers regarding public relations focus (r = −.155), telephone calls (r = −.154), unscheduled meetings (r = .184), and sources of demands—especially, emergencies (r = .285) and citizen-, mayor-, or council-selected tasks (r = .176)—than it did on their counterparts.

Responses of city managers indicate a significant, negative correlation between the percent of time consumed by citizen-, mayor-, or council-selected tasks and the perception that managers control their own workweek (r = −.302). Similar relationships were found for assistant city managers and mayoral assistants, but not for mayors (r = −.026) despite a strong negative correlation between time spent on citizen- or council-selected tasks and the amount devoted to self-selected tasks (r = −.725).

Summary

Analysis of reported time allocations of city executives reveals a cadre of officials whose efforts to be responsive to the city council and citizens sharply restrict their ability to pursue an agenda of their own making. Although, as reported in Chapter Four, mayors and city managers perceive the majority of their workweek to be under their own control (63% according to mayors and 59% estimated by city managers) rather than under the control of others, the responses of city managers indicate a significant, negative correlation between the percent of time consumed by citizen-, mayor-, or council-selected tasks and the perception that managers control their own workweek (r = −.302). Despite the fact that the responses of mayors also exhibit a strong, negative correlation between time devoted to citizen- or council-selected tasks and time devoted to self-selected tasks (r = −.725), practically no statistical association was detected between citizen- or council-selected tasks and perception of mayoral control of their workweek (r = −.026). Such findings easily lead to speculation about the extent to which mayors participate in formulating even those citizen- or council-selected tasks, relative to city managers, and the degree to which city managers pursue an agenda influenced in part by professional norms and, perhaps, feel a greater sense of frustration when delays or detours occur.

Internal administrative activities consume about one-third of the time of municipal executives and compete with all other foci for the attention of those executives. Additional time for internal administration tends to be drawn not simply from one other work focus, but from all other work foci.

A few distinctive patterns were detected in the work activities of executives pursuing particular foci. Those emphasizing public relations to a greater degree than their counterparts tended to devote more time to the telephone and less to desk work. Those emphasizing either policy development or internal administration, on the other hand, tended to minimize telephone use. Furthermore, policy development was positively associated with scheduled meetings and negatively associated with desk work. In contrast, an emphasis on internal administration was positively correlated with desk work and negatively correlated with scheduled meetings. Executives responding to greater-than-average demands from council and citizens, intergovernmental demands, or emergencies tend to spend more time on the telephone than do those freer to pursue self-selected tasks.

Mayors emphasizing public relations tend to devote more time to scheduled meetings and telephone calls, and less to desk work. City managers with less time consumed by boss-selected tasks and more time for self-selected tasks tend to spend more time interacting with city work crews and inspecting city projects.

Greater city population tends to be linked to executive emphasis of a policy development focus, more time devoted to scheduled meetings, and less to desk work. Mayors and city managers serving larger cities tend to devote less time to internal administrative activities.

Long working hours are associated with an emphasis on intergovernmental relations, public relations, policy development, scheduled meetings, intergovernmental demands, emergencies, and citizen- or council-selected demands. Shorter working hours tend to be reported by executives who emphasize desk work and internal administrative activities.

Chapter Six

EXPLAINING VARIATIONS IN THE WORK OF LOCAL GOVERNMENT EXECUTIVES

Henry Mintzberg has proposed a "contingency theory" for explaining variations in the content and characteristics of managerial work. Based upon his systematic observation of five executives, he concludes that such variations may be explained by four sets of variables:

> . . . environmental variables, including characteristics of the milieu, the industry, and the organization; job variables, including the level in the organization and the function supervised; person variables, including the personality and style of the incumbent; and situational variables, including a host of time-related factors.[1]

This judgment, as plausible for the public-sector executive as for those in the private sector, is the first of 22 enumerated propositions about variations in managerial work suggested by Mintzberg, the first providing a framework for most of the subsequent 21. Five propositions from Mintzberg's list can be examined in some detail for their validity relative to municipal executives from data compiled in this study. Those five propositions are as follows:

1. The level of the job and the function supervised appear to account for more of the variation in managers' work than any other variables.

2. Top managers of public organizations and institutions spend more time in formal activity (such as scheduled, clocked meetings) and more time meeting directors and outside groups than do managers of private organizations.

3. The larger the overall organization, the more time the top manager spends in formal communication (memos, scheduled meetings), . . . the greater his involvement with external work (ceremony, external

board work), the less his involvement with internal operations, and the less time he spends substituting for subordinates.

4. Senior managers work longer hours than others, both on the job and in their off-hours.

5. In some organizations top managers informally create executive teams of two (dyads) or three (triads) that share responsibility for the performance of the . . . roles of a single managerial job . . . . Most common is the dyad in which the chief executive concentrates on the external roles (figurehead, liaison, spokesman, negotiator), leaving much of the responsibility for the internal roles (leader, disseminator, resource allocator, disturbance handler) to his second in command.[2]

Each of these five explanations offered by Mintzberg for variation in managerial work will be examined in light of the survey data from municipal executives. Alternate explanations for variations in the nature of executive work will also be considered.

Level of the Job

According to Mintzberg, "the level of the job and the function supervised appear to account for more of the variation in managers' work than any other variables."[3] In making this statement, Mintzberg places job level and function, which he termed "job variables," ahead of the other three sets of variables in his contingency theory for explaining variations in the nature of managerial work. Relegated to secondary status are environmental variables, person variables, and situational variables. This ordering of variables by Mintzberg reflects a somewhat unorthodox use of contingency terminology if one considers the preeminence accorded situational variables in the literature of contingency theory reviewed in Chapter Two. Some other contingency theorists, however, do include job and situational variables together.

The primacy Mintzberg grants to job variables is plausible but difficult to support on the strength of data obtained from municipal executives. For that matter, his statement would appear equally difficult to substantiate on the basis of a sample of only five executives, as Mintzberg attempted to do in his own study. The relative importance of job variables in comparison to situational variables, the environment, and the executive's personality and style must, from our perspective, remain an open question, although we are inclined to suspect that Mintzberg is correct. The importance of job level, independent of other variables, in explaining variation in the work of municipal executives may be demonstrated. We simply cannot rank its importance relative to the other three.

The most evident pattern of variation in demands imposed on municipal chief executives and their assistants is the substantially greater percentage of time directed toward self-selected tasks by the chief executives than by their subordinates (Table 6–1). Mayors report an average of 37% of their time devoted to self-selected tasks, compared to 29% for their assistants. City managers report an average of 43% of their time spent on self-selected tasks in contrast to 27% for assistant city managers.

Many variations exist in the foci of work of municipal executives, but a rather clear pattern suggests greater emphasis on internal administration by seconds-in-command. Mayors and city managers report spending an average of 30% and 34% of their time, respectively, on internal administration compared to 39% and 45% for mayoral assistants and assistant city managers, respectively. Furthermore, the assistants are likely to spend more time in the specialist/technologist role, performing technical work themselves, than are the chief executives.

Patterns of variation in work activities are generally less marked. Reported time allocation averages differ rather consistently but by only a few percentage points.

As noted above, mayors and city managers report greater time allocations to self-selected tasks than do their assistants. Not surprisingly then, chief executives also tend to perceive greater control over their own time than do their assistants. A particular task does not have to have been chosen personally in order for the executive to maintain a sense of control. However, there is little doubt that the amount of time spent on self-selected tasks influences the perception of executives regarding the percentage of their workweek that they believe to have under their own control (correlations between self-selected tasks and perceived control range from .221 for mayors to .421 for mayoral assistants). Mayors and city managers report an average of 63% and 59% of their workweek under their own control, respectively, rather than under the control of others, compared to 59% and 55% for mayoral assistants and assistant city managers, respectively.

In apparent contradiction to his proposition regarding the primacy of job variables—including job level—in accounting for variation in a manager's work, Mintzberg expresses a "personal belief that managerial jobs are not inherently constrained or inherently open-ended simply because they are at a particular organizational level." He contends, "all managerial jobs are constraining; only the strong-willed managers control their jobs, whether they be chief executives or

Table 6-1

TIME ALLOCATIONS IN EXECUTIVE WORK: APPORTIONED BY DEMANDS, FOCI, AND ACTIVITIES

	Mayors	Mayoral Assistants	City Managers	Assistant City Managers
DEMANDS				
● Citizen-, Mayor-, or Council- Selected Tasks	31.6%[a]	41.3%	33.0%	19.0%
● Intergovernmental Demands	20.8%	18.2%	14.3%	9.6%
● Emergencies	10.4%	12.0%	10.1%	9.7%
● City Manager-Selected Tasks	NA	NA	NA	34.7%
● Self-Selected Tasks	37.2%	28.7%	42.7%	26.9%
Total[b]	100.0%	100.2%	100.1%	99.9%
N	70	100	149	199
FOCI				
● City Council Relations	15.4%	17.4%	26.6%	19.0%
● Intergovernmental Relations	11.6%	10.6%	9.0%	7.5%
● Public Relations	25.5%	15.6%	13.1%	13.5%
● Policy Development	17.7%	17.1%	17.5%	15.4%
● Internal Administration...	[30.0%]	[39.3%]	[33.9%]	[44.5%]
...as manager	17.1%	19.7%	20.3%	22.8%
...as mentor	7.1%	10.3%	8.2%	10.0%
...as specialist/technologist	5.7%	9.3%	5.4%	11.6%
Total[b]	100.1%	100.0%	100.1%	99.8%
N	72	100	150	200
ACTIVITIES				
● Desk Work	25.2%	27.7%	26.8%	32.8%
● Telephone Calls	17.4%	19.8%	15.2%	16.2%
● Scheduled Meetings	32.3%	28.5%	34.1%	28.3%
● Unscheduled Meetings	14.3%	15.5%	13.9%	13.9%
● Inspection of Municipal Activities	10.8%	8.5%	10.0%	8.9%
Total[b]	100.0%	100.0%	100.0%	100.1%
N	71	100	151	199

[a] Includes only citizen- and council-selected tasks in the case of mayors.
[b] Some columns do not add to 100.0% due to rounding.

foremen."[4] Mintzberg does, however, concede the possibility of some exceptions and notes that an executive possesses "two important degrees of freedom—the latitude to develop certain long-term commitments (for example, to establish information channels or initiate projects), and the right to turn obligations to his own advantage."[5] The patterned responses of municipal executives, however, suggest the existence of real distinctions between the work of chief executives and their assistants—something much more fundamental than "strong-willed" determination to control their jobs.

Public versus Private

A second proposition advanced by Mintzberg is that "top managers of public organizations and institutions spend more time in formal activity (such as scheduled, clocked meetings) and more time meeting directors and outside groups than do managers of private organizations."[6]

The five categories of work activity identified by Mintzberg and adopted for this study (i.e., desk work, telephone calls, scheduled meetings, unscheduled meetings, and tours) address the dimensions of this proposition only in a general sense. While his category "scheduled meetings" is clearly identified as a "formal activity" in the proposition, the proposition's second dimension—"meeting directors and outside groups"—is less easily matched. Such meetings could be encompassed in part in "telephone calls" and "unscheduled meetings," but those activities may include many other things as well. On the other hand, two of Mintzberg's work activities, "desk work" and "tours," may be juxtaposed against "formal activity" because they seem neither to be a part of that category nor a factor in meeting directors and outside groups. To operationalize the proposition, it seems reasonable to expect the municipal executives to spend more time in scheduled meetings and less time on the informal activities of desk work and tours than do their private sector counterparts if Mintzberg's premise is correct.

Comparison of the responses of mayors and city managers with the evidence compiled in three studies focusing primarily upon private-sector executives reveals little support for this proposition (Table 6–2). Because each of the private-sector studies focuses upon executives in organizations of a particular size, such comparison requires that the responses of city executives be grouped accordingly. Cities with populations of fewer than 50,000 were excluded from the survey, so "small cities" are those with populations of at least 50,000 but fewer than 75,000. "Intermediate cities" have populations of 75,000 to 100,000 people and "large cities" are defined as having more than 100,000 people. The composite scores reported for municipal executives consist of the mean responses of mayors and city managers serving cities in a specified population range. The responses of mayoral assistants and assistant city managers, although collected in the survey, were excluded from the tabulations in Table 6–2.

Municipal executives in cities of more than 50,000 but fewer than 75,000 people do report spending a greater percentage of their time in scheduled meetings than was found by Irving Choran in an observation of three presidents of small companies, but mayors and city managers in medium and large cities report lower time allocations than were found for executives in medium and large organizations by Lance Kurke and Howard Aldrich and Mintzberg, respectively.[7] Municipal executives report only slightly lower time allocations for desk work in the small organization comparison and virtually identical allocations to managers in intermediate and large organizations. Contrary to expectations, municipal executives report spending virtually as much time on tours as was observed for their private-sector counterparts in small organizations and substantially greater percentages of time than their private-sector counterparts in intermediate and large organizations.

Organization Size

Another of Mintzberg's propositions suggests that organization size is likely to influence the activities and focus of managerial work.

> The larger the overall organization, the more time the top manager spends in formal communication (memos, scheduled meetings), . . . the greater his involvement with external work (ceremony, external board work), the less his involvement with internal operations, and the less time he spends substituting for subordinates.[8]

The evidence displayed in Table 6–2 provides modest support for at least part of this proposition via the separate studies of Choran, Kurke and Aldrich, and Mintzberg.[9] The findings of the study of municipal executives, however, present a different picture in some instances.

Some of the relationships suggested by the findings of Choran, Kurke and Aldrich, and Mintzberg are supported rather clearly by the responses of municipal executives. The pattern of the earlier studies indicates a decline in time allocation to desk work from about one-third of the managers' time in small organizations to less than one-fourth in large organizations. The composite time allocation for desk work by municipal executives in small cities is 29%; in intermediate cities, 25%; and in large cities, 23%.

Table 6-2

PERCENTAGE OF EXECUTIVE TIME DEVOTED TO VARIOUS ACTIVITIES, BY ORGANIZATION SIZE—COMPARISON WITH PREVIOUS MANAGERIAL TIME ALLOCATION STUDIES

	Small Organizations				Intermediate Organizations					Large Organizations			
Category	Choran Composite[a]	Ammons & Newell[b] Composite	Mayors	City Mgrs.	Kurke & Aldrich Composite[c]	Ammons & Newell[b] Composite	Mayors	City Mgrs.	Mintzberg Composite[d]	Ammons & Newell[b] Composite	Mayors	City Mgrs.
Desk Work	35%	29%	30%	29%	26%	25%	24%	26%	22%	23%	21%	25%
Telephone Calls	17%	16%	16%	15%	8%	17%	20%	16%	6%	16%	17%	15%
Scheduled Meetings	21%	30%	26%	32%	50%	34%	35%	34%	59%	37%	38%	36%
Unscheduled Meetings	15%	14%	15%	14%	12%	15%	13%	15%	10%	14%	14%	13%
Tours	12%	11%	12%	10%	3%	9%	9%	9%	3%	11%	10%	11%

[a]Choran data are based on observation of three company presidents for two days each. Irving Choran, "The Manager of a Small Company," MBA thesis, McGill University, 1969; cited in Henry Mintzberg, *The Nature of Managerial Work* (Englewood Cliffs, N.J.: Prentice-Hall, 1980) and Lance B. Kurke and Howard E. Aldrich, "Mintzberg was Right!" *Management Science*, 29 (August 1983), pp. 975-984.
[b]Ammons and Newell data are based on questionnaire responses from 222 mayors and city managers. "Small organizations" are those serving populations of fewer than 75,000; "intermediate organizations" serve cities of 75,000-100,000 people; and "large organizations" serve cities of more than 100,000 people.
[c]Kurke and Aldrich data are based on observation of four managers for one week each. Kurke and Aldrich, "Mintzberg was Right!"
[d]Mintzberg data are based on observation of five chief executives for one week each. Mintzberg, *The Nature of Managerial Work*.

The time allocation pattern for municipal executives' involvement in scheduled meetings follows the general pattern evident in the previous studies, but to a much less dramatic degree. While the previous studies found time allocations for scheduled meetings growing from about one-fifth of the executives' time in small organizations to more than one-half in large organizations, the composite range for municipal executives runs from 30% of the executives' time in small cities to only 37% in large cities. Still, the general pattern is in conformance with that suggested by the earlier studies. Mayors and city managers in larger cities tend to spend a greater portion of their workweek in scheduled meetings than do their counterparts in smaller cities.

The time allocation patterns for the other three executive work activities are more ambiguous—at least for municipal executives. The findings of previous studies suggested a smaller allocation of time to telephone calls, unscheduled meetings, and tours by executives in large organizations compared to their counterparts in intermediate and small organizations. Among municipal executives, however, no clear pattern of time allocation to these executive work activities emerges. The composite time allocation for each of these three executive work activities varies by no more than two percentage points among the three size categories (i.e., 16% to 17% for telephone calls, 14% to 15% for unscheduled meetings, and 9% to 11% for tours). Organization size apparently makes little difference in municipal executive time allocation to telephone calls, unscheduled meetings, and inspections of municipal activities.

If it appears that organization size is relevant to time allocation for only some of the work activities of municipal executives, the same may be said for the relationship between city size and the focus of executive work in city government. Considerable fluctuation from one population category to the next is evident in the average time devoted to several of the foci (for details, see Table A–9 in appendix); e.g., city managers in the smallest population group report devoting 25.5% of their time to city council relations, compared to 28.1% in the intermediate category and 27.0% reported by city managers serving the largest cities. The pattern moving from the small to the intermediate population category begins upward, but fails to maintain that direction as the largest jurisdictions are taken into consideration. In fact, consistent upward or downward time allocation patterns for the various foci are the exception.

Mayors in smaller cities tend to allocate greater percentages of their time to city council relations and slightly smaller percentages to public relations than do their counterparts in larger cities. Mayoral assistants in larger cities tend to allocate more of their time to policy development and more of their time in internal administration to the role of manager and less to the role of specialist/technologist than do mayoral assistants in intermediate and small cities.

Assistant city managers serving large cities are likely to allocate less of their time to public relations and less of their time in internal administration to the role of specialist/technologist than do assistant city managers in smaller jurisdictions. Assistant city managers in large cities are likely to allocate more of their internal administration time to the role of manager than are their smaller city counterparts. No clear pattern of time allocation to a given work focus with consistently greater or lesser allocations according to city size is evident for city managers.

Managerial Level

Yet another proposition by Mintzberg contends that executives devote more time to their work than do other employees. "Senior managers work longer hours than others, both on the job and in their off-hours."[10]

A thorough examination of working hours for the full range of municipal occupations is not possible from the data collected. No information was obtained regarding the working hours of department heads, middle managers, supervisors, and lower-level employees in city government. However, the contention that executive-level employees devote more time to the job than others appears as plausible for municipal government as for private industry.

The typical workweek in city government conforms to the nation's 40-hour week standard. Some employees deviate from that norm, working fewer hours if the nature of their skill and a modest or fluctuating demand for their service permit it (e.g., some lifeguards and craft instructors) or more hours than the norm if sufficient demand exists and overtime expenses are less costly than hiring an additional employee. However, it is safe to assume that most lower-level employees and most supervisors adhere to the 40-hour week standard.

The information collected from municipal executives clearly demonstrates that top managers devote considerably more than 40 hours per week to their jobs. The mean reported workweek for the 514 executives responding to that question is 56.8 hours. The 70 responding mayors reported an average of 66.4 hours per week.[11] An average of 59 hours per week was reported by the 98 responding mayoral assistants.

Workweeks somewhat shorter than those reported for mayors and mayoral assistants in mayor-council cities but still well in excess of the standard 40-hour week were reported by executives in council-manager cities. The 149 responding city managers reported an average workweek of 56.5 hours. An average workweek of 52.7 hours was reported by the 197 responding assistant city managers.

Not only do municipal executives report working hours well in excess of the standard assumed for most other categories of employees, but they also adhere to the Mintzberg proposition among their own ranks. Chief executives report longer working hours than do their assistants.

Managerial Dyads

A final proposition offered by Mintzberg of relevance to this study of municipal executives and testable through its data suggests the existence of executive teams with a patterned, complementary allocation of roles.

> In some organizations top managers informally create executive teams of two (dyads) or three (triads) that share responsibility for the performance of the . . . roles of a single managerial job . . . . Most common is the dyad in which the chief executive concentrates on the external roles (figurehead, liaison, spokesman, negotiator), leaving much of the responsibility for the internal roles (leader, disseminator, resource allocator, disturbance handler) to his second in command.[12]

The applicability of the managerial dyad concept to municipal government could well focus upon the relationship between the mayor and city manager in council-manager cities.[13] The focus in this study, however, is upon the relationship between the chief executive and the primary assistant—the mayor-mayoral assistant and city manager-assistant city manager relationships.

Mintzberg describes executive arrangements featuring an "inside man" and an "outside man" in which the former is typically the organization's second-in-command and the latter is the chief executive. He suggests that such relationships are found in many government organizations.[14]

Is such a management dyad common in city government? Certainly, such an arrangement would seem logical. It makes sense to divide duties and specialize to a degree, rather than "double-teaming" projects. A division of duties allowing the chief executive to concentrate on relationships beyond the administrative machinery and the assistant to concentrate on internal administration seems reasonable. An arrangement of that sort is claimed in many cities, the comments of city manager Donald A. Blubaugh of Hayward, California, being typical of those who prefer such a division of duties:

> In my own case, because I have available only 20 percent of my time to devote to internal operations of the city government, such as personnel, day-by-day budget decisions, and the like, I have turned over responsibility for these tasks to my assistant city manager. The assistant's primary function is to see that the complex organization is running smoothly and providing the services decided on by the policymakers.
>
> . . . [A] manager today with traditional values may find himself or herself frustrated. Good professional staff work no longer 'cuts it'. I suspect that even being labeled an efficient, professional person will not work to one's best advantage in dealing with the myriad of comments about government being unresponsive, too businesslike, and uncaring of the people it serves.[15]

City governments often purport to have such an external-internal operations arrangement, but does the empirical evidence confirm the widespread existence of managerial dyads in city government?

Some of the recent management literature on local government leads to the assumption that management dyads should be readily apparent. One recent ICMA publication reminded city managers that they cannot simply delegate community relations to a subordinate in hopes of removing their responsibility for setting the community relations tone of the organization; nor can they absolve themselves of "taking primary responsibility for working with the governing body."[16] Their role in those arenas is presumably nontransferable, even if managers choose, on the advice of ICMA, to allow subordinates to assume major roles in other activities. The same publication quoted a city manager as saying,

> The most effective managers over the long haul are the ones who surround themselves with talented people and know how to get the best performance out of them. Managers fail when they feel they have to be front and center at all times—when they take a 'follow me over the top' approach. It is the manager's job to provide an organizational atmosphere or ambience where talented people can excel.[17]

The prescription, then, is not for the manager to attempt to do everything personally. Major roles in various administrative functions can and should be delegated. However, the effective manager recognizes that, while assistants and others have important parts to play in community and council relations, the primary role in those functions cannot be delegated.

ICMA's Committee on Future Horizons has predicted an acceleration of the projected trend toward inside-outside specialization:

> A new profession within the profession—that of internal manager—will emerge in some places.
>
> The manager as broker and negotiator, or unobtrusive leader, will dominate the time and resources of the top professional in the future. The more traditional internal management functions—that often require entirely different skills, knowledge, and experience—will fall to a new group of specialists.
>
> And the requirements of the two functions will diverge so much over the next two decades that it is expected that more people will specialize in internal management. Already this specialization is common within single jurisdictions, where an assistant manager or several assistants serve under a number of successive managers. In the future, this will be even more common, and there will be more interjurisdictional mobility for internal managers.[18]

Mixed Evidence on Dyads

Yet, the empirical evidence on the existence of managerial dyads in city government is mixed. Grouped data provide general support. As a group, city managers allocate more of their time to city council relations (26.6%) and scheduled meetings (34.1%) and less to internal administration (33.9%) and desk work (26.8%) than do assistant city managers (19%, 28.3%, 44.5%, and 32.8%, respectively) (see Table 6–1). Although mayors as a group report spending slightly less of their time on city council relations than do mayoral assistants, the expected dyadic pattern otherwise prevails, although modestly in most cases. Mayors spend an average of 32.3% of their time on scheduled meetings compared to 28.5% for mayoral assistants, 30% on internal administration compared to 39.3% by mayoral assistants, and 25.2% on desk work compared to 27.7% by mayoral assistants.

Like private-sector executives, chief executives in city government are likely to differ substantially from their assistants in the way they allocate their time among various roles. In a survey in which 1,369 private-sector managers were asked to indicate their allocation of time to three roles identified by Philip Marvin, top-level executives reported devoting more time to the managerial role, less time to the specialist/technologist role, and nearly the same as their managerial subordinates to the mentor role (see Table 6–3).[19] That pattern prevails for municipal executives, as well.

Despite the generally supportive evidence from grouped data, a statistical analysis that could provide the most compelling evidence of a managerial dyad in city government falls short of such confirmation. By matching responding chief executives with responding assistants from the same cities it is possible to examine the degree to which time allocations for particular activities or foci vary in a positive or negative way. Strong, positive correlations for activities and foci would indicate similar emphases and deemphases, perhaps even hinting at double-teaming. Such correlations would indicate that chief executives who allocate more time than their counterparts to a particular function tend to have assistants who also allocate more time than their counterparts to that function. Strong negative correlations, on the other hand, would indicate the existence of Mintzberg's dyads. Executives with greater allocations of time to a particular function would tend to have assistants with lower allocations than the norm to that function.

Data from the 183 cities from which both the chief executive and assistant responded provides scant evidence to confirm the existence of municipal managerial dyads (for details, see Table A–10 in appendix). Moderately strong positive correlations were found for time allocations to city council relations and scheduled meetings, indicating that chief executives and assistants in the same city tend to vary together in their relative emphasis or deemphasis of those functions—e.g., if the city manager devotes a relatively great deal of time to city council relations, so does the assistant. This pattern, of course, is contrary to the notion of managerial dyads. The overriding message of an examination of correlations, however, is that there is very little systematic variation— very little correlation between the emphases of the municipal chief executives and their assistants when examined on a paired basis over many cities.

Dyads? Assessing the Mixed Evidence

At least two explanations are possible. First, perhaps relatively few truly dyadic relationships exist in municipal management. John Kotter

Table 6-3
PERCENTAGE OF INTERNAL ADMINISTRATIVE TIME DEVOTED TO MANAGERIAL, MENTOR, AND SPECIALIST/TECHNOLOGIST ROLES: COMPARISON WITH PREVIOUS RESEARCH

	Marvin Survey[a]					Ammons and Newell[b]				
	Com-posite	Presidents	Vice Presidents	Managers	Super-visors	Com-posite	Mayors	Mayoral Assistants	City Managers	Assistant City Mgrs.
Managerial Role	47	60	49	44	39	54.3	57.1	50.1	59.8	51.3
Mentor Role	16	17	14	16	15	23.9	23.7	26.3	24.3	22.6
Specialist/Technologist Role	31	19	28	34	40	21.7	19.1	23.6	15.9	26.1
Other[c]	6	4	9	6	6	NA[c]	NA[c]	NA[c]	NA[c]	NA[c]

[a] Marvin data are based on survey responses from 1,369 private sector managers. Philip R. Marvin, *Executive Time Management* (New York: AMACOM, 1980).
[b] Ammons and Newell data are based on survey responses from 521 municipal executives.
[c] Marvin's respondents were asked to divide all work activities among the three roles, with provision of an "other" category for exceptions. Ammons and Newell's respondents were asked only to divide their "internal administrative activities" among the three roles, with no provision of an "other" category.

and Paul Lawrence note that the great uncertainty and little control over the situation in the life of a mayor create a powerful incentive "to select a staff based primarily on loyalty, not skills, thereby removing at least one source of uncertainty."[20] An executive who succumbs to this temptation and chooses loyalty over extraordinary competence is likely, subsequently, to feel great pressure to double-team any particularly important projects nominally assigned to an assistant.

On the other hand, it is possible that too much could be made of the absence of strong negative correlations for time allocations to particular functions. The evidence of major overall variations in time allocation by differing executive positions is perhaps much more telling than the absence of systematic variation by managerial tandems. Strong negative correlations would have provided seemingly irrefutable evidence of managerial dyads. It may be unreasonable, however, to leap to the conclusion that a city manager and assistant city manager, both of whom devote more time to city council relations than most of their counterparts, are working on the same projects or that the relative emphases of the city manager on outside matters and the assistant city manager on internal matters is upset. Perhaps the most relevant evidence of possible dyads is the clear distinctions between chief executives and their assistants in the amount of time reportedly allocated to internal administration, presumed to be the principal domain of the assistants. True to form, mayoral assistants report 39% of their time devoted to internal administration compared to 30% for mayors, and assistant city managers report 45% compared to 34% for city managers.

Alternate Explanations for Work Variations

The propositions examined above are dominated by what Mintzberg calls "environmental variables" and "job variables." While it would be difficult from the data collected to assess the relevance of "situational variables," a third element in Mintzberg's suggested four-variable model for explaining variation in managerial jobs, it is possible at least to scratch the surface on a fourth element, "person variables," defined to include "the personality and style of the incumbent."[21]

Among the personal characteristics of potential relevance to the manner in which an executive approaches the job are the age of the executive, level of education, years of experience in that line of work, and number of years of service in their current position. Although this set of characteristics only begins to tap the vast array of possible "person variables," these variables were selected for their relevance and data availability. Conceivably, each of these factors could influence the executive's outlook, sense of priorities, and choice of options in attacking problems and pursuing opportunities.

Roughly one-half of the respondents in each position—mayor (47%), mayoral assistant (52%), city manager (56%), and assistant city manager (55%)—were in the 36 to 50 years of age group (for detailed age profiles, see Table A–11 in appendix). As might be expected, mayors and city managers had higher percentages in the 51 to 65 age category than did mayoral assistants and assistant city managers. Although young executives were numerous, with about one-tenth of the mayors and city managers and more than one-fourth of the mayoral assistants and assistant city managers in the 35 or younger age category, very few of the respondents were 66 years of age or older.

More than one-half (59%) of the respondents reported possessing a graduate degree (Table A–12 in appendix). The overall percentage, however, was boosted by extremely high percentages of city managers (69%) and assistant city managers (68%) holding graduate degrees. One-third of the mayors and 44% of the mayoral assistants reported having earned graduate degrees.

In terms of possessing an MPA degree or its equivalent (e.g., Master of Government Administration), a graduate degree especially tailored to the needs of government executives, the distribution of degree holders is even more skewed toward executives from reform governments—city managers and assistant city managers (Table A–13 in appendix). Only 3% of the mayoral respondents and 15% of the mayoral assistants reported possessing an MPA, compared to 49% of the city managers and 41% of the assistant city managers.

Relevance of Age and Education to Work Patterns

What evidence exists that the age or graduate education of a particular municipal executive influences the nature of that executive's work? No statistically significant correlations could be found between those variables and various time allocation dimensions for mayors.[22] Neither age nor formal education appears to have much bearing on how mayors allocate their time.

For mayoral assistants, possessing an MPA degree is positively correlated, although modestly, to the reported allocation of time to emergencies (Kendall's tau = .188). Possessing a graduate degree (not necessarily an MPA) by mayoral assistants is also positively correlated with the allocation of time to emergencies (tau = .204) and negatively correlated to the percentage of their time consumed in responding to intergovernmental demands (tau = −.174). One possible interpretation of these findings is that graduate education has not only failed to equip mayoral assistants with the organizational and planning skills necessary to avoid, or at least minimize the frequency of, emergency situations, it has somehow increased their vulnerability to such situations. A more likely possibility, however, is that mayoral assistants with advanced training are more often trusted to deal with emergencies. Similarly, such persons are perhaps more adept in intergovernmental relations, abler to anticipate demands in that realm, and abler to avoid many of the time-consuming pitfalls encountered by officials unfamiliar with the latest regulations governing application procedures and recordkeeping requirements for a particular federal or state grant program.

Younger city managers and assistant city managers tend to work longer hours and devote more time to policy development than do their older counterparts. Age is negatively correlated to working hours per week and time allocation to policy development for city managers (tau = −.170 and −.259, respectively) and for assistant city managers (tau = −.172 and −.159, respectively). Furthermore, older assistant city managers, apparently operating with greater independence, are likely to devote a smaller percentage of their time to city manager-selected tasks than do their younger counterparts. Age and the allocation of time to city manager-selected tasks are negatively correlated (tau = −.160).

Assistant city managers with advanced formal education tend to work longer hours than their counterparts without graduate degrees, and also to devote greater percentages of their time to policy development, scheduled meetings, and emergencies. They tend to devote less time to desk work. Specifically, possession of a graduate degree is positively correlated with working hours per week (tau = .143), time allocated to policy development (tau = .211), and time allocated to scheduled meetings (tau = .127), and negatively correlated to desk work (tau = −.129). Possession of an MPA degree—as opposed to simply any graduate degree—is also negatively correlated with time allocation to desk work (tau = −.150) and positively correlated to hours per week (tau = .170), policy development (tau = .132), and, similar to the case for mayoral assistants, time allocated to emergencies (tau = .163).

Advanced academic training appears to have little influence on the time allocations of city managers. No systematic distinctions could be made between the work foci of city managers with graduate degrees, on the one hand, and those without graduate degrees, on the other. Similarly, no significant distinctions could be found for time allocations to desk work, scheduled meetings, unscheduled meetings, or inspections of municipal activities. Only time allocated to telephone calls is significantly correlated with possession of an MPA degree by city managers (tau = .180).

Relevance of Experience

Experience influences time allocation factors differently from one position to another. Years of service correlates negatively with a perception of personal control of the workweek by mayors (tau = −.190). In other words, respondents with more years of service as mayor or city council member tend to perceive lower percentages of their workweek to be under their own control as opposed to the control of others. Furthermore, such respondents tend to allocate lower percentages of their time to city council relations (tau = −.204).

The experience level of mayoral assistants seems to have its greatest influence on the role they adopt in their internal administrative activities, and on their overall working hours. Those with more years of service tend more than their counterparts to emphasize the specialist/technologist role (tau = .162). More years in their current position correlates negatively with working hours per week (tau = −.156).

City managers with relatively little experience are more likely than their long-tenured counterparts to work long hours and to devote higher percentages of their time to policy development, emergencies, and telephone calls, and lower percentages to desk work. Furthermore, they are more likely to perceive major portions of their workweek to be under the control of others, rather than under their own control. This finding is in sharp contrast to that for mayors, where the perception of personal control of the workweek declines with increasing tenure. Longer-tenured mayors perceive less personal control of their time; longer-tenured city managers, more. Specifically, years of service as a city manager correlates negatively with working hours (tau = −.234), and time allocation to policy development (tau = −.138) and emergencies (tau = −.153), and positively with desk work (tau = .125) and perception of personal control of the workweek (tau = .113). Years of service in their current position as city manager is negatively correlated with working hours (tau = −.186) and time allocation to emergencies (tau = −.209) and telephone calls (tau = −.141) and positively correlated to perception of personal control of the workweek (tau = .131).

In contrast to mayoral assistants, relatively short-tenured assistant city managers—not those with more years of experience—are more likely to emphasize the specialist/technologist role in internal administration. Furthermore, they tend to allocate more time to desk work and city manager-selected tasks, and less time to scheduled meetings. Those who are relatively new to their current positions tend to work longer hours. Specifically, years of service in local government are negatively correlated with time allocation to the specialist/technologist role (t = −.145), desk work (t = −.110), and city manager selected tasks (tau = −.100), and positively correlated to time allocated to scheduled meetings (tau = .123). Years of service in their current position correlate negatively with working hours (tau = −.123) and city manager-selected tasks (tau = −.143).

Assessing the Importance of Personal Characteristics

Each of the correlations reported above meets the conventional level of statistical significance (p<.05). The relatively small magnitude of these correlations, however, reflects the complexity involved in attempting to explain variation in the nature of executive work. Variation in background and personal characteristics, although important, can be expected to account for only a relatively small portion of the variation in work activities and time allocations from one municipal executive to another.

Contributions of Related Studies

Several writers have offered thoughts on managerial style, community type, and the interrelationship of those factors—thoughts that address obliquely the "person variables" and "situational variables" in Mintzberg's contingency theory. Consideration of two works is especially instructive.

In their study of mayors, Kotter and Lawrence review the

agenda-setting process and postulate the existence of a continuum encompassing four general patterns of agenda-setting behavior.[22] Pattern #1 is characterized by a reactive, short-run orientation and "muddling through" tendencies.[24] Pattern #4 is characterized by "rational-deductive" or "rational-comprehensive" planning, the textbook approach to pro-active, middle- and long-run oriented management. Patterns #2 and #3 fall along the continuum, incorporating bits of the rational-comprehensive and muddling through patterns in different degrees.

In addition to identifying agenda-setting patterns, Kotter and Lawrence categorize cities according to the variety and analyzability of information pertinent to those cities (Figure 6-1). For example, cities with a great variety of highly analyzable information tend to be large, heterogeneous, stable cities, according to Kotter and Lawrence. Various combinations of information variety and analyzability, then, are postulated to be of relevance to ideal agenda-setting behavior (Figure 6-2). Planning is futile where information variety and analyzability are both low (point A); rational planning is especially useful where both dimensions are high (point B); agenda-setting approaching the rational-comprehensive is appropriate where information variety is relatively high and analyzability is moderate (point C); and agenda-

Figure 6-1
INFORMATION COMING FROM A CITY

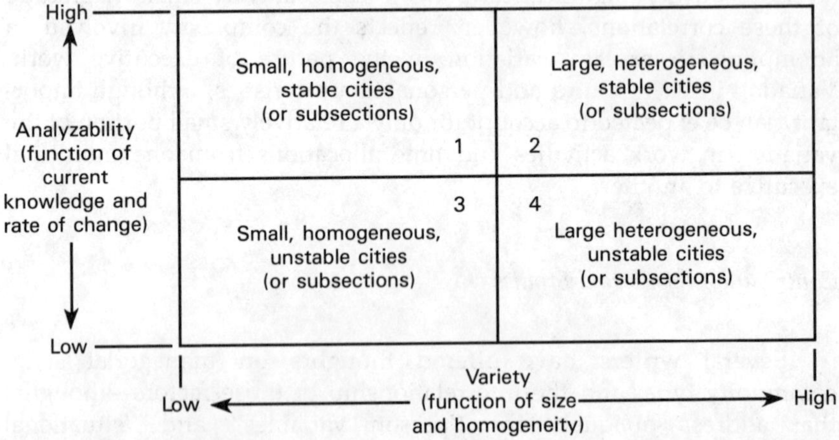

Analyzability (function of current knowledge and rate of change) High → Low	Small, homogeneous, stable cities (or subsections) 1	Large, heterogeneous, stable cities (or subsections) 2
	Small, homogeneous, unstable cities (or subsections) 3	Large heterogeneous, unstable cities (or subsections) 4

Low ← Variety (function of size and homogeneity) → High

SOURCE: John P. Kotter and Paul R. Lawrence, *Mayors in Action: Five Approaches to Urban Governance* (New York: John Wiley & Sons, 1974), p. 129. Copyright © 1974 by John Wiley & Sons, Inc. Reprinted by permission of John Wiley & Sons, Inc.

Variation of Local Government Executives 137

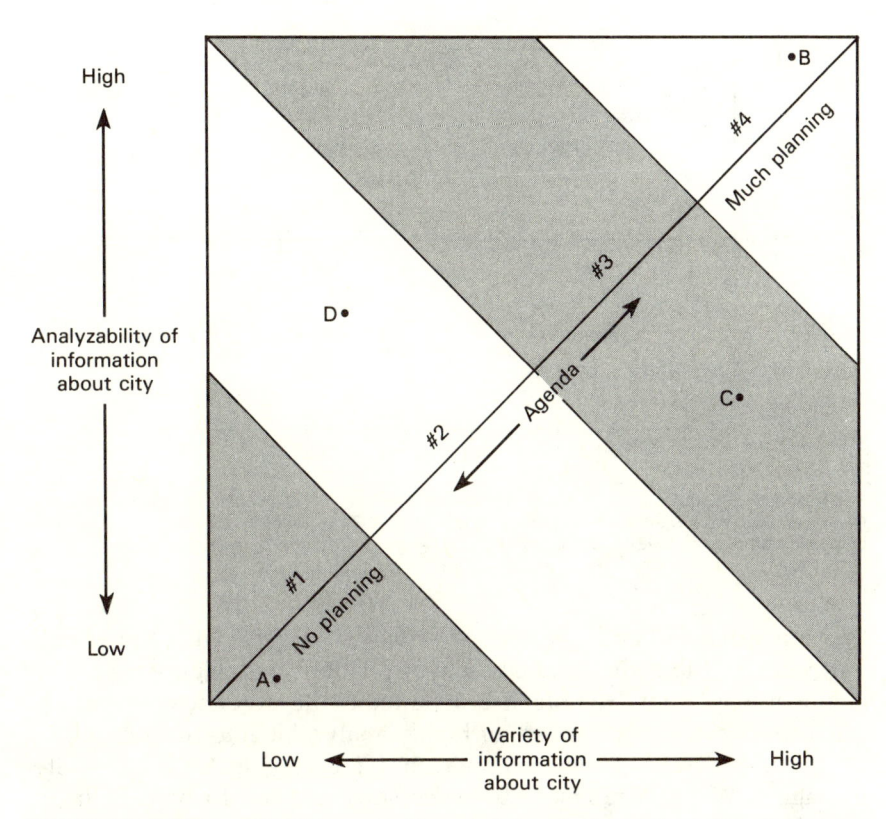

Figure 6-2
IDEAL AGENDA-CITY RELATIONSHIP

[Figure 6-2: A diagram showing the ideal agenda-city relationship. The vertical axis is "Analyzability of information about city" ranging from Low to High. The horizontal axis is "Variety of information about city" ranging from Low to High. The diagram shows diagonal bands labeled "No planning" (#1), "#2", "Agenda", "#3", "#4", and "Much planning". Points A, B, C, and D are plotted: A at lower left, B at upper right, C at middle right, D at upper middle-left.]

SOURCE: John P. Kotter and Paul R. Lawrence, *Mayors in Action: Five Approaches to Urban Governance* (New York: John Wiley & Sons, 1974), p. 130. Copyright © 1974 by John Wiley & Sons, Inc. Reprinted by permission of John Wiley & Sons, Inc.

setting approaching the reactive posture is pragmatic where analyzability is moderate but information variety is low (point D).

Kotter and Lawrence further postulate that mayors may be categorized according to different cognitive orientations (Figure 6–3). A mayor tends to be either preceptive or receptive in bringing information to mind and either systematic or intuitive in using that information. Those who are systematic and preceptive, for example, are labeled "engineer mayors." These personal characteristics combined with a city's information characteristics—factors that Mintzberg would call

Figure 6-3
DIFFERENT COGNITIVE ORIENTATIONS OF MAYORS

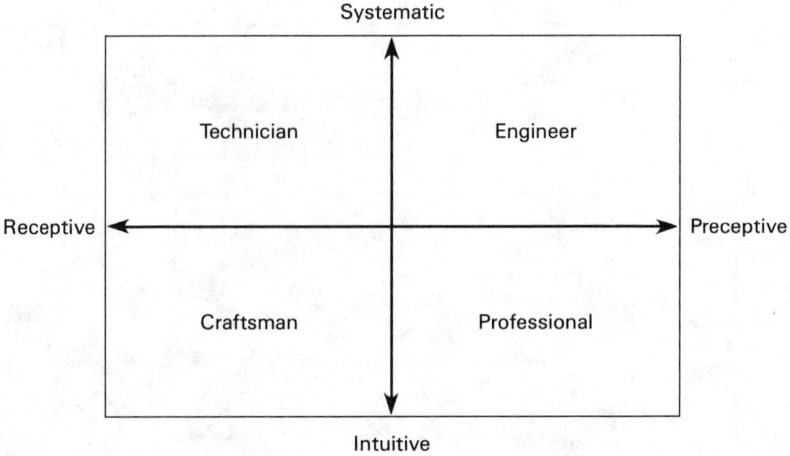

```
                    Systematic
         ┌─────────────┬─────────────┐
         │             │             │
         │  Technician │   Engineer  │
         │             │             │
Receptive├─────────────┼─────────────┤Preceptive
         │             │             │
         │  Craftsman  │ Professional│
         │             │             │
         └─────────────┴─────────────┘
                     Intuitive
```

SOURCE: John P. Kotter and Paul R. Lawrence, *Mayors in Action: Five Approaches to Urban Governance* (New York: John Wiley & Sons, 1974), p. 133. Copyright © 1974 by John Wiley & Sons, Inc. Reprinted by permission of John Wiley & Sons, Inc.

"person variables" and "situational variables"—reveal what Kotter and Lawrence consider the ideal city-mayor relationships (Figure 6–4). The engineer mayor, for example, is best-suited to the large, heterogeneous, stable city with a great variety of highly analyzable information.

In a generally similar manner, but focusing instead upon city managers, Wayne Anderson, Chester Newland, and Richard Stillman postulate an ideal matching of managerial types and community types.[25] Drawing on the work of Oliver Williams, they identify four community types for their high or low people orientation and high or low technical orientation.[26] According to this typology, communities tend to be "arbiter communities," "growth communities," "caretaker communities," or "consumption communities" (Figure 6–5). Anderson and associates speculate that these community types may then be matched beneficially with managerial types identified by the same dimensions as "community leader," "chief executive," "administrative caretaker," and "administrative innovator" (Figure 6–6).[27]

If particular management styles are best-suited for particular communities, as suggested by these authors in well-reasoned arguments consistent with the views of the contingency theorists reviewed in Chapter Two, it should be anticipated that different management

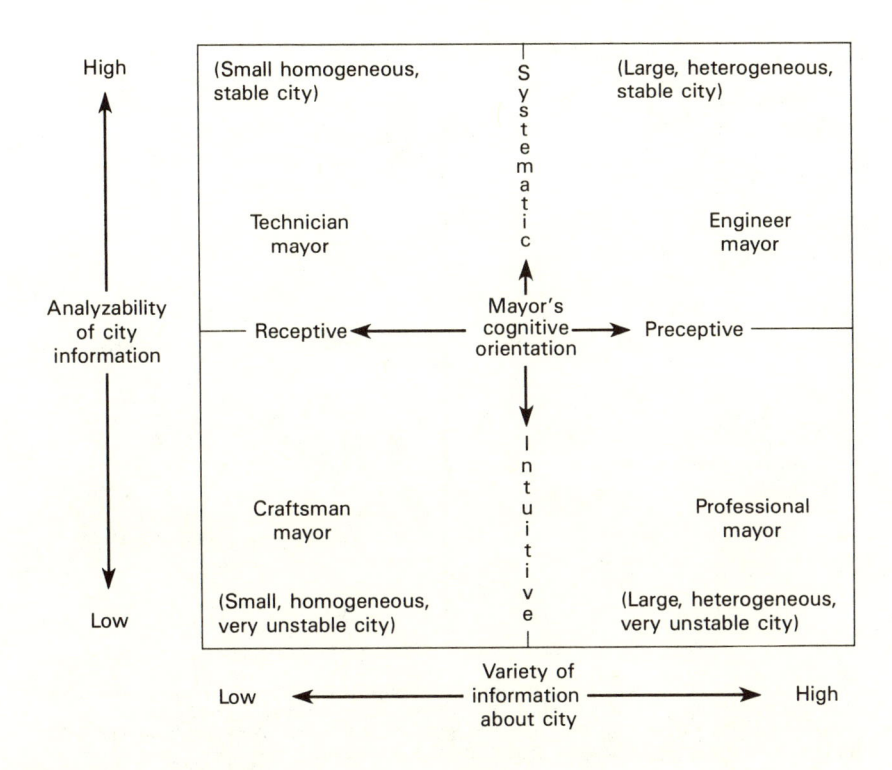

Figure 6-4
IDEAL CITY-MAYOR RELATIONSHIP

	Systematic ↑	
(Small homogeneous, stable city)		(Large, heterogeneous, stable city)
Technician mayor		Engineer mayor
Receptive ←	Mayor's cognitive orientation →	Preceptive
Craftsman mayor	↓ Intuitive	Professional mayor
(Small, homogeneous, very unstable city)		(Large, heterogeneous, very unstable city)

Analyzability of city information: High ↑ / Low ↓

Variety of information about city: Low ← → High

SOURCE: John P. Kotter and Paul R. Lawrence, *Mayors in Action: Five Approaches to Urban Governance* (New York: John Wiley & Sons, 1974), p. 132. Copyright © 1974 by John Wiley & Sons, Inc. Reprinted by permission of John Wiley & Sons, Inc.

styles would be manifested in distinctive patterns of executive work demands, foci, and activities. Such distinctions, presumably, would be driven by differences in managerial background and characteristics (e.g., personal factors predisposing a manager to behave as a community leader, chief executive, administrative caretaker or administrative innovator) and by situational factors varying from one city to another. Personal characteristics of age, education, and length of experience, however, appear to have only modest power for explaining variations in the work of city executives, suggesting either that other personal characteristics are more relevant or that situational variables associated with each job and each city—the identification of which lies beyond the scope of this study—join environmental variables and job

Figure 6-5
PEOPLE/TECHNICAL ORIENTATIONS DEMANDED BY COMMUNITIES

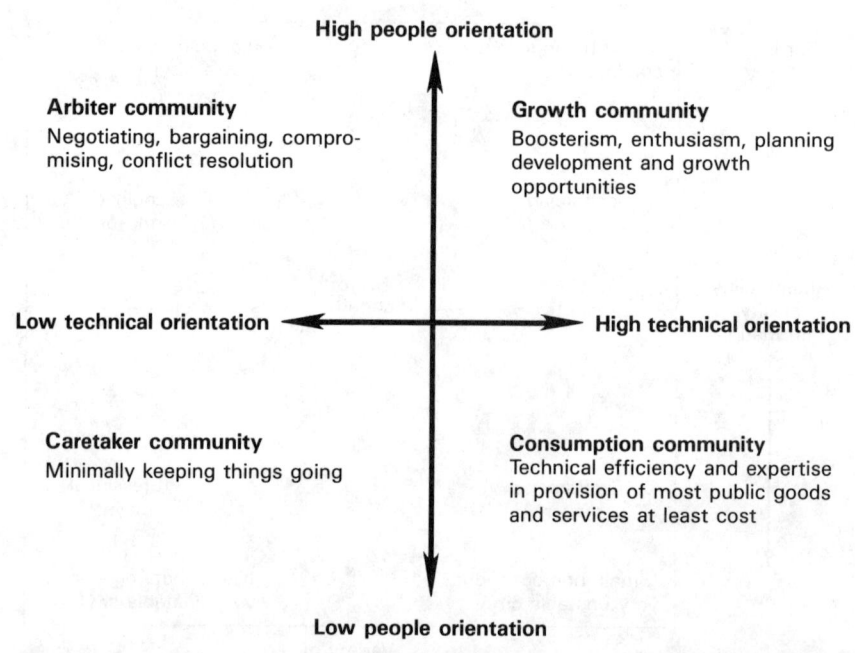

High people orientation

Arbiter community
Negotiating, bargaining, compromising, conflict resolution

Growth community
Boosterism, enthusiasm, planning development and growth opportunities

Low technical orientation ←——————→ High technical orientation

Caretaker community
Minimally keeping things going

Consumption community
Technical efficiency and expertise in provision of most public goods and services at least cost

Low people orientation

SOURCE: Wayne F. Anderson, Chester A. Newland, and Richard J. Stillman, II, *The Effective Local Government Manager* (Washington, D.C.: International City Management Association, 1983), p. 26, based upon Oliver P. Williams, "A Typology for Comparative Local Government," *Midwest Journal of Political Science*, 5 (May 1961), pp. 150-164. Reprinted with permission.

variables as more important than person variables in explaining the variation in municipal executive work. The latter interpretation would be consistent with contingency theorists' criticism of attempts to analyze leadership solely according to a given manager's orientations toward people and tasks.

Summary

Five of the major propositions Mintzberg posited regarding the nature of managerial work following his study of five executives may be examined for their applicability to local government executives, using

Figure 6-6
MANAGERIAL TYPES IN TERMS OF PEOPLE ORIENTATION VERSUS TECHNICAL ORIENTATION

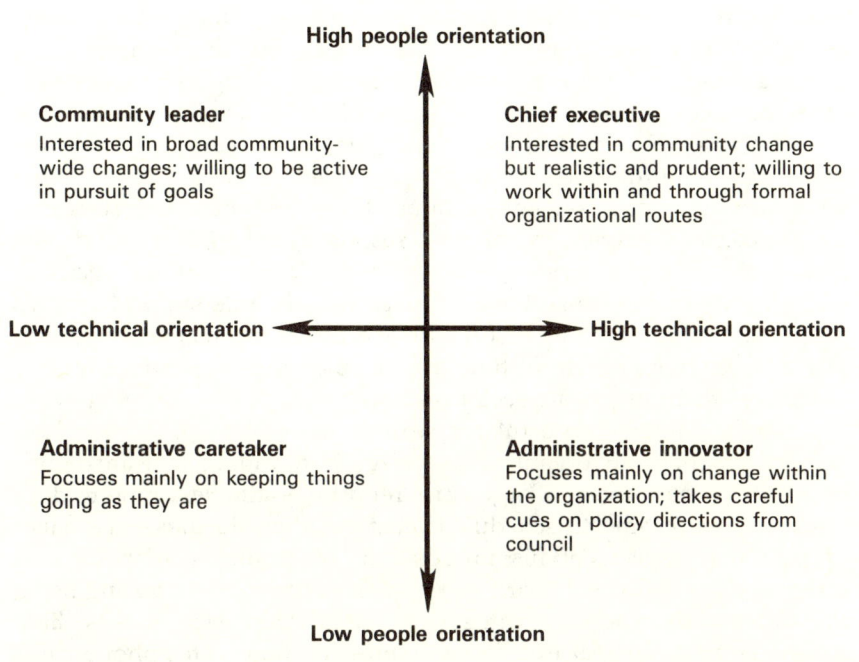

High people orientation

Community leader
Interested in broad community-wide changes; willing to be active in pursuit of goals

Chief executive
Interested in community change but realistic and prudent; willing to work within and through formal organizational routes

Low technical orientation ←→ High technical orientation

Administrative caretaker
Focuses mainly on keeping things going as they are

Administrative innovator
Focuses mainly on change within the organization; takes careful cues on policy directions from council

Low people orientation

SOURCE: Wayne F. Anderson, Chester A. Newland, and Richard J. Stillman, II, *The Effective Local Government Manager* (Washington, D.C.: International City Management Association, 1983), p. 22. Reprinted with permission.

data compiled for this study. General support is found for two of the propositions. Senior managers do appear to work longer hours than others in city government, with the most senior working more hours than their immediate subordinates. Furthermore, the dyadic relationship identified by Mintzberg in which chief executives focus on external relationships and their seconds-in-command concentrate on internal matters is evident for local government, as mayoral assistants report 39% of their time devoted to internal administration compared to 30% for mayors, and assistant city managers report 45% compared to 34% for city managers. Such evidence provides rather strong support for the dyadic contention, despite the virtual absence of negative correlations for paired chief executive-assistant comparisons.

Three other propositions receive much less support. Mintzberg contended that job level and functions supervised are more relevant than any other variable in explaining variation in managerial work. The data on city executives clearly show the importance of job level in defining the nature of their work. Mayors and city managers, for example, report substantially higher percentages of their time devoted to self-selected tasks than do their assistants. But demonstrating the importance of job level is not the same as establishing its primacy over other variables, a task beyond the scope of this research.

Mintzberg also posited a tendency for public managers to devote more time to formal activity (e.g., scheduled meetings) and dealing with directors and outside groups than do their private-sector counterparts. Comparison of the responses of mayors and city managers with the evidence compiled in three studies focusing primarily upon private-sector executives reveals little support for this proposition. Only in comparison with executives in small organizations was a larger commitment of time to scheduled meetings found for city executives than for private-sector officials.

Finally, Mintzberg postulated several time-allocation relationships tied to variations in organizational size. Conforming to Mintzberg's proposition, executives in large cities report devoting less time to desk work and more time to scheduled meetings than do those in smaller cities. Other aspects of his proposition, regarding such matters as ceremonies and external board work, are less amenable to testing using Mintzberg's five activity categories. Jurisdiction size makes little difference in municipal executives' time allocation to telephone calls, unscheduled meetings, and inspections of municipal activities.

Alternate explanations for variations in the nature of the work of city executives suggest the importance of person variables and management style preferences unique to the incumbent, and situational variables which distinguish the organization and its environment. While statistically significant correlations ($p<.05$) were found between some of the background and personal characteristics of the city executives and various time-allocation factors, most correlations were relatively small. A potentially more fruitful, although more difficult, area of inquiry may be situational variables and their impact on executive work.

Chapter Seven

TIME MANAGEMENT

Henry David Thoreau once remarked that "Time is but the stream I go a-fishing in."[1] Time, in other words, flows by quickly in our brief outing in life. Most executives are keenly aware of that commodity's value even if they view time in a less philosophical manner and express its value in terms different than Thoreau's. Modern managers, moreover, lead a far more harried life than did the contemplative nineteenth-century essayist and often find their "stream" polluted with paper, people, and problems.

The last three chapters have portrayed municipal chief executive officers (CEOs) as individuals who work long hours, many of which are perceived to be beyond their own control (37% of the time of mayors is thought to be controlled by others; 41% for city managers). More than one-half of the time of the typical mayor or city manager is spent in a combination of desk work, telephone contacts, and unscheduled meetings or unplanned encounters (see Table 6–2). The proportion of time reportedly expended on these activities by city executives is somewhat greater than the proportions found in other research on CEO allocation of time.[2]

The workload of the typical mayor and city manager is heavy; demands, extensive; interruptions, frequent; and expectations, high. The price of executive responsiveness is expensive; long-term projects of high priority frequently yield to short-run, even penny-ante, political crises. But responsiveness is an important measure of performance in local government. Failure to pay the price may doom an administrator.

Says Dianne Feinstein, former mayor of San Francisco:

> Mayors are still expected to do the ribbon cuttings and speechmaking, of course. But that's the easy part—getting away from the desk and out of the meetings.
>
> I submit to you that America's busiest executives today are no

longer in the private sector; they are modern American mayors, city managers, controllers, treasurers and finance directors, beset and beleaguered by an infinite variety of concerns, considerations and complaints.

With so much going on, most mayors today are financially short, understaffed and overworked. Their daily schedules look like television logs. They overdose on meetings. The press is pounding them for glib answers to imponderable issues. The public is protesting outside city hall.

Let's face it: Today's mayors have to be good managers, hands-on executives with whom the buck stops. It is an exhilarating but frustrating opportunity to make a difference by doing more with a lot less.[3]

If mayors and city managers hope to be more than the proverbial marionette, hopelessly vulnerable to tugs on their strings by the forces that threaten to rob them of every modicum of control of their work, they must find ways to gain at least a degree of control over the time demanded by others and more substantial mastery of remaining discretionary time. Otherwise, any similarity between the relative priorities they would assign to their management role, their policy role, and their political role in a given situation and the relative time allocations to those roles or to priority projects will be more a matter of coincidence than control. Effective use of time is an organizational problem,[4] and like other organizational problems is amenable to the application of executive skills. The major causes of ineffective use of time may be identified and prescriptions offered for curing some of the time-management ills of public executives, even if the manager in question may be skeptical of the super-efficiency of "one-minute management."[5]

To a large extent, the overall prescription is self-management. "To manage our time means to manage ourselves. Time control is self control. One of the reasons many of us find the management of time so frustrating is because it means we need to manage *ourselves* more effectively."[6]

This chapter will identify many of the principal time wasters that plague managers. It will then suggest ways to eliminate or mitigate against those time wasters, and briefly review the long-term consequences of failing to gain control of one's time.

Where Does the Time Go?

The literature on time management points to a series of persistent problems as the chief culprits in the theft of executive time. The worst offenders include telephone interruptions, erratic crisis management, drop-in visitors, a failure to delegate properly, poorly managed meetings, and procrastination. Other time wasters in the public sector include attempting to do too much at once; a lack of objectives, priorities, and planning; personal disorganization and a cluttered desk; and an inability to say "no."[7] Leo Moore's study of almost 3,000 private-sector managers suggests that report preparation, special requests, delays, and an overload of superfluous reading should be added to the list of time wasters.[8] Yet another infringement on time is business travel.[9]

These time wasters are not mutually exclusive. For example, too-frequent telephone interruptions may be due to failure to delegate adequate authority to subordinates who subsequently feel the need to check frequently with the executive before taking any action. Too many meetings may be linked to an inability to say no. A cluttered desk may be linked to a failure to set priorities. Individual managers plagued by most of the 15 time wasters cited above may recognize themselves in the scenario below.

Anne Davis is the mayor and chief executive of Metro, a bustling mayor-council city of one-quarter of a million people on the edge of the oil belt. She arrives at her office at 7:30 a.m. before other staff members with the hope of 30 minutes of "quiet time" to study a proposal for a major new planned development that is on tonight's council agenda. Having wasted five minutes looking for the proposal in the clutter on her desk, she has just begun to read it when her administrative assistant saunters into her office (the door was left ajar). They talk briefly about the schedule for the day, and, then, she resumes reading. At 8:05 a.m., the first telephone call of the day is put through to her.

The call is from the director of the streets and sanitation department who wants to know if he can come up to discuss the problems he sees with the long-range transportation plan being developed by the planning department. His visit is not among the morning's anticipated activities, but the mayor tells him to come on in.

They chat for a few minutes—it turns out that he really wants some political leverage to use against the planning director—until the mayor dashes off to a meeting of the economic development committee at 8:30 a.m. The committee is a joint city-chamber of commerce effort and is chaired by a prominent citizen. The meeting drones on until 10:30 a.m., seemingly without resolving any of the issues carried over from last week's meeting. The mayor then goes straight to a meeting with the local school superintendent, the administrator of a large public hospital, and the president of the community college to discuss possible cooperative ventures.

Forty-five minutes into the meeting, the mayor's secretary slips into the room and tells the mayor that she had better excuse herself, that a major problem is brewing. Outside the conference room, Mayor Davis presses for more information, only to find that the transit authority drivers are being stricken by the "flu" at a highly improbable rate. She asks the secretary to get the transit director on the phone for a briefing on the extent of the problem. Before that call could be completed, however, her phone rings. Her teenage son is just calling to say that he made an "A" on his algebra exam.

It's only 11:30 a.m. The day's schedule is "blown." Mayor Davis doesn't have a hope of having lunch (darn, she knew she shouldn't have skipped breakfast) or of reading the planned development proposal. It looks as if she'll have to face the city council and the proposal's opponents unprepared. Unhappily, it won't be the first time—or the last—that has happened. Her temples are beginning to pound, signaling the advent of a headache and resurrecting the lingering doubts about whether she should run for reelection.

Mayor Davis needs to learn how to manage her time. It's her only hope for survival.

Is There a Better Way?

In Chapter Three, scientific management's "one-best-way" legacy was described, as well as its influence on the development of notions of managerial roles. In this chapter, we are not so much looking for one best way to do things as for a variety of options for improvement. A number of techniques and tactics can be recommended for gaining control of one's time. While it is unlikely the one individual would use all of them—that individual could spend more time getting organized and trying out new gimmicks than is spent doing the substantive work he or she was hired or elected to perform—individual managers/executives may select the ones that best seem to address the time-waster problems confronting them. While some of the tactics directly address a specific time waster—for example, telephone interruptions—others address several time wasters.

Controlling the Telephone

The telephone is both a boon and bane for all managers. While communications advances have expanded immeasurably the capabilities of the modern executive, the telephone can be an unrelenting and insistent intruder. Mayors report spending 17% of their 66-hour workweek on the telephone, while city managers report spending 15% of their 57-hour workweek on the telephone. Those figures amount to more than two hours each day for the mayors and one and one-half hours for the city managers. Those time allocations are in keeping with Alec Mackenzie's observations: "Nine out of ten executives spend at least an hour each day on the phone and four out of ten spend more than two hours per day, so the urgent need for telephone discipline is evident."[10]

The *problem* includes call frequency, length, being put on hold, and an assortment of other telephone-related interruptions and time wasters, such as telephone tag and receiving calls placed by secretaries for their bosses who then turn out to be unavailable for the conversation.[11] Suggested *solutions* include the following:

1. Keep calls short and relevant—guide the caller to the point by asking "What may I do for you?" after a brief exchange of pleasantries: "Conversations longer than 10 minutes turn into a meeting or gossip."[12]
2. Let the secretary intercept calls, making it clear who has automatic entree to the executive, who will be called back, and who should be referred to someone else (perhaps the secretary).[13]
3. Establish a call-back system, that is, a set time each day for returning calls, and a means of keeping track of such calls.[14]
4. Time return calls—return calls during periods when others are less likely to want to chat, such as shortly before lunch or at the end of the day.[15]
5. Carefully limit the scope of the call: "Hi, Sam; I need brief answers to two questions."[16]

Deciding What's Most Important

For most executives, there is almost always too much to do, a situation exacerbated by the tendency of many managers to agree to take on even more tasks. Consequently, it is imperative for these individuals to set priorities and determine which activities must be accomplished, which are desirable but not mandatory, and which could fall by the wayside if need be.[17] The *problem* is the misallocation of time and perhaps other resources in the absence of clear objectives and priorities.

Suggested *solutions* include the following:

1. Plan. Achievers plan; things do not happen by chance, and they "write things down," including a daily and weekly plan of action.[18] Assigning priorities to tasks as part of the planning process enables the determined executive to ensure that adequate time is devoted to those of greatest importance rather than simply to those with the closest deadline or most insistent advocate. Edwin Bliss offers two supplementary suggestions in this regard: (a) activities of secondary importance should not be scheduled for specific times, and (b) if the same items are carried over repeatedly from one day to the next, it is either an indicator that the item is low priority or a sign of procrastination.[19]
2. Use spare time wisely/do two compatible things at once: Perhaps more than any other group, the manufacturers of "executive tapes" seem to understand this suggestion. Mayors can hear market analyses, listen to news interpretations, or polish their Spanish for that impending trip to their sister city in Costa Rica while taking their morning jog or driving to city hall. This remedy is also one that is compatible with business travel: instead of spending four hours on a jet airplane focused on the mundane food, liquor, and the latest movie, the efficient city manager uses the time to complete some small, specific projects or catch up on that growing mountain of reading material.[20]
3. Satisfice. Insisting on perfection can only result in frustration. An important principle for the busy executive to understand is that a marginal utility exists with regard to the expenditure of time: for many tasks, most of the desired objective can be accomplished with the first expenditure of effort, but refining the product to claim the last 10% of the objective may require more effort than the other 90%. Thus, the advice is "don't bother" unless refinement is critical; spend the time on another project.[21]
4. Set personal objectives with deadlines. Mayors perceive that 63% of their workload consists of self-selected tasks; city

managers, 59%. An executive should not let projects in this category drift, even if the only "deadlines" are self-imposed.

Avoiding Procrastination

At some point, almost everyone has probably had a teacher, parent, or other authority figure recite the admonition, "Procrastination is the thief of time."[22] Indeed it is. The *problem* is putting off work. "Procrastination wears many disguises—laziness, indifference, forgetfulness, overwork—but behind the mask," writes one time management expert, "is usually a single emotion, fear of embarrassment, rejection or failure."[23] Jane Burka and Lenora Yuen devised this Procrastinator's Code:

> I must be perfect.
> Everything I do should go easily and without effort.
> It's safer to do nothing than to take a risk and fail.
> I should have no limitations.
> If it's not done right, it's not worth doing at all.
> I must avoid being challenged.
> If I succeed, someone will get hurt.
> If I do well this time, I must *always* do well.
> Following someone else's rules means I'm giving in and I'm not in control.
> I can't afford to let go of anything or anyone.
> If I expose my real self, people won't like me.
> There is a right answer, and I'll wait until I find it.[24]

According to Burka and Yuen, "A procrastinator plays games with the clock, trying to outsmart it."[25] Unfortunately, it is a game they rarely, if ever, win and the penalty for even playing may be to invite further interruptions because colleagues understand that the person is easily distracted and even enjoys delay.[26]

What can be done about procrastination? Suggested *solutions* include the following:

1. Break tasks into manageable components, or what Thomas Peters and Robert Waterman call "chunking"; chunking also involves delegation.[27]
2. Attack problems at one's "best time of day," when the mind is keenest: " . . . work on the most difficult or unpleasant tasks

at the time of the day when . . . [you] are freshest and most creative."[28]
3. Assess the reasons for and consequences of past procrastination behavior, then set specific goals for accomplishment, and announce those goals publicly: "You may take more seriously a commitment you've made to someone else than if you just think to yourself that you need to do something."[29]
4. Never look back. "Needless worry makes people into terrible procrastinators."[30]

Procrastination is a fault with few apparent redeeming features. However, for managers who despair of ever overcoming that malady, Helen Reynolds and Mary Trammel offer a "calculated procrastination" strategy that, though admittedly risky, may produce some beneficial results if applied only to low-priority problems.

> Some problems, if left alone, will resolve themselves. Why not keep a desk drawer for such problems?
>
> If a problem in your procrastination drawer becomes urgent, you can always say you've had it under study, pull it out, and go to work on it. It's risky but, on the other hand, you may save hours not doing some jobs that will never need to be done anyway.[31]

Gaining Control of Drop-ins

While the telephone represents one significant intrusion on managerial concentration, another major source of interruption is the drop-in visitor. Municipal executives report spending 14% of their time in unscheduled meetings; presumably, only a portion of these meetings are initiated by the executive. The *problem* is that "visitors, particularly those who arrived unannounced, prove difficult for the manager who must decide how to handle the conversation and how and when to finish the interview."[32] A policy of a totally closed door is not a solution because it cuts off the manager from important information and promotes an image of detached management, but no executive is obliged to have a continual open house in the office. Suggested *solutions* for dealing with such interruptions include the following:

1. Stand during information exchanges. A stand-up encounter issues a subtle cue, without being rude, that a lengthy visit is

not anticipated and does not invite visitors to become too comfortable; in more extreme cases, it is hard for even a determined visitor to chat aimlessly or at length when the boss begins to pace or otherwise demonstrates eagerness to get on with pending tasks.[33]
2. Take cover. The cooperation of the secretary in shielding against intrusions, a closed door with a note indicating the need to work "in peace" for a set time, or relocation to a "hideout" are suggested tactics.[34]
3. Go to the subordinate's office. If the manager tells the unscheduled visitor that he or she will stop by in a few minutes, the manager thus controls the beginning and the ending point of the conversation. [35]
4. Make the secretary an accomplice, even asking for innocent white lies. Robert Heller advises, "Be mean with your time—and even Machiavellian . . . in your own office, there's always the time-honored subterfuge of having your secretary remind you of some fictitious but desperately urgent next appointment."[36]
5. Have a clear policy of appointments and a specific time for open house. The consolidation of appointments and the reception of drop-in visitors during a particular part of each day, permitting few exceptions, while steadfastly preserving uninterrupted time, will provide an inoffensive means of reducing disruptions to the manager's concentration during prime times.[37]

Meeting Meetings Head-On

The life of the executive sometimes appears to be nothing more than a string of seemingly endless meetings. Municipal executives report spending slightly more than one-third of their work time in formal meetings, a figure somewhat below those reported by other groups of executives;[38] but combining scheduled and unscheduled meetings pushes the figure for mayors and city managers to almost one-half of their workweeks. Another recent report states that executives spend 16.5 hours a week in meetings, but consider 30% of them a waste of time.[39] Many local government executives voice the same complaints as their colleagues in other fields: the *problem* is meetings that are too many, too long, too indecisive, too ineffective.[40]

One observer assessed the phenomenon of organizational meetings by saying that they "have become our national pastime, yet one is hard put to see any advantage to them other than someone's decision to hold a meeting so the group can for a time avoid doing the job it is paid to do."[41] Another observer notes, "Meetings are a necessary part of public administration. But, if allowed to grow unattended, they can spread like crabgrass and choke an agency."[42]

Meetings can be an effective decisionmaking tool if managed properly and if appropriate participants are involved and properly motivated. On the other hand, unproductive meetings can be incredible time wasters. So desperate have some meeting attenders become that an enterprising firm has reportedly found a market for a "false alarm," a gadget resembling a real paging device but that is triggered by the individual being "beeped," deftly extricating the owner from a boring meeting.[43] More conventional *solutions* include the following:

1. Establish a meeting policy that discourages unnecessary meetings and encourages having meetings only when a better option is not available.[44]
2. Organize the meeting, including an agenda, a fixed time for convening and adjourning, and a format for follow-up,[45] and adhere to that organization, including beginning the meeting promptly, following the agenda, and ending the session at the prearranged time.
3. Establish a review process to ensure that committees do not outlive their usefulness.[46]
4. Control participation, including all participants whose input is crucial and excluding those whose time does not need to be spent in a given meeting.[47]
5. Schedule meetings with adequate time but close enough to lunch or quitting time to discourage dawdling.
6. Discourage rambling, off-target speeches or discussions.
7. Avoid outside interruptions that keep all other participants waiting while a key member deals with, say, a telephone call or office visit.

Managing Paper Work

Another aspect of effective time management is gaining control of paper work. The *problem* has two major components. First is the volume of correspondence and reports to be both read and written. "The ever-increasing stream of forms, records, memos, mail, and simple informational notes [is] continually usurping time."[48] Mayors and city managers report spending slightly more than one-quarter of their time on desk work, about average for executives. Second is the effect of clutter on efficiency. A recent survey indicates that managers spend three hours a week searching for paper that has gone astray.[49] Suggested *solutions* include the following:

1. Clear the desk and establish a system for handling paper work: Time management experts suggest that the manager develop a system for keeping close at hand material needed regularly for reference while clearing the desk of any other materials not germane to the current project. If possible, a "projects" desk or table is a good idea.[50] The system should also ensure that the same piece of paper (letter, memorandum, report, etc.) is not handled repeatedly. It is an all-too-common practice for the executive/manager to take an item from the "in" basket, read it, put it back for later reference, then read it again to act on it. The secretary can be crucial in helping the executive avoid such wasted effort by organizing incoming material into several folders so that the executive knows which ones are most important and which can be read later. An important component of the paper-handling system is to adopt "don't read junk mail" as a cardinal rule.
2. Speedy reading: A speed reading "industry" has developed in recent years, producing instructional tapes and classroom courses that have been beneficial to many busy executives wishing to move through mounds of reading material more rapidly. Short of formal instruction, other speed reading tips include the following: (a) Executives should force themselves to read rapidly, especially if the material is not highly technical, and resist the temptation to reread sentences or phrases already passed. (b) They can, for use on noncrucial items, develop skimming skills such as reading only the first paragraph, the first and last sentences of subsequent paragraphs unless the material being covered seems crucial, and the last paragraph in its entirety. (c) Executives may avoid spending time on irrelevant material by using the table of contents to decide whether a book or journal contains anything of use to them. If it does not, the material should be bypassed.[51]

3. Take advantage of modern technology: Dictating equipment, the personal computer for form letters and "boilerplate" (material that is reproduced frequently such as general facts about the city, standard contracts, and bid invitations), and multipart, no-carbon-required (NCR) reply forms are examples.[52] Dictating equipment allows the adept executive to work through a stack of correspondence, memoranda, and even lengthy reports more rapidly than does any other option. Hand-held units often have more limited capabilities but offer the advantage of being useful not only at a desk but also in many other place, e.g., in the car driving to work. Their use allows the busy executive to record ideas and instructions as they are conceived and often to consolidate various types of paper work tasks. Technology, however, does not always deliver on all its promises. Some managers are beginning to observe that the advent of the desk-top computer may have done more to free their secretaries' time than their own.
4. Take legitimate shortcuts: An example is jotting a response on the bottom of a letter or memo rather than originating a new letter whenever a formal reply is not mandatory (a photocopy can be made if it is necessary to keep a record). Another example is making use of the ubiquitous Post-it® note pads.
5. Insist that subordinates provide information in a succinct fashion and that lengthy reports be accompanied by a one-page summary: Local government executives, like executives everywhere, are deluged by paper produced within their own organizations. If they do not insist that this material be presented in an efficient manner, they are adding immeasurably to their own paperwork load.

Letting "Joe" Do It

Delegation has always been a fundamental component of management, and assigning tasks to others not only may enrich their jobs (assuming that the tasks are meaningful ones) but also will free the executive to consider larger projects. The *problem* is failure to delegate duties to subordinates and provide them sufficient authority to accomplish the tasks that are assigned. The *solution* is obvious: delegate. The boss does *not* have to do everything, although many executives fail to understand this point. Some, for example, refuse to turn loose of favorite tasks they enjoyed doing on their way up the organizational ladder or think that only they can handle most matters that reach their desks. Yet, failure to delegate is poor management indeed because it maximizes personnel costs. The following are some ground rules for delegating authority and tasks to others:

1. Delegate properly, that is, "give the delegate full day-to-day responsibility."[53]
2. Delegate to the lowest level capable of handling the tasks competently.
3. Make effective use of one's secretary, who not only controls access to the executive but who can probably do much more.[54]
4. Make the best of mentoring; doing so not only helps to develop that bright young newcomer in the organization but also frees executive time for more important projects.[55]

Psychologist Perry Buffington recommends what he calls the "A-B-C Method" of delegation. The label for his system refers to a shorthand code that the manager assigns to a given project prior to routing it to a subordinate. The code indicates the intended level of executive involvement and, correspondingly, the level of subordinate discretion in completing the project.

> . . . [a]n 'A' project is a 'Don't do anything until I've authorized it'; 'B' means 'Get on with it, and let me know afterwards what you did'; and 'C' is 'Get on with it, and I don't need to know what happened'. This method stops interruptions before they happen. Anything you can do to avoid interruptions means improved time management. It has been estimated that a one-minute interruption can cost as long as 20 minutes to rebuild your momentum.[56]

The effective use of subordinates is a significant element in executive time management; however, it is important to anticipate that, while some subordinates will welcome increased responsibilities, others will attempt to shift the work back to the executive. Delegation resisters often request frequent conferences or "briefing sessions" where they will elaborate on the problem or describe the data they have collected, asking for "direction" but secretly hoping that the executive will make a decision without insisting on a recommendation from the subordinate. Executives who allow such a pattern to persist deny themselves the full value of their staff and commit a major time management sin. By insisting that any subordinate completing a project or merely informing the executive of a problem make a recommendation for dealing with it, the executive sends a clear message regarding the important role of the subordinate and executive expectations, increases the likelihood that adequate time and consideration will be given to the project, and takes a major step toward effective time management. In ideal instances, the executive will be able to simply approve the recommendation.[57]

Stress: The Product of Failed Time Management

Other than spending unnecessary time on the job or directing too much to low-priority projects, what are the consequences for the executive who fails to manage time effectively? Very often, the answer is stress—higher doses than the amounts inevitable in an inherently stressful line of work. Stress is a state of mental and, sometimes, bodily tension brought about by pressures that psychologists call "stressors." The term "stress" is also used to apply to the stressors themselves. While some stress may actually promote creativity and peak performance, too much has the opposite effect. In fact, "the bad news is that too much stress can be fatal and you may well be unaware of how much is too much"[58] until the heart attack or ulcer makes its appearance. In describing "Type A" behavior, conventionally regarded since the 1960s as the type most likely to lead to coronary disease, Meyer Friedman and Ray Rosenman observe that the primary behavioral pattern of heart-attack-prone individuals is that the person "is *aggressively* involved in a *chronic, incessant* struggle to achieve more and more in less and less time" [emphasis in original].[59] Later research has drawn into question the precise nature of the cause-and-effect relationship between Type A behavior and heart disease, but has indicated that Type A personalities who do suffer a heart attack are more likely than Type B personalities to avoid a second one because they are more likely than their "laid-back" counterparts to follow doctor's orders regarding such matters as nutrition and exercise.[60] While the medical community is now divided about the linkage between personality and coronary illness, agreement still exists that lifestyle—including the stressful emotions of anger and hostility—does contribute to heart disease.

Mayors, especially, place a high priority on their role in community leadership, their political role. Even if they absolutely love the speechmaking, the meetings with community groups, and all the related duties, it is a love affair that can be deadly.

Mayor John P. Rousakis of Savannah, Georgia, a veteran of bypass surgery, knows the demands but remains undaunted:

> It's the circuit that stresses you out. The banquet circuit, the lunch circuit, the church groups, the speeches, the meetings, the appointments. If you don't go it's an insult.
>
> I still attend 90% of the major conventions and functions in this city. If you don't enjoy your city and doing what you are doing, then you should get out. Being under stress is part of the job.
>
> Sure, it takes its toll psychologically; it's like being in charge of a big family. It's a tough task to do what we do, so you [sic] got to love it.[61]

Many causes of stress, such as a death in the family, divorce, the arrest of a child, or building a new house are personal. Others, such as the loss of a job or a change in economic conditions, are related to the job but not to time allocation.[62] Our concern, however, is with the stress caused by the mismanagement of executive time.

Heller characterizes executives who maintain a frenetic pace as having "run-down batteries" that negatively affect judgment and performance. He terms them "jet-lagged," and charges them with not only failing to control their own time but also potentially causing other organizational members to suffer time management problems. "The jet-lagged dynamos can easily carry great bundles of stress and anxiety around as presents for their subordinates, making it difficult, if not impossible, for the latter to gain control over the most critical element in their lives, working or not: time."[63] Because lower-level employees subjected to tedious tasks and removed from decisions and much, if any, control over their own environment have been found to suffer considerable stress,[64] the stress-laden executive who restricts subordinate discretion and whose manner intensifies feelings of pressure creates a serious organizational problem. Although frenzied behavior may be symptomatic of an imbalanced management style overwhelmingly favoring "task orientation" over "people orientation," to use popular leadership style terminology, no particular style marks the stressful executive. Even the democratic leader, for example, can develop anxieties about an approaching deadline, prompting stress-induced reactions that may or may not be visible to subordinates.

Executives are by nature doers. Thus, they induce stress in

themselves by their willingness to assume more and more responsibility. Contrary to the stereotypical assertiveness and "thick skin" assumed to be characteristics of an individual in a leadership position, executives are extremely sensitive to the goal of responsiveness, even when a particular request is unreasonable or would overburden their staff, and are, therefore, often victims of the "guilt" syndrome for even contemplating saying "no."[65] What, then, can an executive do to cope with stress?

One suggestion is to engage in one of the mind-over-matter techniques that have a calming effect. Richard Stein describes four of these techniques:

1. the Jacobson deep muscle relaxation procedure, which is a series of mild bending, clenching, and flexing maneuvers done in a set order;
2. meditation exercise, which involves relaxing the body and clearing the mind, thinking only of a serene picture; in order to clear the mind, a chant (mantra) may be recited;
3. deep-breathing exercises; and,
4. biofeedback techniques, which involve an effort to gain voluntary control over bodily functions through the use of a mechanical aid, usually electronic.[66]

In addition, vigorous physical exercise, such as jogging, is often suggested, as is good nutrition.[67] Such advice, however, is often thwarted by the tendency of high achievers—including leaders—to opt for spectator rather than participant sports,[68] and to indulge in less-than-nutritious executive lunches (or fast food in the office).

Another suggestion for dealing with stress is the maintenance of an interpersonal support network.[69] Because a city has only one mayor and only one city manager, if any at all, municipal executives may find it particularly helpful to be active in organizations such as the National League of Cities, the International City Management Association, or state or substate groups affiliated with those or similar associations in order to develop contacts with others in similar positions who can best empathize with local executives.

All of these techniques—mind control, physical exercise, good eating habits, a network of friends and colleagues—help to alleviate stress, but they do not eliminate its causes. Effective time management, on the other hand, attacks a major cause of stress.

A Matter of Style

Suggestions for reducing stress include a variety of techniques potentially influencing lifestyle. Another style issue—work style—is also important to this discussion. Hans Selye has commented on one dimension of style that could apply equally to lifestyle or work style in saying: ". . . decide whether you're a racehorse or a turtle and live your life accordingly."[70] Some individuals thrive on pressure, excitement, constant activity, being needed, making decisions; they are adrift at sea (without the joys of a relaxing sailboat) if left with nothing to do. Others need to work at a slower, more deliberative, and more controlled pace. While no one is immune to negative stress, the dividing line between positive and negative stress varies greatly among individuals. Thus, time-related stress may affect some individuals more negatively than it does others.

Another dimension of work style relevant to time management stems from research on brain dominance. Brain researchers have found that one hemisphere or the other tends to be dominant in most individuals. The left side controls linear thinking, logic, organization, discipline; the right, creativity, intuition, fantasy. This type of research has led to various prescriptions such as exercises for helping managers and entrepreneurs use both sides of their brain and advice that a manager would do well to balance his or her own brain dominance (i.e., left side or right side) by selecting subordinates with a different predilection.[71]

Ann McGee-Cooper has specifically applied brain-dominance research to time management. Based on teaching time-management skills and observing when her advice was taken and when it was not, she concludes that the standard prescriptions may be inappropriate for large numbers of individuals. Essentially, the solutions to time problems, including the ones suggested in this chapter, assume that an individual is left-brained and would more likely thrive in an orderly, logical environment that promotes sequential thinking. McGee-Cooper has found that right-brained people do not respond positively to suggestions such as "finish one task before starting another" or establish a clean, uncluttered work environment. Instead, these individuals like to work on several projects simultaneously, often at a messy work table, and perform much better in that setting.[72]. If McGee-Cooper is correct, standard time-management suggestions can be expected to work well only for executives whose brains are dominated by the left hemisphere.

Summary

This chapter has provided an overview of some of the leading time wasters that plague modern executives and suggested specific remedies for dealing with telephone interruptions, a lack of priorities, procrastination, drop-in visitors, unproductive meetings, excessive paper work, and failure to delegate. When the executive's time is too constrained, stress may result. Mind-control techniques, physical exercise, nutrition, and an adequate support system are all potentially useful mechanisms for coping with stress.

The chapter ends on a cautionary note. Different individuals are affected differently by stress, including that produced by seemingly inadequate time. Some individuals thrive on frantic activity and are not upset by disorder. Others, however, are prone to become upset and may create dysfunctional stress among subordinates. Time-management advice is useful for both groups, allowing the former to pack even more activity into a frantic pace and introducing order in the work world of the latter. Brain-dominance research, however, suggests that not all executives will be equally attracted to time-management prescriptions.

Chapter Eight

CONCLUSIONS

Orchestra conductors or puppets on a string? In reality, neither is a very accurate depiction of chief executives, whether operating in the private sector or the public sector. The previous seven chapters have shown executives in city government to differ from their corporate counterparts in some important respects and to be similar in many, many others.

Not all municipal chief executives view their jobs in the same light; substantial differences exist even among officials holding the same title. Some mayors are deeply grateful for the public trust bestowed upon them and pursue their agendas with almost evangelical zeal. Others, like the former mayor of Baltimore quoted in the first chapter, see the job as just one "plate of crap" after another.[1] Some see problems as opportunities; others, no doubt, would be satisfied to ride out an uneventful tour of duty.

All city executives recognize common roles, demands, work foci, and activities. Not one of the respondents to the 1985 survey expressed great discomfort in accounting for the totality of his or her time within the role dimensions developed by Deil Wright,[2] the work activities enumerated by Henry Mintzberg,[3] or the demand and foci categories that we developed. They differed substantially, however, in their allocations of time to various aspects of their work and in their assessments of the relative importance of municipal executive roles.

The modern history of city government and the evolution of four distinct forms of local government structure provide an important backdrop for understanding not only some of the fundamental functional differences between executive posts, but perhaps more importantly, many of the basic perceptual differences. An awareness of the corruptness of many turn-of-the-century cities and the subsequent platforms of the various reform groups aids in understanding, for example, why chief executives in reformed cities (i.e., city managers) are so much more likely than their counterparts in unreformed cities (i.e., mayors) to think their "political role" to be relatively unimportant to the successful performance of their job.

Perceptual and functional differences are in many ways overshadowed by similarities that transcend forms of government and even the boundary between the public and private sectors. Scholars studying the work of executives have been struck by its fragmented nature, its variety, its brevity, and its sheer magnitude. The uniformity of such observations is striking, whether gained through case studies or any of a variety of methods for investigating time-allocation patterns, and whether they had as their focus public-sector or private-sector executives. Virtually all executives, it seems, exhibit most of the same superficial tendencies—they function at a relentless pace, are frequently interrupted in their work, and are generally overburdened. Fundamental distinctions between executives in different industries, different sectors, or different forms of government appear subtle, at first, when juxtaposed against the obvious similarities that cannot escape even the most undiscerning eye.

Public-sector and private-sector executives alike work long hours. Eight-hour workdays are a privilege for most of their mid- and lower-level subordinates, but not for them. The surveyed mayors report an average workweek of 66 hours; city managers, 57. Immediate subordinates follow the executive pattern, with mayoral assistants reporting an average workweek of 59 hours and assistant city managers reporting 53.

Although the work activities of city executives fit within the categories identified by Mintzberg, fairly substantial differences are evident between time allocations of city executives and those previously reported for other managers, primarily from the private sector, for some work activity categories. Mayors and city managers report spending considerably greater percentages of their time on telephone calls and tours or inspections than do their predominately private-sector counterparts and less on scheduled meetings. Only for desk work and unscheduled meetings are the time allocations relatively uniform across sectors.

The executive function calls for an action orientation and typically thrusts a fast-paced, fragmented, even incremental, mode of operation onto the occupant of the executive chair, even if that occupant would occasionally prefer a more deliberative pace. Management scholars frequently criticize executives for their failure to allocate sufficient time and energies for personally contemplating their organization's future and personally designing elaborate plans to ensure maximum advantage for their organization and its clients or constituents—in other words, for their reactive posture or their failure to adhere to the principles of rational-comprehensive decisionmaking and formal planning. In doing so, they exhibit a fundamental naivete regarding the nature of executive work. As discovered by Mintzberg:

> Trying to keep some time open for contemplation or for general 'planning' will not work. The manager is not a planner in a reflective sense, and no amount of admonition in the literature will make him so. His milieu is one of stimulus-response. The manager must schedule those specific things he wants to do. Then he will be obliged to do them. If he wishes to innovate, he must initiate a project and involve others who will report back to him . . . .[4]

Rational planning processes make magnificent sense, but they suffer mightily under the "real world" pressures that impinge on the temporal, financial, and political resources of city executives. In their study of the agenda-setting processes of 20 mayors, John Kotter and Paul Lawrence found not a single mayor following the rational planning model.[5] Almost one-half were incrementalists, behaving in a muddling through manner, and the rest fell at various points along the incremental-rational continuum, exhibiting characteristics from each model.

Aspects of Managerial Work

If the absence of reflective planning by executives frustrates the writers of scholarly and popular management literature, what frustrates the executives themselves? Responses to a 1980 ICMA survey reveal three primary sources of frustration among local government managers: general job pressures, lack of time for themselves and their families, and dealing with citizens' feelings about local government.[6] Almost two-thirds of the nearly 2,000 local government managers who participated in the survey indicated that they had thought seriously of resigning, many citing long hours and lack of privacy among other concerns.

The job of municipal chief executive would be difficult even without the special environmental factors that subject crucial elements of the decisionmaking process to media scrutiny, restrict the range of practical or legal options for addressing operational problems, and rob the mayor and city manager of the privacy that most of their private-sector counterparts enjoy. Functioning in the local government arena does all of that. Intergovernmental demands, emergencies, and the demands of citizens and legislative officials leave mayors and city managers only a minority of their time for tasks that they undertake as a matter of personal choice. For most, their focus on internal administration consumes only about one-third of their time, with matters of policy development, public relations, city council relations, and intergovernmental relations commanding the remaining two-thirds.

The nature of the work of city executives is defined by work activities, as well as by demands and foci. They report spending one-third of their time in scheduled meetings, followed in descending order of time allocation by desk work, telephone calls, unscheduled meetings, and tours or inspections of municipal operations. Meetings are clearly an important mode of operation for most mayors and city managers. When scheduled and unscheduled meetings are combined, meetings capture virtually one-half of the workday of the typical city executive.

Some local government observers, and even some mayors and city managers themselves, think the key to successful mastery of the demands, competing work foci, and activities lies in the adoption of a particular operating style—perhaps one that has proven effective for some renowned city executive. Unfortunately, mastery of the job of chief executive in a city government is much more complicated than that. Following their study of mayors, Kotter and Lawrence concluded, "The notion that one approach to the mayor's job is best (given any definition of "best") is a fallacy. The same approach, under different conditions, can lead to very different results."[7] The crucial element for Kotter and Lawrence is not the adoption of a particular style, but instead something they call "coalignment."[8]

Kotter and Lawrence's observations about mayors are applicable to other municipal executives as well. Each city executive has (1) a network of groups and individuals with whom they interact, (2) a set of problems and opportunities confronting their organization or community, (3) an agenda of some type for action (or inaction) regarding those problems and opportunities, and (4) an array of personal assets and liabilities. The effective executives are those who can inventory those four key elements and find them to be in general alignment; that is, their personal and interpersonal resources and plans are sufficient to address the problems and opportunities at hand. Imbalance—too much of one element and not enough of another—is likely to cause problems for the executive. According to Kotter and Lawrence, "A large nonalignment sooner or later leads to a crisis situation for the mayor and is almost always responsible for his defeat in the next election. No less than 8 of the 20 mayors in this study suffered these consequences."[9]

Understanding the nature of the work of mayors and city managers—the demands they face, the foci of their efforts, and the activities in which they are engaged—should help to educate an interested student of local government. An awareness of time allocation norms among their counterparts may be revealing to an executive who suspects that his or her own efforts are maldistributed. A grasp of the nature of the work of city executives may even persuade or dissuade a potential mayoral candidate or managerial prospect. But effectiveness in performing the job requires much more than simply understanding its composition. The effective executive is the one who can respond to demands, overcome problems, seize opportunities, motivate subordinates, and, in essence, master the job not only as a technician but as a leader.

Prospects for Time Management

The demands of executive work in city government take a heavy toll on the time of the incumbents. "Free" time—that commodity that management experts tell executives to spend planning, academicians tell them to spend keeping abreast of the latest thinking in the field, physicians tell them to spend exercising, therapists tell them to spend meditating, kids tell them to spend camping, and they promise themselves to spend reading that good book they have been saving for years—is rare. As Mintzberg notes, " 'Free' time is made, not found, in the manager's job. The manager must force it into his schedule."[10]

The quest to "force" some free time into the executive's schedule may take several forms. Some simply schedule a block of time for that free time activity that otherwise never would be undertaken. Others use any of the variety of potentially useful time management techniques that they hope will ease the strain on that nonrenewable resource. Regrettably, many executives fall into neither camp, remaining victims of their own personal time crunch and persisting in their hope for a miraculous discovery of some free time.

The truth of the matter is that while time management is important to city executives, it can help only so much. Some time-consuming functions can be streamlined and made more effective, but cannot be eliminated. Take meetings, for example. Mayors and managers report spending an average of 34% of their time in scheduled meetings and 14% in unscheduled meetings—almost one-half of their time in one form of meeting or another. And meetings are notorious time wasters. Many disgruntled meeting attendees in countless organizations have vented their frustration by reporting the result of their calculation of the salary costs incurred in holding this worthless meeting or that. Discussions ramble; points are repeated; assignments are not made; and elusive conclusions continue to elude. Executives—at least those who are action-oriented—leave such meetings with a sense of frustration. Meetings as a whole cannot be eliminated inasmuch as they represent not only an important means of communication and decisionmaking, but also an important means of group involvement in the decisionmaking process and, thereby, a means of achieving employee acceptance of organizational decisions.[11] But meetings do not have to be poorly organized; they do not have to waste time.

Death, Taxes, and . . . Interruptions?

Perhaps even more intriguing to the time management specialist than the many meetings that executives attend are the myriad odds and ends with which they contend—apparent interruptions in the "real" work of chief executives. Improved priority-setting systems, telephone and visitor screening, uninterruptable blocks of work time, concentrated dictation, concentrated returning of telephone calls, improved delegation of duties, and a wide assortment of other techniques seem to offer opportunities for enormous time savings. Each technique has much to commend it and, indeed, proper application could effect time management gains. It would be a mistake, however, to expect too much.

There is ample reason to believe that fragmentation, brevity, and interruptions are no only facts of executive life, but the preferred operating mode for most executives. Mintzberg reports:

> The five chief executives of my own study appeared to be properly protected by their secretaries, and there was no reason to believe that these men were inferior delegators. In fact, there was

evidence that they *chose* not to free themselves of interruption or to give themselves much free time. To a large extent, it was the chief executives themselves who determined the durations of their activities. For example, the tours that they chose to take could not be interrupted by the telephone, yet they lasted, on an average, only 11 minutes. Furthermore, the managers, not the other parties, terminated many of the meetings and telephone calls, and the managers frequently left meetings before they ended. They frequently interrupted their desk work to place telephone calls or to request that subordinates come by. One chief executive located his desk so that he could look down a long hallway. The door was usually open, and his subordinates were continually coming into his office. He fully realized that by moving his desk, closing his door, or changing the rules his secretary used to screen callers, he could easily have eliminated many of these interruptions.[12]

Mintzberg concluded that executives tolerate fragmentation, brevity, and interruptions for four reasons. First, they value current information and wish to do nothing to damage its flow to them. Second, they grow to enjoy great variety in their work and would be bored by anything less. Third, they become sensitive to the opportunity costs of their time allocation decisions; i.e., a decision to do one thing, even something of considerable value, denies the executive the opportunity to do other things also of value. Fourth, they are acutely aware of the obligations that come with their job—the things that only they, as chief executive, can do—and they race against the clock to fulfill those obligations.[13]

> In effect, the manager is encouraged by the realities of his work to develop a particular personality—to overload himself with work, to do things abruptly, to avoid wasting time, to participate only when the value of participation is tangible, to avoid too great an involvement with any one issue. To be superficial is, no doubt, an occupational hazard of managerial work. In order to succeed, the manager must, presumably, become proficient at his superficiality.[14]

The Urgency of Time Management

Mintzberg's description conveys primarily a strong sense of the frenetic pace of modern executives; somewhat more subtle is the time management message. Executives abhor the wasting of time. Those who are successful develop a keen sense of priorities, involving themselves only when tangible benefits are likely to be achieved from such involvement. Furthermore, they are adept at delegating work to subordinates, making such assignments carefully so as to minimize the need for subsequent personal involvement.

The importance of managing their time to the extent possible is intensified for city executives by their feeling that much of that commodity is already being controlled by persons other than themselves. On average, mayors report a perception that 37% of their workweek is controlled by others, leaving 63% under their own control. For city managers, the average perception is that 41% of their workweek is controlled by others. Persons who have built a career on the strength of demonstrable performance, as have most executives, take pride in their ability to set targets and to achieve them. They, more than others, are likely to be frustrated by interference and distractions, regardless of the source. Public pronouncements of their allegiance to basic democratic principles notwithstanding, mayors and city managers cannot possibly avoid the feeling that progress on their own agenda is threatened when city councils, citizen groups, chambers of commerce, and other interests place major unanticipated demands on their shoulders. Time is a precious resource to such persons, and methods for achieving even marginal gains in its effective use are of considerable value.

Overwork and Frustration

The delegating of work to subordinates seems an obvious solution—and much delegation does, in fact, take place. But delegating is only a partial answer, limited as the practice is by practical constraints. As Mintzberg points out, the executive is "damned . . . either to a life of overwork or to one of frustration."[15] Either the executive attempts to do all the work personally or work is delegated to persons who do not have benefit of all the knowledge, all the insights, and all the possible information sources that the executive has. To attempt to convey all of that knowledge and special insight, and to attempt to funnel each bit of relevant information as it enters the system would negate much of the advantage of delegating the work in the first place. The executive must either direct the work personally or accept the imperfections that inevitably accompany the performance of work attempted without the benefit of full information—hence the choice, overwork or frustration.

For most city executives, it seems, the decision is clear—overwork *and* frustration. Anecdotal evidence strongly suggests a tendency, especially well-documented among mayors, to be extremely demanding both on themselves and on subordinates. San Antonio's Mayor Henry Cisneros, for example, is known as an intense, hard-driving boss. Quoting the director of his political support organization: "He's a perfectionist. Excellent is merely the status quo. He's friendly with staff, but he expects staff to meet his standards. And they're tough. If we work 100 hours a week, he works 120."[16]

Such sentiments are reiterated by others associated with Cisneros. According to a high-ranking city official in San Antonio, "He can't accept flaws in himself or others. For Henry, being human is a weakness."[17]

Donald Schaefer of Baltimore was also known as an extremely demanding mayor. He surrounded himself with capable people and he delegated considerable work to them, but his operating style would hardly be described as "detached." He insisted on getting the desired results and his outbursts, when those results were not forthcoming, were legendary:

> He didn't want to hear 'I'm not sure how . . . .' He'd snap, 'If you don't know how to do it, then do it MY WAY.' He didn't want to hear 'We can't . . . .' [His face] would get red and he'd scream, 'If you can't, I'll get someone else. What the hell have I got YOU for?'
>
> When they got it done, he wanted to know, 'What's *new?* NEW!'
>
> It worked, too. They busted their butts. They wracked their brains. When it came time to talk, they credited 'his inspiration, drive . . . .' Curiously, it was only the oldest, who went back with him the longest, who wondered, 'Why so desperate?' But they didn't wonder aloud.[18]

Why so desperate? The answer appears to lie in the intense pride characteristic of mayors, and perhaps other chief executives as well, and in the recognition of an inevitable linkage between the perceived accomplishments of their administration and their personal stature as a leader. In the words of Mayor Dianne Feinstein of San Francisco, "Always you feel you've got to do better because if you don't, you're not going to succeed." [19]

Cisneros' elaboration cuts to the point:

> Rewards go to those who are relentless in their pursuit[s] and

work with intensity to achieve them. Very few people understand the importance of intensity, of single-mindedness.

And you must keep in mind always that the possibility exists we could have done a better job.[20]

The management of performance and the management of time, whether pursued consciously or subconsciously, are not distinctly separable matters for such executives. They go hand in hand.

The Future

If the predictions of many local government observers come true, many of the distinctions between mayors and city managers found in this study will begin to blur in the years ahead. The premise of a politics-administration dichotomy, a proposition that anchored the call for a professional manager as chief executive in local government, continues to erode in practice, long after academic pronouncements of its demise. In part, that erosion is a reflection of the constant quest for the leadership necessary to solve the problems of the nation's cities.

James Banovetz predicted in 1971 that a "preoccupation with problems of a policy nature" would replace concentration on traditional line management functions as the primary concern of urban administrators.[21] That such a forecast was logical is seemingly borne out by the fact that modern city managers ascribe to the "policy role" greater importance for job success than they do to either the "management role" or the "political role." More than one-third of the mayors in this study also named the policy role as most important, second only to the 42% reserving that status for the political role. Yet, a difference persists between the logic that would propel policy concerns to top priority status and the reality of actual time allocations. City executives continue to report spending more time on the management role than on either of the other two.

David Welborn predicted an increasingly external focus for city managers in the future, requiring larger doses of political skill and social sensitivity.[22] A 1980 ICMA survey, however, revealed a split in perceptions among local government managers on this issue, some predicting greater responsibility for "brokering and negotiation" and others envisioning a "technical managerial role" involving "pure management, leaving politics to 'the politicians'."[23] In reporting the results of the ICMA survey, Richard Stillman identified a "Back-to-the-Fundamentals School" and a "Forward-to-the-New-Horizons School":

The first school, by and large, tends to see the profession moving toward a more technical, specialized, "pure management" (in the words of one manager) in which fewer local services will be provided and the narrower traditional values of economy, efficiency, and effectiveness will tend to predominate . . . .

But an equal number of managers took the opposite view, namely, that city managers will be pressed into dealing with far broader issues and concerns, and therefore will be compelled to adopt new roles. This will require a greater understanding of human needs, skills, and values in order to function effectively.[24]

The views of the "Forward-to-the-New-Horizons School" coincide most closely with predominant academic views and with those most prominently advanced by the ICMA itself.[25] According to such a forecast, managers increasingly will become involved in significant matters of community leadership, policy formulation and advocacy, negotiation, and brokering, leaving greater shares of their internal administrative duties to subordinates.

If the "New Horizons" predictions materialize, many of the heretofore sharp differences between the roles of the city manager and the mayor in mayor-council cities will fade. At least three factors, however, militate against the likelihood of a complete blurring of the distinctions:

1. The educational backgrounds and, hence, the orientations of mayors and city managers tend to differ. Although managers increasingly are obtaining formal education in graduate programs of public administration that stress the importance of policy analysis, leadership, and political astuteness, as well as competence in more technical functions, their orientation to the former and their grounding in the latter are likely to produce a different type of executive than one ascending to the office of mayor.
2. City managers will continue to serve at the pleasure of city councils under the council-manager form of government. City council members will continue to be motivated to seek office by a variety of factors including not only community service, civic obligation, and altruism, but ego gratification, as well. The spotlight can become crowded if too many star performers move to center stage. After they have been elected to office, council members have the authority to name the few remaining key members of the cast and to determine who the

stars will be and who will hold supporting roles. They are likely to continue to guard against encroachments by appointees on their role, their prerogatives, and their status.
3. The fundamental differences that have existed in the past between the roles of mayor and city manager, including especially the lesser constraints placed on the former in a "strong" mayor setting, are likely to continue to attract persons of differing personalities and skills to the two positions. This self-selection process will contribute to the preservation of many of the fundamental differences.

The evolution of the roles of chief executive in city government, some of which is chronicled herein, is undeniable. Change is inevitable. The nature of the change in the city manager's role is toward greater involvement in the policy process, yet it would be a mistake to convey a false image of abandonment of internal administration as a major activity and a continuing responsibility. The facts simply do not yet bear out such a development.

The degree to which the roles of city executives will change and the speed at which that change will occur are matters of conjecture. The likelihood that the work of these municipal leaders will remain burdensome, fragmented, characterized by brevity and interruption, and fodder for time management seems assured.

APPENDIX

Table A-1

PROFILE OF RESPONDENTS, BY FORM OF GOVERNMENT, POSITION CATEGORY, AND CITY POPULATIONS

Form of Government	Position Category	City Population 50,000 to 74,999	75,000 to 100,000	Greater than 100,000	TOTAL
Council-Manager	Chief Executive	63	30	60	153
	Assistant	73	43	84	200
Mayor-Council or Commission	Mayor/Chief Executive	29	14	30	73
	Assistant	27	20	54	101
TOTAL		192	107	228	527[a]

[a] N excludes missing data and responses not completed by the official personally, but by an aide.

Table A-2

GENERAL LINEAR MODEL (GLM) TABLES FOR REPORTED TIME ALLOCATIONS OF MAYORS, MAYORAL ASSISTANTS, CITY MANAGERS, AND ASSISTANT CITY MANAGERS

Dependent Variable: Working Hours per Week
Explanatory Variables: Position, Population, Interaction of Position and Population

Source	Degrees of Freedom	Sum of Squares	Mean Squares	F-ratio	Significance	R-square
Model	11	11,410.6	1,037.3	15.90	0.0001	0.258
Error	502	32,747.0	65.2			
Corrected Total	513	44,157.5				

Dependent Variable: Percentage of Time Devoted to the Management Role
Explanatory Variables: Position, Population, Interaction of Position and Population

Source	Degrees of Freedom	Sum of Squares	Mean Squares	F-ratio	Significance	R-square
Model	11	22,034.9	2,003.2	8.07	0.0001	0.151
Error	499	123,900.2	248.3			
Corrected Total	510	145,935.1				

Dependent Variable: Percentage of Time Devoted to the Policy Role
Explanatory Variables: Position, Population, Interaction of Position and Population

Source	Degrees of Freedom	Sum of Squares	Mean Squares	F-ratio	Significance	R-square
Model	11	6,199.4	563.6	3.97	0.0001	0.080
Error	499	70,858.1	142.0			
Corrected Total	510	77,057.5				

Table A-2--Continued

Dependent Variable: Percentage of Time Devoted to the Political Role
Explanatory Variables: Position, Population, Interaction of Position and Population

Source	Degrees of Freedom	Sum of Squares	Mean Squares	F-ratio	Significance	R-square
Model	11	16,334.2	1,484.9	13.06	0.0001	0.224
Error	499	56,732.4	113.7			
Corrected Total	510	73,066.6				

Table A-3

SUMMARY OF SIGNIFICANT EXPLANATORY VARIABLES IDENTIFIED THROUGH STEPWISE REGRESSION FOR WORKING HOUR AND TIME ALLOCATION VARIATION AMONG MAYORS AND CITY MANAGERS

(N = 205)

Dependent Variable	Explanatory Variable	B-Value sign (+/-)	Partial R^2	Cumulative R^2	F	Significance
Working Hrs. Per Week	MAYOR[a]	+	.184	.184	45.6	.000
	AGE[b]	-	.022	.206	5.6	.019
Percentage of Time Devoted to Management Role	MAYOR[a]	-	.040	.040	8.5	.004
	MPA[c]	-	.040	.080	8.8	.003
	POPULATION[d]	-	.025	.106	5.7	.018
	AGE[b]	+	.028	.133	6.4	.012
Percentage of Time Devoted to Policy Role	MAYOR[a]	-	.066	.066	14.4	.000
	AGE[b]	-	.039	.105	8.8	.003
	POPULATION[d]	+	.034	.139	7.8	.006
Percentage of Time Devoted to Political Role	MAYOR[a]	+	.242	.242	64.9	.000
	MPA[c]	+	.015	.258	4.1	.044

[a] MAYOR variable is coded "1" for mayors and "0" for city managers.
[b] AGE variable is coded "1" for 35 or younger, "2" for 36 to 50, "3" for 51 to 65, and "4" for 66 or older.
[c] MPA variable is coded "1" for master of public administration degrees or equivalent (e.g., MGA); "0" for other degrees or levels of education.
[d] POPULATION variable is the 1980 census population.

NOTES:
(1) Variables included in the analysis of the dependent variable "working hours per week" were: years employed in current position, percentage of time allocated to the management role, percentage of time allocated to the policy role, percentage of time allocated to the political role, and the four variables described above--mayor, age, MPA, and population.

(2) Variables included in the analysis of the dependent variables dealing with percentage of time allocations were: working hours per week, years employed in current position, and the four variables described in footnotes a-d.

(3) Only variables significant at the 0.05 level are included in the models.

Table A-4

PEARSON CORRELATION COEFFICIENTS FOR SOURCES OF DEMAND ON EXECUTIVE WORKWEEK IN CITY GOVERNMENT

Pearson's r
(N)

	Citizen-, Mayor-, or Council-Selected Tasks	Intergovernmental Demands	Emergencies	City Manager-Selected Tasks[a]	Self-Selected Tasks
Citizen-, Mayor-, or Council-Selected Tasks	1.000** (518)				
Intergovernmental Demands	.046 (518)	1.000** (518)			
Emergencies	-.030 (518)	.027 (518)	1.000** (518)		
City Manager-Selected Tasks[a]	0.284** (199)	-.172* (199)	-.189** (199)	1.000** (199)	
Self-Selected Tasks	-.493** (518)	-.319** (518)	-.222 (518)	-.567** (199)	1.000** (518)

[a]This category pertains only to assistant city managers.

*p < .05
**p < .01

Table A-5

PEARSON CORRELATION COEFFICIENTS FOR FOCI OF MUNICIPAL EXECUTIVE WORK

Pearson's r
(N)

	City Council Relations	Inter-governmental Relations	Public Relations	Policy Development	Internal Administrative Activities
City Council Relations	1.000** (522)				
Intergovernmental Relations	.010 (522)	1.000** (522)			
Public Relations	-.182** (522)	.067 (522)	1.000** (522)		
Policy Development	-.113** (522)	.025 (522)	-.097* (522)	1.000** (522)	
Internal Administrative Activities	-.497** (522)	-.424** (522)	-.485** (522)	-.396** (522)	1.000** (522)

*p < .05
**p < .01

Table A-6

PEARSON CORRELATION COEFFICIENTS FOR ACTIVITIES IN MUNICIPAL EXECUTIVE WORK

Pearson's r
(N)

	Desk Work	Telephone Calls	Scheduled Meetings	Unscheduled Meetings	Inspections of Municipal Activities
Desk Work	1.000** (521)				
Telephone Calls	-.185** (521)	1.000** (521)			
Scheduled Meetings	-.617** (521)	-.296** (521)	1.000** (521)		
Unscheduled Meetings	-.365** (521)	-.094* (521)	-.131** (521)	1.000** (521)	
Inspections of Municipal Activities	-.164** (521)	-.152** (521)	-.237** (521)	-.001 (521)	1.000** (521)

*p < .05
**p < .01

Table A-7

PEARSON CORRELATION COEFFICIENTS FOR WORK ACTIVITIES, FOCI, AND DEMANDS ON EXECUTIVE TIME IN CITY GOVERNMENT

Pearson's r
(N)

ACTIVITIES	FOCI					DEMANDS				
	City Council Relations	Intergovernmental Relations	Public Relations	Policy Development	Internal Administrative Activities	Citizen, Mayor, or Council-Selected Tasks	Intergovernmental Demands	Emergencies	City Manager-Selected Tasks[a]	Self-Selected Tasks
Desk Work	-.004 (516)	-.090* (516)	-.166** (516)	-.150** (516)	.219** (516)	-.075 (514)	-.086 (514)	-.204** (514)	.011 (198)	.016 (514)
Telephone Calls	.027 (516)	.091* (516)	.303** (516)	-.111* (516)	-.185** (516)	.151** (514)	.193** (514)	.091* (514)	-.104 (198)	-.196** (514)
Scheduled Meetings	.048 (516)	-.043 (516)	.001 (516)	.183** (516)	-.113* (516)	.035 (514)	-.032 (514)	.008 (514)	.144* (198)	.053 (514)
Unscheduled Meetings	-.059 (516)	.067 (516)	-.046 (516)	.088* (516)	-.003 (516)	-.031 (514)	.011 (514)	.201** (514)	-.125 (198)	.008 (514)
Inspections of Municipal Activities	-.055 (516)	.080 (516)	.013 (516)	-.025 (516)	.012 (516)	-.069 (514)	-.011 (514)	.064 (514)	-.036 (198)	.096* (514)

[a] This column pertains only to assistant city managers.

*p < .05
**p < .01

Table A-8

PEARSON CORRELATION COEFFICIENTS FOR POPULATION, WORKING HOURS, PERCEIVED EXECUTIVE CONTROL OF TIME, AND CHARACTERISTICS OF MUNICIPAL EXECUTIVE WORK

Pearson's r
(N)

	FOCI				ACTIVITIES					DEMANDS				
	City Council Relations	Inter-governmental Relations	Public Relations	Policy Development	Internal Administrative Activities	Desk Work	Telephone Calls	Scheduled Meetings	Un-scheduled Meetings	Inspections of Municipal Activities	Citizen-, Mayor-, or Council-Selected Tasks	Inter-governmental Demands	Emergencies	City Manager-Selected Tasks[a]	Self-Selected Tasks
1980 Population	-.031 (522)	.005 (522)	-.035 (522)	.121** (522)	-.022 (522)	-.143** (521)	-.031 (521)	.138** (521)	.070 (521)	-.026 (521)	.009 (518)	.031 (518)	.080 (518)	.139* (199)	.018 (518)
Work Hours of Executive	-.054 (510)	.157** (510)	.164** (510)	.159** (510)	-.204** (510)	-.171** (508)	.037 (508)	.144** (508)	-.031 (508)	.047 (508)	.091* (505)	.201** (505)	.117** (505)	-.014 (196)	.062 (505)
Perceived Extent to which Workweek is Controlled by Executive	-.076 (517)	.048 (517)	-.046 (517)	.028 (517)	.048 (517)	.112* (516)	-.102* (516)	-.045 (516)	-.089* (516)	.088* (516)	.144** (514)	-.028 (514)	-.234** (514)	-.180* (196)	.363** (514)
Perceived Extent to which Workweek is Controlled by Others	.076 (517)	-.048 (517)	.046 (517)	-.028 (517)	-.048 (517)	-.112* (516)	.102* (516)	.045 (516)	.089* (516)	-.088* (516)	.144** (514)	.028 (514)	.234** (514)	.180* (196)	-.363** (514)

[a]This column pertains only to assistant city managers.

*p < .05
**p < .01

Table A-9

FOCUS OF EXECUTIVE WORK IN CITY GOVERNMENT, BY POSITION AND CITY SIZE--
PERCENTAGE OF TIME DEVOTED TO VARIOUS FOCI

Focus of Work/ City Size	Mayors	N	Mayoral Assistants	N	City Managers	N	Asst. City Managers	N
City Council Relations/								
greater than 100,000	13.5	30	16.2	53	27.0	59	21.3	84
75,000 - 100,000	14.2	14	21.3	20	28.1	29	18.5	43
50,000 - 74,999	18.0	28	16.8	27	25.5	62	16.6	73
All cities	15.4	72	17.4	100	26.6	150	19.0	200
Intergovernmental Relations/								
greater than 100,000	13.5	30	11.0	53	8.9	59	7.0	84
75,000 - 100,000	8.7	14	9.1	20	11.3	29	8.0	43
50,000 - 74,999	10.9	28	11.1	27	8.0	62	7.8	73
All cities	11.6	72	10.6	100	9.0	150	7.5	200
Public Relations/								
greater than 100,000	26.7	30	14.8	53	13.3	59	11.5	84
75,000 - 100,000	26.4	14	16.3	20	14.0	29	15.0	43
50,000 - 74,999	23.7	28	16.7	27	12.4	62	15.0	73
All cities	25.5	72	15.6	100	13.1	150	13.5	200
Policy Development/								
greater than 100,000	20.0	30	19.1	53	18.0	59	16.9	84
75,000 - 100,000	15.4	14	16.5	20	16.1	29	12.7	43
50,000 - 74,999	16.3	28	13.8	27	17.6	62	15.5	73
All cities	17.7	72	17.1	100	17.5	150	15.4	200

Table A-9--Continued

Internal Administration.../								
greater than 100,000	[26.4]	30	[39.0]	53	[32.7]	59	[43.4]	84
75,000 - 100,000	[35.3]	14	[36.9]	20	[30.6]	29	[45.8]	43
50,000 - 74,999	[31.1]	28	[41.6]	27	[36.5]	62	[45.1]	73
All cities	[30.0]	72	[39.3]	100	[33.9]	150	[44.5]	200
...as manager/								
greater than 100,000	15.0	30	21.2	53	19.1	59	24.3	84
75,000 - 100,000	21.6	14	18.0	20	18.4	29	23.9	43
50,000 - 74,999	17.2	28	17.4	27	22.2	62	20.5	73
All cities	17.1	72	19.7	100	20.3	150	22.8	200
...as mentor/								
greater than 100,000	6.2	30	10.4	53	8.6	59	9.7	84
75,000 - 100,000	7.7	14	9.9	20	6.5	29	10.7	43
50,000 - 74,999	7.7	28	10.6	27	8.7	62	10.1	73
All cities	7.1	72	10.3	100	8.2	150	10.0	200
...as specialist/technologist/								
greater than 100,000	5.2	30	7.4	53	5.0	59	9.4	84
75,000 - 100,000	6.0	14	9.0	20	5.6	29	11.3	43
50,000 - 74,999	6.1	28	13.6	27	5.6	62	14.5	73
All cities	5.7	72	9.3	100	5.4	150	11.6	200
Total (all cities)[a]	100.1	72	100.0	100	100.1	150	99.8	200

[a] Some columns do not add to 100.0% due to rounding.

Table A-10

PEARSON CORRELATION COEFFICIENTS FOR TIME ALLOCATION BY CHIEF EXECUTIVES AND ASSISTANTS IN THE SAME CITY

Time Allocation	Mayors & Mayoral Assistants (N = 45 pairs)	City Managers & Asst. City Managers (N = 138 pairs)
Hours of Work per Week	.072	-.025
City Council Relations	.245	.275**
Intergovernmental Relations	-.129	.104
Public Relations	.014	.062
Policy Development	.075	.071
Internal Administrative Activities	-.015	.076
Managerial Role	.131	.034
Mentor Role	.014	.108
Specialist/Technologist Role	-.031	.044
Desk Work	.217	.062
Telephone Calls	.098	.059
Scheduled Meetings	.336*	.344**
Unscheduled Meetings	.060	-.116
Inspections of Municipal Activities	-.061	-.007

*p < .05
**p < .01

Table A-11

PERCENTAGES OF EXECUTIVE RESPONDENTS IN SPECIFIED AGE CATEGORIES, BY POSITION HELD AND POPULATION OF JURISDICTION SERVED

Position/Age	50,000-74,999	Population Served 75,000-100,000	Greater than 100,000	Total
Mayor	(N=29)	(N=13)	(N=30)	(N=72)
35 or younger	13.8	15.4	13.3	13.9
36 to 50	51.7	38.5	46.7	47.2
51 to 65	34.5	30.8	33.3	33.3
66 or older	0.0	15.4	6.7	5.6
Total	100.0	100.1	100.0	100.0
Mayoral Assistant	(N=27)	(N=20)	(N=54)	(N=101)
35 or younger	37.0	20.0	24.1	26.7
36 to 50	51.9	50.0	51.9	51.5
51 to 65	7.4	30.0	24.1	20.8
66 or older	3.7	0.0	0.0	1.0
Total	100.0	100.0	100.1	100.0
City Manager	(N=63)	(N=30)	(N=60)	(N=153)
35 or younger	7.9	13.3	8.3	9.2
36 to 50	55.6	53.3	56.7	55.6
51 to 65	36.5	33.3	35.0	35.3
66 or older	0.0	0.0	0.0	0.0
Total	100.0	99.9	100.0	100.1
Assistant City Manager	(N=73)	(N=42)	(N=82)	(N=197)
35 or younger	34.2	40.5	20.7	29.9
36 to 50	50.7	45.2	64.6	55.3
51 to 65	13.7	14.3	14.6	14.2
66 or older	1.4	0.0	0.0	0.5
Total	100.0	100.0	99.9	99.9

Table A-12

PERCENTAGES OF EXECUTIVE RESPONDENTS POSSESSING GRADUATE DEGREES, BY POSITION HELD AND POPULATION OF JURISDICTION SERVED

Position	50,000-74,999 (N=192)	75,000-100,000 (N=107)	Greater than 100,000 (N=227)	Total (N=526)
Mayor (N = 72)	27.6	14.3	48.3	33.3
Mayoral Assistant (N = 101)	29.6	30.0	55.6	43.6
City Manager (N = 153)	65.1	73.3	71.7	69.3
Assistant City Manager (N = 200)	63.0	60.5	75.0	67.5
Total (N = 526)	53.6	52.3	66.1	58.7

Table A-13

PERCENTAGES OF EXECUTIVE RESPONDENTS POSSESSING MPA DEGREE, BY POSITION HELD AND POPULATION OF JURISDICTION SERVED

Position	50,000-74,999 (N=192)	75,000-100,000 (N=107)	Greater than 100,000 (N=228)	Total (N=527)
Mayor (N = 73)	3.4	7.1	0.0	2.7
Mayoral Assistant (N = 101)	14.8	15.0	14.8	14.9
City Manager (N = 153)	50.8	50.0	46.7	49.0
Assistant City Manager (N = 200)	38.4	37.2	45.2	41.0
Total (N = 527)	33.9	32.7	32.5	33.0

NOTES

Chapter One

1. See, for example, Peter F. Drucker, *The Practice of Management* (New York: Harper and Row, 1954), pp. 341–42; and Sune Carlson, *Executive Behavior: A Study of the Work Load and the Working Methods of Managing Directors* (Stockholm: Strombergs, 1951).

2. See, for example, "A Rust-Belt Relic's New Shine," *Newsweek*, 106 (September 9, 1985), p. 26.

3. Henry Mintzberg, *The Nature of Managerial Work* (New York: Harper & Row, 1973).

4. Ibid., pp. 1–6.

5. Henri Fayol, *Administration Industrielle et Generale* (Paris: Dunod, 1916); Luther H. Gulick, "Notes on the Theory of Organization," in L.H. Gulick and L.F. Urwick (eds.), *Papers on the Science of Administration* (New York: Columbia University Press, 1937).

6. Mintzberg, *The Nature of Managerial Work*, p. 4.

7. Drucker, *The Practice of Management*, pp. 341–42.

8. Leonard R. Sayles, *Managerial Behavior: Administration in Complex Organizations* (New York: McGraw-Hill, 1964), p. 162.

9. Carlson, *Executive Behavior*, p. 52.

10. Former Mayor Erik Jonsson of Dallas, quoted in John P. Kotter and Paul R. Lawrence, *Mayors in Action: Five Approaches to Urban Governance* (New York: John Wiley and Sons, 1974), p. 175. Copyright © 1974 by John Wiley & Sons, Inc. Reprinted by permission of John Wiley & Sons, Inc. Although the mayor of Dallas, a council-manager city, is a legislative rather than executive position, the analogy is clearly appropriate for chief executives.

11. Remark attributed to Mayor Tommy D'Alesandro in Richard Ben

Cramer, "Can the Best Mayor Win?"*Esquire*, 102 (October 1984), p. 64. Copyright © 1984. Reprinted by permission of Sterling Lord Literistic, Inc.

12. See, for example, Kotter and Lawrence, *Mayors in Action;* and Ronald O. Loveridge, *City Managers in Legislative Politics* (Indianapolis, Ind.: Bobbs-Merrill, 1971.)

13. Richard Daley was the long-time mayor of Chicago who operated with immense power, despite Chicago's "weak mayor" charter. See, for example, Milton L. Rakove, *Don't Make No Waves; Don't Back No Losers* (Bloomington, Ind.: Indiana University Press, 1975).

14. See, for example, Thomas W. Fletcher, "What is the Future for Our Cities and the City Manager?" *Public Administration Review*, 31 (January/February 1971), pp. 14–20; and David N. Ammons and Joseph C. King, "Productivity Improvement in Local Government: Its Place Among Competing Priorities," *Public Administration Review,* 43 (March/April 1983), pp. 113–20.

15. Two of the many publications addressing the topic of desirable skills are Richard J. Stillman, II, "Local Public Management in Transition: A Report on the Current State of the Profession," in *Municipal Year Book 1982* (Washington, D.C.: International City Management Association, 1982), pp. 171–72; and John Kerrigan and David Hinton, "Knowledge and Skill Needs for Tomorrow's Public Administrators," *Public Administration Review*, 40 (September/October 1980), pp. 469–73.

16. Such a model for mayoral behavior is advanced in Kotter and Lawrence, *Mayors in Action.*

17. Deil S. Wright, "The City Manager as a Developmental Administrator," Chapter 6 in Robert T. Daland (ed.), *Comparative Urban Research* (Beverly Hills, Calif.: Sage Publications, 1969), pp. 203–48.

18. Mintzberg, *The Nature of Managerial Work.*

Chapter Two

1. "Perot to Smith: GM Must Change," *Newsweek,* 108 (December 15, 1986), p. 62.

2. James McGregor Burns, *Leadership* (New York: Harper & Row, 1978), especially pp. 42–45.

3. Harold F. Gortner, Julianne Mahler, and Jeanne Bell Nicholson, *Organization Theory: A Public Perspective* (Chicago: Dorsey, 1987), Chapter 8. Their schema of differentiating among levels of leadership follows the

classification of Daniel Katz and Robert L. Kahn, *The Social Psychology of Organizations* (New York: John Wiley & Sons, 1966).

4. Thomas J. Peters and Robert H. Waterman, Jr., *In Search of Excellence: Lessons from America's Best-Run Companies* (New York: Harper & Row, 1982), pp. 81–86.

5. Luther Gulick, "Notes on the Theory of Organization," in Luther Gulick and L. Urwick (eds.), *Papers on the Science of Administration* (New York: Augustus M. Kelley, 1969, originally published by Institute of Public Administration, 1937), p. 13. Gulick's conceptualizations were based on those of Henri Fayol, *General and Industrial Management*, trans. Constance Storrs (London: Sir Isaac Pitman and Sons, 1949, originally published in Paris by Dunod in 1925). While classical notions dominated thinking about organizations until after World War II, they were successfully challenged. See, for example, Herbert A. Simon, "The Proverbs of Administration," *Public Administration Review*, 4 (Winter 1946), pp. 53–67, and *Administrative Behavior: A Study of Decision-Making Processes in Administrative Organization*, 2d ed. (New York: Macmillan, 1957).

6. See, for example, William G. Scott, "Organization Theory: An Overview and an Appraisal," in Joseph A. Litterer (ed.), *Organizations: Structure and Behavior* (New York: John Wiley & Sons, 1965), pp. 13–26, who provides a helpful review of classical, neoclassical, and modern organization theory.

7. Henry Mintzberg, *The Nature of Managerial Work* (New York: Harper & Row, 1973), pp. 59–62.

8. Ibid., Chapter 4.

9. Ibid., pp. 92–93; quotation on p. 92.

10. Michael D. Cohen and James G. March, *Leadership and Ambiguity: The American College President,* 2d ed. (Boston: Harvard Business School Press, 1986), pp. 37–39.

11. Chester I. Barnard, *The Functions of the Executive* (Cambridge, Mass.: Harvard University Press, 1962; originally published in 1938).

12. Ibid., pp. 217–34, 258–84; quotation on p. 283. For a capsule version of Barnard's thinking, see Michael M. Harmon and Richard T. Mayer, *Organization Theory for Public Administration* (Boston: Little, Brown, 1986), pp. 102–18.

13. Burns, *Leadership*, p. 45.

14. Phillip Selznick, *Leadership in Administration* (New York: Harper & Row, 1957), pp. 56–64.

15. Gortner, Mahler, and Nicholson, *Organization Theory*, p. 292.

16. See, for example, Peter F. Drucker, *Managing in Turbulent Times* (New

York: Harper & Row, 1980); Warren Bennis and Philip E. Slater, *The Temporary Society* (New York: Harper & Row, 1968); Warren Bennis and Burt Nanus, *Leaders: The Strategies for Taking Charge* (New York: Harper & Row, 1985); *Leadership for Dynamic State Economies* (New York: Committee for Economic Development, 1986); and Donald C. Hambrick and Phyllis A. Mason, "Upper Echelons: The Organization as a Reflection of Its Top Managers," *Academy of Management Review*, 9 (April 1984), pp. 293–306. The first four volumes focus on the need for strategic management while the Hambrick and Mason article focuses on predicting strategic outcomes.

17. See, for example, Joyce D. Ross, "City Management and Leadership: A Necessary Partnership," *Public Management*, 68 (August 1986), pp. 14–15; John F. Azzaretto, "Integrating Management and Leadership," *Public Management*, 68 (August 1986), pp. 15–16, and George P. Barbour and George A. Sipel, "Excellence in Leadership: Public Sector Model," *Public Management*, 68 (August 1986), pp. 3–5.

18. Mintzberg, *The Nature of Managerial Work*, p. 61.

19. John D. Millett, *Organization for the Public Service* (Princeton, N.J.: D. Van Nostrand, 1966).

20. John Rehfuss, "The Convergence of Public and Private Management Environments," paper presented at the Annual Conference of the American Society for Public Administration, Honolulu, March 1982.

21. Michael A. Murray, "Comparing Public and Private Management: An Exploratory Essay," *Public Administration Review*, 35 (July/August 1975), pp. 364–71.

22. See, for example, Katz and Kahn, *The Social Psychology of Organizations*, and James D. Thompson, *Organizations in Action* (New York: McGraw-Hill, 1967).

23. See, for example, David B. Truman, *The Governmental Process* (New York: Alfred A. Knopf, 1951), and Robert T. Golembiewski, "Organization Development in Public Agencies: Perspectives on Theory and Practice," *Public Administration Review*, 29 (July/August 1969), pp. 367–77.

24. James D. Thompson and William J. McEwen, "Organization Goals and Environment: Goal Setting as an Interaction Process," *American Sociological Review*, 28 (February 1958), pp. 23–31.

25. Gortner, Mahler, and Nicholson, *Organization Theory*, p. 300.

26. Francis E. Rourke, *Bureaucracy, Politics and Public Policy*, 2d ed. (Boston: Little, Brown, 1976, originally published in 1969).

27. Richard E. Neustadt, *Presidential Power: The Politics of Leadership* (New York: John Wiley & Sons, 1961).

28. John D. Millett, *Organization for the Public Service* (Princeton, N.J.: D. Van Nostrand, 1966), pp. 9–15. Emmette S. Redford, *Democracy in the Administrative State* (New York: Oxford University Press, 1969), pp. 6, 31–35, adds to Millett's nation of social responsibility by positing that only government is responsible for public morality.

29. Louis C. Gawthrop, *Bureaucratic Behavior in the Executive Branch: An Analysis of Organizational Change* (New York: The Free Press, 1969), p. 190.

30. W. Michael Blumenthal, "Candid Reflections of a Businessman in Washington," *Fortune*, January 29, 1979, pp. 36–49.

31. Donald Rumsfeld, "A Politician-Turned-Executive Surveys Both Worlds," *Fortune*, September 10, 1979, pp. 88–94.

32. Hal G. Rainey, Robert W. Backoff, and Charles H. Levine, "Comparing Public and Private Organizations," *Public Administration Review*, 36 (March/April 1976), pp. 233–34.

33. Don McLeod, "Affairs of State Turn Corporate," *Insight*, December 22, 1986, p. 9.

34. Graham T. Allison, Jr.,"Public and Private Management: Are They Fundamentally Alike in All Unimportant Respects," paper presented at the Public Management Research Conference, Brookings Institution, Washington, D.C., November 1979, p. 25; the edited version of this paper appears in James L. Perry and Kenneth L. Kraemer (eds.), *Public Management: Public and Private Perspectives* (Palo Alto, Calif.: Mayfield, 1983), pp. 72–92.

35. Warren Bennis, "Leaders: The Strategies for Taking Charge," *Public Management*, 69 (January 1987), pp. 11–12.

36. Christopher Bellavita, "The Organization of Leadership," *The Bureaucrat*, 15 (Fall 1986), p. 13.

37. John W. Gardner, *The Nature of Leadership* (Washington, D.C.: Independent Sector, 1986), p. 7.

38. Rodd Zolkos, "The Leader Who Stands Where the Buck Stops," *City and State*, 4 (September 1987), p. 15.

39. Thomas Carlyle, *On Heroes and Hero-Worship* (London: Oxford University Press, 1959; originally published in 1841), p. 1.

40. Friedrich Nietzsche, *The Use and Abuse of History*, trans. Adrian Collins (New York: Liberal Arts Press, 1957, originally published in a series of essays, 1873–76).

41. Colleen O'Connor, "High Profile: Jack Evans," *Dallas Morning News*, January 11, 1987, pp. 1E–3E.

42. Ralph M. Stogdill, "Personal Factors Associated with Leadership: A

Survey of the Literature," *Journal of Psychology,* 25 (1948), pp. 35–71. See also Bernard M. Bass (ed.), *Stodgill's Handbook of Leadership* (New York: Free Press, 1981), and Bernard M. Bass, *Leadership, Psychology, and Organizational Behavior* (Westport, Conn.: Greenwood Press, 1960).

43. E.E. Jennings, "The Anatomy of Leadership," *Management of Personnel Quarterly,* (Autumn 1961), as cited in Grover Starling, *Managing the Public Sector,* 3rd ed., (Chicago: Dorsey, 1986), pp. 418, 547.

44. Vincent Vinci, "What It Takes," *Sky,* November 1986, pp. 34–37. A longer but complementary list can be found in Thomas R. Horton, "Qualities of a Successful CEO," *Hyatt Magazine,* Fall 1987, pp. 22–27.

45. Robert Heller, *The Super Managers: Managing for Success, the Movers and the Doers, The Reasons Why* (New York: Dutton, 1984), p. 388.

46. Ibid., and Michael Maccoby, *The Leader: A New Face for American Management* (New York: Simon and Schuster, 1981), p. 221.

47. Chris Argyris, *Executive Leadership: An Appraisal of a Manager in Action* (New York: Harper and Brothers, 1953), p. 4, and *Giants in Management,* ed. Robert L. Haught (Washington, D.C.: National Academy of Public Administration, 1985), pp. 119–20.

48. Argyris, *Executive Leadership,* p. 4.

49. Maccoby, *The Leader,* p. 221, and Heller, *The Super Managers,* p. 388.

50. Bennis, "Leaders: The Strategies for Taking Charge," pp. 11–12, and *Giants in Management,* pp. 119–20.

51. Ibid., and Peters and Waterman, *In Search of Excellence,* p. 84.

52. Argyris, *Executive Leadership,* p. 4, and *Giants in Management,* pp. 119–20.

53. Maccoby, *The Leader,* p. 221, and Heller, *The Super Managers,* p. 388.

54. Maccoby, *The Leader,* p. 221.

55. Peters and Waterman, *In Search of Excellence,* p. 84.

56. See, for example, William B. Eddy, *Public Organization Behavior and Development* (Cambridge, Mass.: Winthrop, 1981), p. 153.

57. Fred E. Fiedler and Martin M. Chemers, *Leadership and Effective Management* (Glenview, Ill.: Scott, Foresman, 1974), p. 40.

58. "What Managers Can Learn from Manager Reagan," *Fortune,* September 15, 1986, cover.

59. This chapter limits discussion of authority to its relationship to leadership style. Individuals interested in more extensive discussions of

authority, influence, and power should see, for example: Max Weber, *The Theory of Social and Economic Organization*, trans. and ed. A.M. Henderson and T. Parsons (New York: Free Press, 1947), Chapter 3; Peter M. Blau, *Bureaucracy* (New York: Random House, 1956); John R.P. French and Bertram Raven, "The Bases of Social Power" in *Studies in Social Power*, ed. Dorwin Cartwright (Ann Arbor, Mich.: Institute for Social Research, 1959), pp. 150–67; and Amatai Etzioni, *A Comparative Analysis of Complex Organizations*, rev. ed. (New York: Free Press, 1975). Related material on transactional analysis can be found in George Graen and Steven Ginsburgh, "Job Resignation as a Function of Role Orientation and Leader Acceptance: A Longitudinal Investigation of Organizational Assimilation," *Organizational Behavior and Human Performance*, 19 (June 1977), pp. 1–17; Eric Berne, *Games People Play: The Psychology of Human Relationships* (New York: Grove Press, 1964); and Thomas A. Harris, *I'm OK— You're OK* (New York: Avon, 1967).

60. Dorwin Cartwright and Alvin Zander, "Leadership and Performance of Group Functions," in Dorwin Cartwright and Alvin Zander (eds.), *Group Dynamics: Research and Theory*, 3rd ed. (New York: Harper & Row, 1968).

61. Robert R. Blake and Jane S. Mouton, *The Managerial Grid III* (Houston: Gulf Publishing, 1985).

62. Douglas McGregor, *The Human Side of Enterprise* (New York: McGraw-Hill, 1960), pp. 33–58.

63. William G. Ouchi, *Theory Z: How American Business Can Meet the Japanese Challenge* (Reading, Mass.: Addison-Wesley, 1981), pp. 251–52.

64. Kurt Lewin, Ronald Lippitt, and Ralph K. White, "Patterns of Aggressive Behavior in Experimentally Created Social Climates," *Journal of Social Psychology*, 10 (February 1939), pp. 271–99, and Kurt Lewin, *Resolving Social Conflict* (New York: Harper & Row, 1948).

65. See, for example, Theodore T. Herbert, *Dimensions of Organizational Behavior*, 2d ed. (New York: Macmillan, 1981), pp. 396–97.

66. Rensis Likert, *New Patterns of Management* (New York: McGraw-Hill, 1961), and *The Human Organization: Its Management and Value* (New York: McGraw-Hill, 1967). An analytical scheme similar to that of Likert can be found in Bernard M. Bass, Enzo R. Valenzi, Dana L. Farrow, and Robert J. Solomon, "Management Styles Associated with Organizational, Task, Personal, and Interpersonal Contingencies," *Journal of Applied Psychology*, 60 (December 1975), pp. 720–29.

67. Warren Bennis and Burt Nanus, *Leaders: The Strategies for Taking Charge* (New York: Harper & Row, 1985).

68. Kenneth Blanchard, "Choosing the Right Management Style," *Public Management*, 68 (August 1986), p. 16.

69. The expression "it all depends" forms part of the title of a book by Harvey Sherman. See *It All Depends: A Pragmatic Approach to Organization* (University, Al.: University of Alabama Press, 1966).

70. Herbert Kaufman, *Time, Chance, and Organizations: Natural Selection in a Perilous Environment* (Chatham, N.J.: Chatham House, 1985).

71. "Thousands File Past Chicago Mayor's Body," *Atlanta Journal and Constitution*, November 29, 1987, p. 16E.

72. Fred E. Fiedler, "A Contingency Model of Leadership Effectiveness," in Leonard Berkowitz (ed.), *Experimental Social Psychology* (New York: Academic Press, 1964), pp. 133–53, and Fred E. Fiedler, *A Theory of Leadership Effectiveness* (New York: McGraw-Hill, 1967).

73. Paul Hersey and Kenneth H. Blanchard, *Management of Organizational Behavior: Utilizing Human Behavior*, 4th ed. (Englewood Cliffs, N.J.: Prentice-Hall, 1982).

74. Chris Argyris, "The Individual and Organization: Some Problems of Mutual Adjustment," *Administrative Science Quarterly*, 2 (June 1957), pp. 1–24.

75. William J. Reddin, *Managerial Effectiveness* (New York: McGraw-Hill, 1970), quotation on p. 40.

76. Robert Tannenbaum and Warren H. Schmidt, "How to Choose a Leadership Pattern," *Harvard Business Review*, 36 (March/April 1958), pp. 95–101, especially pp. 96–97.

77. Ibid., pp. 98–101. A somewhat more complex version of the continuum incorporating the impact of societal changes on managerial freedom appeared in a "Retrospective Commentary" by the authors in 1973. See Robert Tannenbaum and Warren H. Schmidt, "How to Choose a Leadership Pattern," *Harvard Business Review*, 51, No. 3 (May–June 1973), pp. 1–10.

78. Kenneth N. Wexley and Gary A. Yukl, *Organizational Behavior and Personnel Psychology*, rev. ed. (Homewood, Ill.: Richard D. Irwin, 1984), Chapter 7, and Gary A. Yukl, *Leadership in Organizations* (Englewood Cliffs, N.J.: Prentice-Hall, 1981).

79. Robert J. House and Terrance R. Mitchell, "Path-Goal Theory of Leadership," *Journal of Contemporary Business*, 3 (Autumn 1974), pp. 81–87. See also Robert J. House, "A Path-Goal Theory of Leadership Effectiveness," *Administrative Science Quarterly*, 16 (September 1971), pp. 321–28.

Chapter Three

1. Herbert Kaufman develops the theme of evolving political values in his

book *Politics and Policies in State and Local Government* (Englewood Cliffs, N.J.: Prentice-Hall, 1963).

2. See Charles R. Adrian and Charles Press, *Governing Urban America,* 3rd ed. (New York: McGraw-Hill, 1968), pp. 71–83, quotation on p. 83.

3. Woodrow Wilson, "The Study of Administration," *Political Science Quarterly,* 2 (June 1887), p. 210.

4. According to Albert Lepawsky (*Administration: The Art and Science of Organization and Management*; New York: Alfred A. Knopf, 1949, p. 444), Albert Stickney called for a separation of politics and administration as early as 1870.

5. Edward C. Banfield and James Q. Wilson, *City Politics* (New York: Vintage Books, Random House, 1963), p. 142.

6. Robert L. Lineberry and Edmund P. Fowler, "Reformism and Public Policies in American Cities," *American Political Science Review,* 61 (September 1967), pp. 701–16, especially pp. 715–16.

7. Robert B. Boynton, "City Councils: Their Role in the Legislative System," *The Municipal Year Book, 1976* (Washington, D.C.: International City Management Association, 1976), pp. 67–77.

8. Adrian and Press, *Governing Urban America,* pp. 71–80.

9. See James H. Svara, "Unwrapping Institutional Packages in Urban Government: The Combination of Electoral Systems in American Cities," *Journal of Politics,* 39 (February 1977), pp. 166–175, and Ronald G. Claunch and Leon C. Hallman, "Ward Elections in Texas Cities," *Municipal Matrix,* 10 (March 1978), pp. 1–5.

10. See Frederick W. Taylor, *The Principles of Scientific Management* (New York: Harper and Brothers, 1911).

11. Luther Gulick, "Science, Values, and Public Administration," in Luther Gulick and L. Urwick (eds.), *Papers on the Science of Administration* (New York: Institute of Public Administration, 1937), p. 192.

12. Richard J. Stillman II provides a useful reminder that the concept of council-manager government had been advocated as early as 1899 by a California newspaper; see *The Rise of the City Manager: A Public Professional in Local Government* (Albuquerque: University of New Mexico Press, 1974), p. 14.

13. Richard S. Childs, *The First 50 Years of the Council-Manager Plan of Municipal Government* (New York: National Municipal League, 1965), pp. 7–8.

14. John Porter East, *Council-Manager Government: The Political Thought of Its Founder, Richard S. Childs* (Chapel Hill: University of North Carolina Press, 1965), p. 92.

15. Ibid., p. 130.

16. Clarence E. Ridley and Orin Nolting, *The City Manager Profession* (Chicago: University of Chicago Press, 1934), and Clarence E. Ridley, *The Role of the City Manager in Policy Formulation* (Chicago: International City Managers' Association, 1958), pp. 3–6.

17. Leonard D. White, *The City Manager* (Chicago: University of Chicago Press, 1931), pp. 181–82.

18. Harold A. Stone, Don K. Price, and Kathryn H. Stone, *City Manager Government in the United States: A Review After Twenty-Five Years* (Chicago: Public Administration Service, 1940), p. 244.

19. Mark Keane, "Foreward," in Bill Gilbert, *This City, This Man: The Cookingham Era in Kansas City* (Washington, D.C.: International City Management Association, 1978), not paginated.

20. Stone, Price, and Stone, *City Manager Government in the United States*, pp. 178–79, 243.

21. Stillman, *The Rise of the City Manager*, pp. 22–23.

22. Dorothy Strauss Pealy, "The Need for Elected Leadership," *Public Administration Review*, 18 (Summer 1958), pp. 214–16, quotation on p. 214.

23. Karl A. Bosworth, "The Manager *Is* a Politician," *Public Administration Review*, 18 (Summer 1958), pp. 216–22, quotation on p. 220.

24. *The Techniques of Municipal Administration*, 4th ed., published for the Institute for Training in Municipal Administration (Chicago: International City Managers' Association, 1958), Chapters 1 and 2.

25. Gladys M. Kammerer, Charles D. Farris, John M. DeGrove, and Alfred B. Clubok, *City Managers in Politics: An Analysis of Manager Tenure and Termination*, University of Florida Monographs, Social Sciences, No. 13 (Gainesville: University of Florida Press, 1962), p. 10. A later but conceptually related study is that of Fremont J. Lyden and Ernest G. Miller, "Why City Managers Leave the Profession: A Longitudinal Study in the Pacific Northwest," *Public Administration Review*, 36 (March/April 1976), pp. 175–81. Salary and council relations were the two most frequent factors.

26. Ibid., p. 83.

27. Norton E. Long, "Politicians for Hire—The Dilemma of Education and the Task of Research," *Public Administration Review*, 25 (June 1965), pp. 115–20, quotation on p. 117.

28. James M. Banovetz, "The City: Forces of Change," Chapter 2 in James M. Banovetz (ed.), *Managing the Modern City* (Washington, D.C.: International City Management Association, 1971), p. 42. Reprinted with permission.

29. David Welborn, "The Environment and Role of the Administrator,"

Chapter 4 in James M. Banovetz (ed.), *Managing the Modern City* (Washington, D.C.: International City Management Association, 1971), p. 85. Reprinted with permission.

30. Frank Aleshire and Fran Aleshire, "The American City Manager: New Style, New 'Game'." *National Civic Review*, 66 (May 1977), p. 239.

31. Wayne F. Anderson, Chester A. Newland, and Richard J. Stillman II, *The Effective Local Government Manager* (Washington, D.C.: International City Management Association, 1983), Chapter 7.

32. For an excellent examination of this problem, see Lawrence J.R. Herson, "The Lost World of Municipal Government," *American Political Science Review*, 51 (June 1957), pp. 330–95.

33. Neal Gross, Ward S. Mason, and Alexander W. McEachern, *Explorations in Role Analysis: Studies of the School Superintendency* (New York: John Wiley & Sons, 1966), pp. 60, 67.

34. Charles R. Adrian, "A Study of Three Communities," *Public Administration Review*, 18 (Summer 1958), pp. 208–13, quotation on p. 209.

35. Jeptha J. Carrell, "The Role of the City Manager: A Survey Report," *Public Management*, 44 (April 1961), pp. 73–78, and John C. Buechner, *Differences in Role Perceptions in Colorado Council-Manager Cities* (Boulder: Bureau of Governmental Research and Service, University of Colorado, 1965).

36. Kammerer et al., *City Managers in Politics*, p. 11.

37. Deil S. Wright, "The City Manager as a Developmental Administrator," Chapter 6 in *Comparative Urban Research*, ed. Robert T. Daland (Beverly Hills, Calif.: Sage Publications, 1969), pp. 203–48.

38. Keith F. Mulrooney, ed., "A Symposium: The American City Manager: An Urban Administrator in a Complex and Evolving Situation," *Public Administration Review*, 31 (January/February 1971), pp. 6–46.

39. Keith F. Mulrooney, "Prologue: Can City Managers Deal Effectively with Major Social Problems?" *Public Administration Review*, 31 (January/February 1971), pp. 6–14.

40. William V. Donaldson, "Continuing Education for City Managers," *Public Administration Review*, 33 (November/December 1973), p. 505.

41. Ibid., p. 507.

42. Ronald O. Loveridge, *City Managers in Legislative Politics* (Indianapolis: Bobbs-Merrill, 1971), especially pp. 51–57.

43. Jerry L. Yeric, Charldean Newell, and Russell L. Smith, "Professional Administrators and Democratic Beliefs: An Exploratory Analysis," paper presented at the annual meeting of the Midwest Political Science Association,

Chicago, May 1975. This study was based on the responses of 179 city managers and 613 mayors and city council members.

44. Fremont J. Lyden and Ernest G. Miller, "Policy Perspectives of the Northwest City Manager, 1966–1974," *Administration and Society*, 8 (February 1977), pp. 469–480. This study included 83 city managers in 1966 and 82 in a 1974 replication.

45. Edward B. Lewis, "Role Behavior of U.S. City Managers: Development and Testing of a Multidimensional Typology," *International Journal of Public Administration*, 4 (No. 2, 1982), pp. 135–65.

46. Timothy J. Almy, "Local-Cosmopolitanism and U.S. City Managers," *Urban Affairs Quarterly*, 10 (March 1975), pp. 243–275.

47. Alvin Gouldner, "Cosmopolitans and Locals: Toward an Analysis of Latent Social Roles—I, II," *Administrative Science Quarterly*, 2 (December 1957 and March 1958), pp. 281–306, 444–480.

48. Robert J. Huntley and Robert J. Macdonald, "Urban Managers: Organizational Preferences, Managerial Styles, and Social Policy Roles," *The Municipal Year Book, 1975* (Washington, D.C.: International City Management Association, 1975), pp. 153–55.

49. David R. Morgan, "Managing the Urban Future," Chapter 12 in *Managing Urban America*, 2d ed. (Monterey, Calif.: Brooks/Cole, 1984), p. 320.

50. Richard J. Stillman II, "Local Public Management in Transition: A Report on the Current State of the Profession," *The Municipal Year Book, 1982* (Washington, D.C.: International City Management Association, 1982), p. 171. See also John Nalbandian, "The Evolution of Local Governance: A New Democracy," *Public Management*, 69 (June 1987), pp. 2–5.

51. Richard J. Stillman II, "Local Public Management in Transition," *Public Management*, 64 (May 1982), p. 4.

52. Robert V. Camuto, "Knight Has Yet to Show His Mettle in Leading Administration of Dallas," *Dallas Times Herald*, June 22, 1987, p. A-10.

53. Ibid., pp. A-1, A-10.

54. Ibid., p. A-10.

55. Ibid.

56. Anderson, Newland, and Stillman, *The Effective Local Government Manager*, p. 49. Reprinted with permission.

57. ICMA Committee on Future Horizons, . . . *New Worlds of Service* (Washington, D.C.: International City Management Association, 1979), pp. 16–20.

58. Donald A. Blubaugh, "The Changing Role of the Public Administrator," *Public Management*, 69 (June 1987), pp. 9–10. See also Clifford J. Wirth and Michael L. Vasu, "Ideology and Decision Making for American City Managers," *Urban Affairs Quarterly*, 22 (March 1987), pp. 454–474, on the importance of ideology to city managers' propensity toward the policy role.

59. James H. Svara, "Political Supremacy and Administrative Expertise," *Management Science and Policy Analysis*, 3 (Summer 1985), pp. 3–7, quotation on p. 3; "Dichotomy and Duality: Reconceptualizing the Relationship Between Policy and Administration in Council-Manager Cities," *Public Administration Review*, 45 (January/February 1985), pp. 221–232; "Sharing the Load of Governance: The Manager's Responsibilities," *Public Management*, 67 (July 1985), pp. 16–19.

60. Pealy, "The Need for Elected Leadership," pp. 215–16.

61. Adrian, "A Study of Three Communities," pp. 210–11.

62. Nelson Wikstrom, "The Mayor as a Policy Leader in the Council-Manager Form of Government: A View from the Field," *Public Administration Review*, 39 (May/June 1979), pp. 273–274.

63. Rexford G. Tugwell, "La Guardia: 'Good Government' Can Be Mismanagement," in Edward C. Banfield (ed.), *Urban Government* (New York: Free Press, 1961), pp. 290–91.

64. Banfield and Wilson, *City Politics*, p. 333.

65. Jane Mobley, "Politician or Professional? The Debate Over Who Should Run Our Cities Continues," *Governing*, 1 (February 1988), pp. 42–48, quotation on p. 43.

66. Edward C. Banfield, *Big City Politics* (New York: Random House, 1965).

67. Robert Paul Boynton and Deil S. Wright, "Mayor-Manager Relationships in Large Council-Manager Cities: A Reinterpretation," *Public Administration Review*, 31 (January/February 1971), pp. 28–36.

68. Thomas W. Fletcher, "What Is the Future for Our Cities and the City Manager?" *Public Administration Review*, 31 (January/February 1971), pp. 14–20, quotation on p. 18.

69. Cortus T. Koehler, "Policy Development and Legislative Oversight in Council-Manager Cities: An Information and Communication Analysis," *Public Administration Review*, 33 (September/October 1973), pp. 433–441.

70. Morgan, *Managing Urban America*, p. 71.

71. John P. Kotter and Paul R. Lawrence, *Mayors in Action: Five Approaches to Urban Governance* (New York: John Wiley & Sons, 1974).

72. Ibid., Chapter 3.

73. Ibid., Chapter 13.

74. Ibid., Chapter 7 and pp. 229–30.

75. Douglas Yates, *The Ungovernable City: The Politics of Urban Problems and Policy Making* (Cambridge, Mass.: MIT Press, 1977), Chapter 6.

76. Ibid., p. 165.

77. James Brady, "Citizen Brady: No Last Hurrah for Flawed Mayors," *City and State*, 4 (June 1987), 10.

78. Janet Wilson, "Vues of Austin: The Short Reign of Mr. Meiszer," *Third Coast*, March 1984, pp. 36–39, quotation on p. 36.

79. Edward B. Lewis, "City Managers in Regional Perspective: Is the South Different?" *Southern Review of Public Administration*, 3 (March 1980), pp. 404–426, quotation on p. 419.

80. John Bartlow Martin, "The Town that Tried 'Good Government'," in Banfield (ed.), *Urban Government*, p. 284.

81. Pealy, "The Need for Elected Leadership," p. 216.

82. Svara, "Unwrapping Institutional Packages in Urban Government," pp. 174–175.

83. Adrian and Press, *Governing Urban America*, pp. 196–98.

84. James B. Hogan, *The Chief Administrative Officer: An Alternative to Council-Manager Government* (Tucson: Institute of Government Research, University of Arizona, 1976), p. 8.

85. Banfield, "Los Angeles: Pre (Civil) War," *Big City Politics*, pp. 80–93, quotation on pp. 82–83; see also, Raphe Sonenshein, " Biracial Coalition Politics in Los Angeles," *PS*, 19 (Summer 1986), pp. 582–90; and Paul Pringle, "Dream of Governorship Fading for Tom Bradley," *Dallas Morning News*, November 16, 1986, p. 8A.

86. Wallace S. Sayre, "The General Manager Idea for Large Cities," *Public Administration Review*, 14 (Autumn 1954), pp. 253–58.

87. Charles R. Adrian, "Recent Concepts in Large City Administration," in Edward C. Banfield (ed.), *Urban Government*, 2d ed. (New York: Free Press, 1969), p. 519.

88. John E. Bebout, "Management for Large Cities," *Public Administration Review*, 15 (Summer 1955), pp. 188–95.

89. Hogan, *The Chief Administrative Officer*, p. 81.

90. Andy Oakley, "A Commanding View from the Top," *City and State*, 4 (September 1987), p. 18.

91. Ibid.

92. With few modifications, the remaining sections in this chapter restate the research reported in Charldean Newell and David N. Ammons, "Role Emphases of City Managers and Other Municipal Executives," *Public Administration Review*, 47 (May/June 1987), pp. 246–53. Reprinted with permission from *Public Administration Review* © 1987 by The American Society for Public Administration, 1120 G Street, N.W., Suite 500, Washington, D.C. All rights reserved.

93. Wright, "The City Manager as a Developmental Administrator."

94. Henry Mintzberg, *The Nature of Managerial Work* (New York: Harper & Row, 1973), p. 131. Copyright © 1973 by Henry Mintzberg. Reprinted by permission of Harper & Row, Publishers, Inc. The importance of a good second in command in the case of mayors is made in Kotter and Lawrence, *Mayors in Action*, pp. 234–36.

95. Much of the literature on the modern city manager cites the growing complexity of the job, including policy and political responsibilities. See, for example, Welborn, "The Environment and Role of the Administrator"; Stillman, "Local Public Management in Transition" in *The Municipal Year Book*; and Morgan, *Managing Urban America*, Chapter 12.

96. Wright, "The City Manager as Developmental Administrator," 236.

97. Mintzberg, *The Nature of Managerial Work*, p. 102. Using Mintzberg's framework, Alan W. Lau, Arthur R. Newman, and Laurie A. Broedling found similar complexities in the work of federal executives; see "The Nature of Managerial Work in the Public Sector," *Public Administration Review*, 40 (September/October 1980), pp. 513–520.

Chapter Four

1. Lance B. Kurke and Howard E. Aldrich, "Mintzberg Was Right!: A Replication and Extension of 'The Nature of Managerial Work'," *Management Science*, 29 (August 1983), p. 978.

2. Richard J. Stillman, II, "Local Public Management in Transition: A Report on the Current State of the Profession." In International City Management Association, *The Municipal Year Book 1982* (Washington, D.C.: ICMA, 1982), p. 168.

3. Alan W. Lau, Arthur R. Newman, and Laurie A. Broedling, "The

Nature of Managerial Work in the Public Sector," *Public Administration Review,* 40 (September/October 1980), p. 517.

4. See, for example, Robert B. Jones, "Executive of the Year: Jorge Carrasco, Austin, Texas," *Public Management,* 68 (June 1986), pp. 22–23; Tom Long, "Work or Play, Normal's Anderson Gives His All," *Public Management,* 68 (July 1986), pp. 17–18; Dave Daley, "Richard Helwig: City Manager, Dayton, Ohio," *Public Management,* 67 (August 1985), p. 19; and Jack Hovelson, "Terri Lea Schroeder: City Manager, Iowa Falls, Iowa," *Public Management,* 66 (December 1984), pp. 20–22.

5. Carol Pogash, "Dianne Feinstein," *Working Woman,* 10 (February 1985), pp. 80–83.

6. Kathryn Means, "Mayor on the Move," *Ultra,* (April 1985), pp. 57–60.

7. "A Mayor Caught Up in a Maelstrom," *U.S. News & World Report,* 98 (May 27, 1985), p. 9.

8. "A Rust-Belt Relic's New Shine," *Newsweek,* 106 (September 9, 1985), p. 26.

9. "All-Pro City Management Team—The Best in the Public Sector," *City & State,* 3 (September 1986), p. 16.

10. Sune Carlson, *Executive Behavior: A Study of the Work Load and the Working Methods of Managing Directors* (Stockholm, Strombergs, 1951).

11. Tom Burns, "The Directions of Activity and Communication in a Departmental Executive Group," *Human Relations,* 7, No. 1 (1954), pp. 73–97; G.H. Copeman, H. Luijk, and F. deP. Hanika, *How the Executive Spends His Time* (London: Business Publications Ltd., 1963); Robert Dubin and S. Lee Spray, "Executive Behavior and Interaction," *Industrial Relations,* 3 (February 1964), pp. 99–108; E. Brewer and J.W.C. Tomlinson, "The Manager's Working Day," *The Journal of Industrial Economics,* 12 (July 1964), pp. 191–97; John R. Hinrichs, "Communications Activity of Industrial Research Personnel," *Personnel Psychology,* 17 (Summer 1964), pp. 193–204; J.H. Horne and Tom Lupton, "The Work Activities of 'Middle' Managers—An Exploratory Study," *Journal of Management Studies,* 2 (February 1965), pp. 14–33; R. Stewart, *Managers and Their Jobs* (London: Macmillan, 1967); and Edward E. Lawler, III, Lyman W. Porter, and Allen Tennenbaum, "Managers' Attitudes Toward Interaction Episodes," *Journal of Applied Psychology,* 52 (December 1968), pp. 432–39.

12. Robert H. Guest, "Of Time and the Foreman," *Personnel,* 32 (May 1956), pp. 478–86; Q.D. Ponder, "The Effective Manufacturing Foreman," in Edwin Young (ed.), *Industrial Relations Research Association Proceedings of the Tenth Annual Meeting,* Madison, Wisconsin, 1957, pp. 41–54; Joe Kelly, "The Study of Executive Behavior by Activity Sampling," *Human Relations,* 17 (August 1964), pp. 277–87; Irving Choran, "The Manager of a Small Company,"

(Montreal: McGill University, 1969), unpublished M.B.A. thesis; and Kurke and Aldrich, "Mintzberg Was Right!"

13. Henry Mintzberg, *The Nature of Managerial Work* (New York: Harper & Row, 1973).

14. Henry Mintzberg, "The Manager's Job: Folklore and Fact," *Harvard Business Review*, 53 (July –August 1975), p. 60.

15. Lau et al., "The Nature of Managerial Work in the Public Sector."

16. Lyman W. Porter and John Van Maanen, "Task Accomplishment and the Management of Time." In James L. Perry and Kenneth L. Kraemer (eds.), *Public Management: Public and Private Perspectives* (Palo Alto, Calif.: Mayfield, 1983), pp. 212–24.

17. Mintzberg, *The Nature of Managerial Work*, p. 30.

18. Ibid., fn. 4, pp. 31–32. Copyright © 1973 by Henry Mintzberg. Reprinted by permission of Harper & Row, Publishers, Inc.

19. John P. Kotter and Paul R. Lawrence, *Mayors in Action: Five Approaches to Urban Governance* (New York: John Wiley & Sons, 1974), pp. 51–54. Copyright © 1974 by John Wiley & Sons, Inc. Reprinted by permission of John Wiley & Sons, Inc.

20. Excerpted from Henry Maier, *Challenge to the Cities* (New York: Random House, 1966), pp. 6–15, as found in Kotter and Lawrence, *Mayors in Action*, pp. 56–59. Copyright © 1966 by Random House, Inc. Reprinted by permission of Random House, Inc.

21. Michelle Kay, "The Prime of Ms. Kathy Whitmire," *Texas Business*, January 1988, pp. 24–29, quotation on p. 25.

22. Stillman, "Local Public Management in Transition," p. 168. A predecessor to the 1980 survey reported by Stillman was a study reported by ICMA in 1958 in which 21 city managers kept time allocation records for one week. The managers reported an average workweek of 54 hours, with average daily time allocations (assuming a nine-hour day, six-day week) as follows:

Talking with citizens in office and over telephone—2 hours
Conferences with department heads—1.5 hours
Planning current activities and future work—1 hour
Handling correspondence—1 hour
Formal and informal meetings with city council—50 minutes
Inspecting municipal activities—50 minutes
Attending meetings and talking before various groups—40 minutes
Preparing official reports—30 minutes
Interviewing candidates for positions—20 minutes
Miscellaneous—20 minutes

See *The Technique of Municipal Administration*, 4th ed. (Chicago: International City Managers' Association, 1958), p. 4.

23. Wayne F. Anderson, Chester A. Newland, and Richard J. Stillman, II, *The Effective Local Government Manager* (Washington, D.C.: International City Management Association, 1983), p. 35. Reprinted with permission.

24. Mintzberg, *The Nature of Managerial Work*, pp.54–99.

25. Ibid., pp. 126–29.

26. Ibid., p. 127. Copyright © 1973 by Henry Mintzberg. Reprinted by permission of Harper & Row, Publishers, Inc.

27. Ibid. Copyright © 1973 by Henry Mintzberg. Reprinted by permission of Harper & Row, Publishers, Inc.

28. Laurence Rutter, *The Essential Community* (Washington, D.C.: International City Management Association, 1980), pp. 126–27.

29. Kotter and Lawrence, *Mayors in Action*, pp. 61, 94, 191–94.

30. ICMA Committee on Future Horizons, . . . *New Worlds of Service* (Washington, D.C.: International City Management Association, 1979), p. 18.

31. Robert Paul Boynton and Deil S. Wright, "Mayor-Manager Relationships in Large Council-Manager Cities: A Reinterpretation," *Public Administration Review* 31 (January/February 1971), p.28.

32. Kotter and Lawrence, *Mayors in Action*, pp. 232–34.

33. David Welborn, "The Environment and Role of the Administrator." In James M. Banovetz (ed.), *Managing the Modern City* (Washington, D.C.: International City Management Association, 1971), p. 96. Reprinted with permission.

34. Ibid., p. 83.

35. Tom Morganthau, "Young: A Knack for City Politics," *Newsweek*, 101 (February 7, 1983), p. 10.

36. Ibid.

37. Carlson, *Executive Behavior*; Guest, "Of Time and the Foreman"; Stewart, *Managers and Their Jobs*; Mintzberg, *The Nature of Managerial Work*; Lau et al., "The Nature of Managerial Work in the Public Sector"; and Kurke and Aldrich, "Mintzberg Was Right!"

38. Mintzberg, *The Nature of Managerial Work*; Kurke and Aldrich, "Mintzberg Was Right!" pp. 978–81.

39. Lenora E. Berson, "The Return of the Big Bambino," *The Nation*, 236 (February 19, 1983), pp. 205–7.

40. Excellent accounts of city managers dealing with strikes, floods, misconduct by subordinates, and a variety of lesser crises are contained in Bill Gilbert, *This City, This Man: The Cookingham Era in Kansas City* (Washington, D.C.: International City Management Association, 1978), and LeRoy F. Harlow, *Without Fear or Favor* (Provo, Utah: Brigham Young University Press, 1977).

41. "A Mayor Caught Up in a Maelstrom," *U.S. News & World Report*, p. 9, and Richard Ben Cramer, "Can the Best Mayor Win?" *Esquire*, 102 (October 1984), pp. 71–72.

42. Pogash, "Dianne Feinstein," *Working Woman*, p. 83.

43. *Washington Post* columnist William Raspberry, cited in "A Mayor Caught Up in a Maelstrom," *U.S. News & World Report*, p. 9.

44. Mark Starr, "Did It Have to Happen?" *Newsweek*, 105 (May 27, 1985), p. 25.

45. Ibid., p. 22.

46. Ibid., p. 24.

47. Gilbert, *This City, This Man*, p. 50.

48. Ibid., p. 148.

49. Ibid., pp. 174, 169–70, quoting Porter Homer, Graham Watt, and E. Robert Turner, respectively.

50. Daley, "Richard Helwig," p. 19 (*Public Management* reprint of *Dayton Daily News* article, January 7, 1985). Reprinted here with permission of the *Dayton Daily News*.

51. "1986 All-Pro City Management Team: City & State Recognizes the Best in the Public Sector," *City & State*, 3 (September 1986), pp. 15, 18.

52. Means, "Mayor on the Move," pp. 59–60.

53. David McLemore, "Henry Cisneros," *Dallas Morning News*, November 9, 1986, p. 2E. Reprinted by permission of the *Dallas Morning News*.

54. Morganthau, "Young: A Knack for City Politics," p. 10.

55. David Maraniss, "Houston's 'Straight Slate'," *The Washington Post National Weekly Edition* (November 4, 1985), p. 14.

56. Mark Starr, "A Macho Mayor vs. His Hometown," *Newsweek*, 101 (June 13, 1983), p. 22.

57. Berson, "The Return of the Big Bambino," p. 205.

58. Cramer, "Can the Best Mayor Win?" pp. 64–66. Copyright © 1984. Reprinted by permission of Sterling Lord Literistic, Inc.

59. Berson, "The Return of the Big Bambino," p. 205.

60. Rob Gurwitt, "The Mayoral Races of '87: What November's Results Say About Urban Politics," *Governing*, 1 (December 1987), p. 27–30.

61. Mintzberg, *The Nature of Managerial Work*.

62. Mintzberg, *The Nature of Managerial Work*; Kurke and Aldrich, "Mintzberg Was Right!"

63. Lau et al., "The Nature of Managerial Work in the Public Sector," p. 519.

64. William G. Ouchi, *Theory Z: How American Business Can Meet the Japanese Challenge* (Reading, Mass.: Addison-Wesley, 1981), pp. 208–9, and Thomas J. Peters and Robert H. Waterman, Jr., *In Search of Excellence: Lessons from America's Best-Run Companies* (New York: Harper & Row, 1982), pp. 121–25.

65. Ben Merritt, "B. Gale Wilson: Fairfield's City Manager," *Public Management*, 68 (August 1986), pp. 18–19.

66. Gilbert, *This City, This Man*, pp. 149–50.

67. "A Mayor Caught Up in a Maelstrom," p. 9.

68. Cramer, "Can the Best Mayor Win?" pp. 58–60. Copyright © 1984. Reprinted by permission of Sterling Lord Literistic, Inc.

69. Ibid., p. 60.

70. Carlson, *Executive Behavior*, p. 52.

71. Peter F. Drucker, *The Effective Executive* (New York: Harper & Row, 1966), p. 100.

72. Porter and Van Maanen, "Task Accomplishment and the Management of Time," p. 218.

73. Kotter and Lawrence, *Mayors In Action*, p. 83.

74. Mintzberg, *The Nature of Managerial Work*, p. 181. Copyright © 1973 by Henry Mintzberg. Reprinted by permission of Harper & Row, Publishers, Inc.

Chapter Five

1. Wayne F. Anderson, Chester A. Newland, and Richard J. Stillman, II, *The Effective Local Government Manager* (Washington, D.C.: International City Management Association, 1983), pp. 8, 63, 49, 68, quoting city managers Albert

G. Ilg, Richard B. Chesney, E.H. Denton, and George W. Pyle, respectively. Reprinted with permission.

2. Ibid., pp. 17-26.

3. Ibid., p. 25.

4. Buddy Baxter, "Blue Ash City Manager: He's Grown with the City," *Public Management*, 68 (January 1986), p. 17.

5. Tom Long, "Work or Play, Normal's Anderson Gives His All," *Public Management*, 68 (July 1968), pp. 17-18.

6. "1986 All-Pro City Management Team: City & State Recognizes the Best in the Public Sector," *City & State*, 3 (September 1986), pp. 15, 18.

7. Elizabeth Voisin, "Andrews: Policies Without Politics," *City & State*, 3 (September 1986), p. 22.

8. Ibid.

9. Ibid.

10. Philip Marvin, *Executive Time Management* (New York: AMACOM, 1980).

11. Thomas J. Meyer and Kathy Jackson, "Suburban Mayor's Duty Calls—Sometimes at 5 a.m.," *Dallas Morning News*, January 19, 1987, p. 16A.

12. Bill Gilbert, *This City, This Man: The Cookingham Era in Kansas City* (Washington, D.C.: International City Management Association, 1978), pp. 68-69.

Chapter Six

1. Henry Mintzberg, *The Nature of Managerial Work* (New York: Harper & Row, 1973), pp. 129-30. Copyright © 1973 by Henry Mintzberg. Reprinted by permission of Harper & Row, Publishers, Inc.

2. Ibid., pp. 130-31. Copyright © 1973 by Henry Mintzberg. Reprinted by permission of Harper & Row, Publishers, Inc. The five listed propositions were included as numbers 2, 4, 5, 10, 15, and 16 in Mintzberg's original set of 22 propositions. Original propositions 15 and 16 have been merged in this treatment.

3. Ibid., p. 130. Copyright © 1973 by Henry Mintzberg. Reprinted by permission of Harper & Row, Publishers, Inc.

4. Ibid., pp. 112–13. Copyright © 1973 by Henry Mintzberg. Reprinted by permission of Harper & Row, Publishers, Inc.

5. Ibid., p. 112. Copyright © 1973 by Henry Mintzberg. Reprinted by permission of Harper & Row, Publishers, Inc.

6. Ibid., p. 130. Copyright © 1973 by Henry Mintzberg. Reprinted by permission of Harper & Row, Publishers, Inc.

7. Irving Choran, "The Manager of a Small Company," MBA thesis, McGill University, 1969; Lance B. Kurke and Howard E. Aldrich, "Mintzberg was Right!" *Management Science*, 29 (August 1983), pp. 975–84; and Henry Mintzberg, *The Nature of Managerial Work*.

8. Mintzberg, *The Nature of Managerial Work*, p. 130. Copyright © 1973 by Henry Mintzberg. Reprinted by permission of Harper & Row, Publishers, Inc.

9. Choran, "The Manager of A Small Company"; Kurke and Aldrich, "Mintzberg was Right!"; and Mintzberg, *The Nature of Managerial Work*.

10. Mintzberg, *The Nature of Managerial Work*, p. 130. Copyright © 1973 by Henry Mintzberg. Reprinted by permission of Harper & Row, Publishers, Inc.

11. The mean of 66.4 work hours per week for mayors actually understates slightly the reported figures. One mayor claimed 126 working hours per week, but that claim is regarded as incredible and, therefore, has been excluded from tabulations. Even with that exclusion, reported working hours range from a low of 35 hours per week to a high of 100, reported by two mayors.

12. Mintzberg, *The Nature of Managerial Work*, p. 131. Copyright © 1973 by Henry Mintzberg. Reprinted by permission of Harper & Row, Publishers, Inc.

13. See, for example, Nelson Wikstrom, "The Mayor as a Policy Leader in the Council-Manager Form of Government: A View from the Field," *Public Administration Review*, 39 (May/June 1979), pp. 270–76. Wikstrom contends that "in a sense, council-manager government has evolved into teamwork governance; mayors and managers need and depend upon each other"(p. 275). See, also, John P. Kotter and Paul R. Lawrence, *Mayors In Action: Five Approaches to Urban Governance* (New York: John Wiley & Sons, 1974), pp. 195–96.

14. Mintzberg, *The Nature of Managerial Work*, pp. 118–19.

15. Donald A. Blubaugh, "The Changing Role of the Public Administrator," *Public Management* 69 (June 1987), p. 10.

16. Wayne F. Anderson, Chester A. Newland, and Richard J. Stillman, II, *The Effective Local Government Manager* (Washington, D.C.: International City Management Association, 1983), pp. 15, 50.

17. Ibid., p. 3, quoting city manager George P. McConnaughey.

18. ICMA Committee on Future Horizons, . . . *New Worlds of Service* (Washington, D.C.: International City Management Association, 1979), p. 19.

19. Philip R. Marvin, *Executive Time Management* (New York: AMACOM, 1980).

20. Kotter and Lawrence, *Mayors in Action*, p. 235. Copyright © 1974 by John Wiley & Sons, Inc. Reprinted by permission of John Wiley & Sons, Inc.

21. Mintzberg, *The Nature of Managerial Work*, pp. 129–30.

22. Small positive or negative correlations, of course, were found in every instance, but none was found to meet the conventional test of statistical significance at the .05 level. The same test of statistical significance was used to determine which correlations to report and which to exclude throughout this section.

23. Kotter and Lawrence, *Mayors in Action*, pp. 188–200.

24. Charles E. Lindblom, "The Science of 'Muddling Through,'" *Public Administration Review*, 19 (Spring 1959), pp. 79–88.

25. Anderson et al., *The Effective Local Government Manager*, pp. 17–26.

26. Oliver P. Williams, "A Typology for Comparative Local Government," *Midwest Journal of Political Science*, 5 (May 1961), pp. 150–64.

27. Anderson et al., note that these "ideal local management types" are drawn from three earlier works: Richard J. Stillman, II, *The Rise of the City Manager* (Albuquerque: University of New Mexico Press, 1974); Ronald O. Loveridge, *City Managers in Legislative Politics* (Indianapolis: Bobbs-Merrill, 1971); and Kotter and Lawrence, *Mayors in Action*.

Chapter 7

1. Henry David Thoreau (1817–1862), as cited in Lawrence J. Peter, *Peter's Quotations: Ideas for Our Time* (New York: William Morrow, 1977), p. 470.

2. See Henry Mintzberg, *The Nature of Managerial Work* (New York: Harper & Row, 1973); Lance B. Kurke and Howard E. Aldrich, "Mintzberg Was Right: A Replication and Extension of 'The Nature of Managerial Work'," *Management Science*, 29 (August 1983), 975–84; and Alan W. Lau, Arthur R. Newman, and Laurie A. Broedling, "The Nature of Managerial Work in the Public Sector," *Public Administration Review*, 40 (September/October 1980), pp. 513–20. The

allocation of time most closely approximating allocations by mayors and city managers was that of the hospital administrator in the Kurke and Aldrich study.

3. Diane Feinstein, "Who Are the Nation's Busiest Execs? Mayors," *City & State*, 4 (November 1987), 12. Reprinted with permission.

4. See Stewart L. Stokes, *It's About Time* (Boston: CBI Publishing, 1982), and Merrill E. Douglass and Donna N. Douglass, *Manage Your Time, Manage Your Work, Manage Yourself* (New York: AMACOM, 1985).

5. Kenneth Blanchard and Spencer Johnson, *The One-Minute Manager* (New York: Berkley, 1983).

6. Stokes, *It's About Time*, p. 9.

7. "Top 10 Time Wasters Cited for Public Administration," *Public Administration Times*, 8 (September 1, 1985), p. 12, quoting Alec Mackenzie in *Office of Employee Relations*, 1 (July 1985), a publication of the New York State Governor's Office of Employee Relations Human Resource Development.

8. Leo B. Moore, "Managerial Time," *Industrial Management Review*, 9 (Spring 1968), pp. 77–86.

9. Stephanie Winston, *The Organized Executive: New Ways to Manage Time, Paper, and People* (New York: Norton, 1983), pp. 154–58, and Robert Heller, *The Supermanagers: Managing for Success, the Movers and the Doers, the Reasons Why* (New York: E.P. Dutton, 1984), p. 38.

10. R. Alec Mackenzie, *The Time Trap* (New York: AMACOM, 1972), p. 93.

11. Moore, "Managerial Time," 78.

12. Bonnie McCollough, "Achievers Tell How They Avoid Wasting Time," *Dallas Morning News*, December 6, 1986, p. 7C,

13. Edwin C. Bliss, *Getting Things Done* (New York: Charles Scribner's Sons, 1976), p. 49, and Winston, *The Organized Executive*, p. 140.

14. Winston, *The Organized Executive*, pp. 141–42.

15. Bliss, *Getting Things Done*, p. 50.

16. Mackenzie, *The Time Trap*, p. 97.

17. Grover E. Starling, *Managing the Public Sector*, 3rd ed. (Chicago: Dorsey, 1986), p. 426, and Alan Lakein, *How to Get Control of Your Time and Life* (New York: Peter H. Wyden, 1975), p. 22.

18. McCollough, "Achievers Tell How They Avoid Wasting Time," p. 7C. One manifestation of the trend toward "getting organized" is the development of various executive organizer folios; during the week of January 19, 1987, the

"Cathy" comic strip, drawn by Cathy Guisewite, spoofed the process of selecting just the right organizer.

19. Bliss, *Getting Things Done,* p. 53.

20. Heller, *The Supermanagers,* p. 39.

21. See Robert D. Rutherford, *Just in Time: Immediate Help for the Time-Pressured* (New York: John Wiley & Sons, 1981), pp. 113–25; Warren K. Schilit, "A Manager's Guide to Efficient Time Management," *Personnel Journal,* 62 (September 1983), pp. 736–42; and Ross A. Webber, *Time Is Money: The Key to Managerial Success* (London: Free Press, 1980), pp. 26–34.

22. Edward Young, "Night Thoughts, Night I," line 393.

23. Bliss, *Getting Things Done,* p. 36.

24. Jane B. Burka and Lenora M. Yuen, *Procrastination: Why You Do It, What to Do About It* (Reading, Mass.: Addison-Wesley, 1983), p. 16.

25. Jane B. Burka and Lenora M. Yuen, "A Procrastinator's Guide to Telling Time," *Working Woman,* 9 (September 1984), p. 78.

26. Mackenzie, *The Time Trap,* p. 35.

27. Thomas J. Peters and Robert H. Waterman, Jr., *In Search of Excellence: Lessons from America's Best-Run Companies* (New York: Harper & Row, 1982), p. 126.

28. Starling, *Managing the Public Sector,* p. 426.

29. Burka and Yuen, *Procrastination,* p. 170.

30. Lou Ann Walker, "How to Make Time Work for You: Getting Organized is Easier than It Seems," *Parade,* May 10, 1987, p. 5.

31. Helen Reynolds and Mary E. Trammel, *Executive Time Management* (Englewood Cliffs, N.J.: Prentice-Hall, 1979), pp. 28–29.

32. Moore, "Managerial Time," 78.

33. Ibid.

34. Winston, *The Organized Executive,* p. 142.

35. Mackenzie, *The Time Trap,* pp. 87–89.

36. Heller, *The Supermanagers,* p. 39.

37. Winston, *The Organized Executive,* p. 143.

38. Mintzberg, *The Nature of Managerial Work;* Kurke and Aldrich, "Mintzberg Was Right"; and Lau et al., "The Nature of Managerial Work in the Public Sector."

39. "Work Facts: Meeting Time," *Dallas Morning News*, December 23, 1986, p. 1C.

40. Moore, "Managerial Time," p. 78.

41. Isadore Barmash, "A New Economic Indicator," *Newsweek*, September 9, 1985, p. 12.

42. Starling, *Managing the Public Sector*, p. 428.

43. "Beep and Run," *Dallas Times Herald*, October 22, 1985, p. 1.

44. Joseph D. Cooper, *How to Get More Done in Less Time* (New York: Doubleday, 1971), pp. 279–80.

45. Moore, "Managerial Time," p. 80, and Bliss, *Getting Things Done*, pp. 57–58.

46. Winston, *The Organized Executive*, p. 150.

47. Ibid.

48. Moore, "Managerial Time," 78.

49. "Work Facts: Paper Chase," *Dallas Morning News*, December 2, 1986, p. 1C.

50. Mackenzie, *The Time Trap*, pp. 66–67.

51. Reynolds and Trammel, *Executive Time Management*, p. 51.

52. Starling, *Managing the Public Sector*, p. 428.

53. Heller, *The Supermanagers*, p. 39.

54. Stephanie Winston, "The Boss/Secretary Team," *Working Woman*, 9 (February 1984), 16.

55. Bliss, *Getting Things Done*, pp. 29–30.

56. Perry W. Buffington, "Getting It Together," *Sky*, May 1987, pp. 138, 141.

57. Reynolds and Trammel, *Executive Time Management*, p. 42.

58. Richard A. Stein, *Personal Strategies for Living with Stress* (New York: John Gallagher Communications, 1983), p. 2.

59. Meyer Friedman and Ray H. Roseman, *Type A Behavior and Your Heart* (New York: Alfred A. Knopf, 1974), p. 67.

60. "Type A Men Deemed More Likely to Survive Heart Disease," *Dallas Morning News*, January 14, 1988, p. 12A.

61. John G. Falcioni, "Stress as an Occupational Hazard," *City and State*, 5 (January 4, 1988), p. 28.

62. Stein, *Personal Strategies for Living with Stress*, pp. 15–22.

63. Heller, *The Supermanagers*, p. 38.

64. Starling, *Managing the Public Sector*, p. 430.

65. See Manuel J. Smith, *When I Say No, I Feel Guilty* (New York: Dial, 1975). Smith's focus is not on the work place, but he does offer advice for both employers and employees on how to be assertive.

66. Stein, *Personal Strategies for Living with Stress*, Chapter 4.

67. Ibid., Chapters 5 and 6, and Wayne F. Anderson, Chester A. Newland, and Richard J. Stillman, II, *The Effective Local Government Manager* (Washington, D.C.: International City Management Association, 1983), pp. 224–28.

68. Christine Brooks, quoted in "Inner-Directed People Likely to Exercise Often," a *Chicago Tribune* article appearing in *Dallas Morning News*, January 26, 1987, p. 5C.

69. Anderson, Newland, and Stillman, *The Effective Local Government Manager*, pp. 228–29.

70. Interview with Hans Selye in Laurence Cherry, "On the Real Benefits of Eustress," *Psychology Today*, (March 1978), p. 70, cited in Ibid., p. 223.

71. See, for example, Jacquelyn Wonder and Priscilla Donovan, *Whole-Brain Thinking: Working from Both Sides of the Brain to Achieve Peak Job Performance* (New York: Morrow, 1984).

72. Interview with Ann McGee-Cooper reported in Barbara Lau, "How to Add an Hour to Your Day," *Family Circle*, 100 (February 10, 1987), pp. 22, 24, 26.

Chapter Eight

1. Richard Ben Cramer, "Can the Best Mayor Win?" *Esquire*, 102 (October 1984), p. 64.

2. Deil S. Wright, "The City Manager as a Developmental Administrator," Chapter 6 in Robert T. Daland (ed.), *Comparative Urban Research* (Beverly Hills, Calif.: Sage Publications, 1969), pp. 203–48.

3. Henry Mintzberg, *The Nature of Managerial Work* (New York: Harper & Row, 1973).

4. Ibid., pp. 181–82. Copyright © 1973 by Henry Mintzberg. Reprinted by permission of Harper & Row, Publishers, Inc.

5. John P. Kotter and Paul R. Lawrence, *Mayors in Action: Five Approaches to Urban Governance* (New York: John Wiley & Sons, 1974), p. 51.

6. Richard J. Stillman, II, "Local Public Management in Transition: A Report on the Current State of the Profession." In *The Municipal Year Book 1982* (Washington, D.C.: International City Management Association, 1982), p. 168.

7. Kotter and Lawrence, *Mayors in Action*, pp. 230–31. Copyright © 1974 by John Wiley & Sons, Inc. Reprinted by permission of John Wiley & Sons, Inc.

8. Ibid., p. 236.

9. Ibid., p. 237. Copyright © 1974 by John Wiley & Sons, Inc. Reprinted by permission of John Wiley & Sons, Inc.

10. Mintzberg, *The Nature of Managerial Work*, p. 181. Copyright © 1973 by Henry Mintzberg. Reprinted by permission of Harper & Row, Publishers, Inc.

11. See, for example, Gene E. Burton, "The Group Process: Key to More Productive Management," in John Matzer, Jr., *Productivity Improvement Techniques: Creative Approaches for Local Government* (Washington, D.C.: International City Management Association, 1986), pp. 132–42.

12. Mintzberg, *The Nature of Managerial Work*, pp. 34–35. Copyright © 1973 by Henry Mintzberg. Reprinted by permission of Harper & Row, Publishers, Inc.

13. Ibid., p. 35.

14. Ibid. Copyright © 1973 by Henry Mintzberg. Reprinted by permission of Harper & Row, Publishers, Inc.

15. Ibid., p. 75. Copyright © 1973 by Henry Mintzberg. Reprinted by permission of Harper & Row, Publishers, Inc.

16. David McLemore, "Henry Cisneros," *Dallas Morning News,* November 9, 1986, p. 2E. Reprinted by permission of the *Dallas Morning News.*

17. Ibid. Reprinted by permission.

18. Cramer, "Can the Best Mayor Win?" p. 68. Copyright © 1984. Reprinted by permission of Sterling Lord Literistic, Inc.

19. Carol Pogash, "Dianne Feinstein," *Working Woman,* 10 (February 1985), p.83.

20. McLemore, "Henry Cisneros," p. 3E. Reprinted by permission of the *Dallas Morning News.*

21. James M. Banovetz, "The City: Forces of Change," in James M.

Banovetz (ed.), *Managing the Modern City* (Washington, D.C.: International City Management Association, 1971), p. 40.

22. David Welborn, "The Environment and Role of the Administrator," in Banovetz (ed.), *Managing the Modern City, p. 107.*

23. Stillman, "Local Public Management in Transition," p. 169.

24. Ibid., p. 172.

25. ICMA Committee on Future Horizons, . . . *New Worlds of Service* (Washington, D.C.: ICMA, 1979), pp. 16–22.

INDEX

Activities, managerial. *See* Time allocated by managerial activities
Adrian, Charles: 35, 46–47, 53, 58
Age. *See* Explanatory variables; Work variations, alternative explanations for
Aldrich, Howard: 73, 85, 96, 122–123
Aleshire, Fran: 45
Aleshire, Frank: 45
Allison, Graham: 17
Almy, Timothy: 49
Anderson, Charles: 50
Anderson, Wayne, on city managers: role ambiguity, 50; typical day, 78; typology, 107, 138, 140–41
Andrews, Marvin: 108
Argyris, Chris: 27
Ashburner, Charles E.: 37
Assistants, municipal: correlations for, 108–10, 113–15; role perceptions of, compared with executives, 60–65

Banfield, Edward: 36, 53–54, 58
Banovetz, James: 170
Barnard, Chester I.: 13–14
Bay Area Study. *See* Loveridge, Ronald
Bebout, John: 58
Bellavita, Christopher: 17
Bennis, Warren: 22, 25
Bilandic, Michael A.: 96
Blake, Robert: 23–24. *See also* Managerial Grid
Blanchard, Kenneth: 22, 25–26
Blubaugh, Donald A.: 51, 127
Blumenthal, Michael: 16
Bosworth, Karl: 44

Boundary-spanning activities: 15, 17
Boynton, Robert: 36, 54, 82
Bradley, Tom: 85
Brady, James: 56
Broedling, Laurie: 96
Buechner, John: 46–47
Buffington, Perry: 155
Burka, Jane: 149
Burns, James McGregor: 10, 13

Carlson, Sune: 72–73, 100
Carlyle, Thomas: 19
Carrell, Jeptha: 46–47
Chief administrative officer form of city government: 58–59
Childs, Richard: 41–42, 44, 46, 52
Choran, Irving: 121
Cisneros, Henry: 72, 85, 92–93, 169
City charters: changes in, 67; roles of mayor and manager related to, 81–85. *See also* Direct election of mayor; District election of city council members
City Manager of: Austin, *see* Meisner, Nick; Cincinnati, *see* Donaldson, William; Dallas, *see* Anderson, Charles, and Knight, Richard; Fairfield, Conn., *see* Wilson, B. Gale; Hayward, Calif., *see* Blubaugh, Donald A.; Kansas City, *see* Cookingham, L. P.; Plano, Tex., *see* Harvard, Jack; Phoenix, *see* Andrews, Marvin; Staunton, Va., *see* Ashburner, Charles E.
City manager performance, council expectations about: 83–84

City manager roles: changes in, over time, 65–67; perceptions of, 61–64; satisfaction with, 63–64. *See also* Typology
Cohen, Michael: 12
Commission form of city government: 37, 39–40
Contextual variables: 47, 54–55
Cookingham, L. P.: 43, 90–91, 98, 113
Correlations: across work dimensions, 111–15; explained, 103–04, 211n.22; of activities, 110–11; of demands, 104–05; of work variations, 119–35; of work foci, 105–10
Council expectations of city managers: 83–84
Council-manager form of city government: 37, 39–40
Council relations. *See* Time allocated by foci of work
Crises. *See* Time allocated by source of demands

Daley, Richard: 4, 56, 190n.13
Delegation. *See* Time management; Time wasters
Desk work. *See* Time allocated by activities
Demands on time. *See* Time allocated by source of demands
Direct election of mayor: 57, 67
District election of city council members: 58, 67
Donaldson, William: 48
Drop-ins. *See* Time management; Time wasters
Drucker, Peter: 99–100
Dyad, managerial: 63, 118, 126–35

East, John Porter: 41
Education. *See* Explanatory variables; Work variations, alternative explanations for
Elbert, Ed: 53
Emergencies. *See* Time allocated by source of demands
Evans, Jack: 19, 50

Executives, managers, and supervisors, distinctions among: 10, 17–18
Experience. *See* Explanatory variables; Work variations, alternative explanations for
Explanatory variables: 64–65, 176

Fayol, Henri: 1
Feinstein, Dianne: 18, 72, 85, 87, 143, 169
Fiedler, Fred: 22, 26
Foci of work. *See* Time allocated by foci of work
Folmar, Emory: 94
Formal meetings. *See* Time management; Time wasters; Work variations, comparison with Mintzberg
Forms of government: 37. *See also* Chief administrative officer, Commission, Council-manager, Strong mayor-council, Weak mayor-council forms of city government; and Structure
Fowler, Edmund: 36
Friedman, Meyer: 156
Frustrations of executives: 163, 168–69

Gardner, John: 18
Gawthrop, Louis: 16
Gilbert, Bill: 43
Good genes. *See* Leadership, great man theory of
Goode, W. Wilson: 72, 87, 98
Gortner, Harold: 10–11
Gross, Neal: 46
Gulick, Luther: 1, 41

Harvard, Jack: 112
Hatcher, Richard: 95
Heller, Robert: 151, 157
Helwig, Richard: 92
Hersey, Paul: 22, 26
Herson, Lawrence: 46
Hogan, James: 58
House, Robert: 29
Hudnut, William H. III: 72

ICMA: Code of Ethics, 42–44; Committee on Future Horizons, 51, 81, 128; "green books," 44–45; and stress management, 158; survey on frustrations and stress, 163, 170, 171. *See also* Keane, Mark; Ridley, Clarence E.
Intergovernmental relations. *See* Time allocated by source of demands
Internal administration. *See* Time allocated by foci of work

Kammerer, Gladys: 44–45, 47
Kaufman, Herbert: 26
Keane, Mark: 43
Kennedy, John: 17, 26
Knight, Richard: 50
Koch, Edward: 56, 85
Kotter, John P., on mayors: agenda-setting patterns, 135–36; approaches, 163–65; cognitive orientations, 137–38; models identified from literature, 55–56; typology, 81–82, 139; uncertainty, 129
Kurke, Lance: 73, 85, 96, 122–123

La Guardia, Fiorella: 53
Lau, Alan: 96
Lawrence, Paul R., on mayors: agenda-setting patterns, 135–36; approaches, 163–65; cognitive orientations, 137–38; models identified from literature, 55–56; typology, 81–82, 139; uncertainty, 131
Leadership, theories of: contingency/situational, 20–21, 25–29, 31; great man, 18, 31; styles, 21–25, 31, 164, 169; traits, 19–21, 31
Leadership: definitions of, 10–11, 13; diffusion of, 40; effective, 18–25, 31, 164–65; people and task relationship in, 23–29, 157; political, 52–59, 63; planning as function of, 162–63; strategic, 14; value setting as function of, 10–11, 14; vision as basic to, 14, 17–18, 25, 50
Lewin, Kurt: 22, 24

Lewis, Edward: 57
Likert, Rensis: 22, 24–25
Lineberry, Robert: 36
Local government reform. *See* Reformism in local government
Long, Norton: 45
Loveridge, Ronald, 48–49

Mackenzie, Alec: 147
McEachern, Alexander: 46
McGee-Cooper, Ann: 159
McGregor, Douglas: 24. *See also* Theory X, Theory Y
Mahler, Julianne: 10–11
Maier, Henry: 75
Management by walking around: 96
Management role. *See* Assistants, municipal; City manager performance, council expectations about; City manager roles; Mayors, roles and duties; Wright, Deil
Managerial Grid: 23–24
Managerial level. *See* Work variations, comparison with Mintzberg
March, James: 12
Martin, John: 57
Marvin, Philip: 109, 129–30
Mason, Ward: 46
Mayor of: Atlanta, *see* Young, Andrew; Baltimore, *see* Schaefer, Donald; Chicago, *see* Bildanic, Michael A.; Daley, Richard; and Washington, Harold; Dallas, *see* Evans, Jack; Strauss, Annette; and Taylor, A. Starke; Dayton, *see* Helwig, Richard; Gary, Ind., *see* Hatcher, Richard; Houston, *see* Whitmire, Kathy; Indianapolis, *see* Hudnut, William H. III; Los Angeles, *see* Bradley, Tom; Milwaukee, *see* Maier, Henry; Montgomery, Ala., *see* Folmar, Emory; New York, *see* La Guardia, Fiorella, and Koch, Edward; Overland Park, Kan., *see* Elbert, Ed; Philadelphia, *see* Goode, W. Wilson, and Rizzo, Frank; San Antonio, *see* Cisneros, Henry; San Francisco, *see* Feinstein, Dianne
Mayors, roles and duties: description of,

52–56; key duties, 82–83; perceptions of, 61–64; satisfaction with, 63–64. *See also* Typology
Meetings. *See* Time management; Time wasters
Meiszer, Nick: 57
Millett, John: 16
Mintzberg, Henry: contingency theory, 68, 117; control of time, 100–101; executive activities, 95–96; executive roles, 1–2, 12, 78–80; hypotheses, 8; leadership, 12; toleration, reasons for, 167; time allocation, 4, 73–74, 85; time management, 165, 166–68; work activities, 161–163
Mitchell, Terrance: 29
Model City Charter: 36, 41
Morgan, David: 55
MOVE and Mayor Goode of Philadelphia: 87–88
Mulrooney, Keith: 48
Mouton, Jane: 22–24. *See also* Managerial Grid

Nanus, Burt: 25
National League of Cities: 158
National Municipal League: 41
Newland, Chester, on city managers: role ambiguity, 50; typical day, 77–78; typology, 107, 138, 140–41
Newman, Arthur: 96
Nicholson, Jeanne: 10–11
Nietzsche, Friedrich: 19

One-minute management: 25, 144
Organizational size. *See* Work variations, comparison with Mintzberg
Organization theory: 11–14, 191n.5, 191n.6
Ouchi, William: 22, 24. *See also* Theory Z
Overwork, executive: 168–69

Paper work. *See* Time management; Time wasters
Pealy, Dorothy: 44, 52–53, 57
Perot, H. Ross: 9

Peters, Thomas: 11, 149
Policy development. *See* Time allocated by foci of work
Policy role. *See* Assistants, municipal; City manager performance, council expectations about; City manager roles; Mayors, roles and duties; Wright, Deil
Political role. *See* Assistants, municipal; City manager performance, council expectations about; City manager roles; Mayors, roles and duties; Wright, Deil
Politics and administration dichotomy: 7, 33, 41–46, 47–52, 106–08
POSDCORB: 1, 11–12, 14
Press, Charles: 35
Price, Don: 43–44
Priorities. *See* Time management, Time wasters
Procrastination. *See* Time management, Time wasters
Public and private managers contrasted: 100, 121–23, 167–168
Public relations. *See* Time allocated by foci of work

Reagan, Ronald: 22
Reddin, William: 27–28
Reform cities. *See* Reformism in local government.
Reformism in local government: characteristics of nonreform cities, 36; characteristics of reform cities, 36; four dimensions of reform movement, 34–35; efficiency as a criterion, 35, 41–42; nonreform elements in reform governments, 54, 57–58, 67; related to education, 132
Research design and methodology: 5–6, 59–61
Research questions: 4, 59–60
Reynolds, Helen: 150
Ridley, Clarence E.: 42
Right stuff. *See* Leadership, theories of
Rizzo, Frank: 86, 94
Role perceptions. *See* Assistants, municipal; City manager performance,

council expectations about; City manager roles; Mayors, roles and duties; Wright, Deil. *See also* Role theory

Role satisfaction. *See* Assistants, municipal; City manager performance, council expectations about; City manager roles; Mayors, roles and duties. *See also* Role theory

Role theory: ambiguity, 83–5; dissonance, 49, 83–85; as explanation of behavior, 46–52

Rosenman, Ray: 156

Rourke, Francis: 15

Rumsfeld, Donald: 16

Sayre, Wallace: 58

Schaefer, Donald: 72, 87, 94–95, 98–99, 169

Scheduled meetings. *See* Time allocated by activities, Time management, Time wasters

Schmidt, Warren: 22, 28

Selye, Hans: 159

Selznick, Phillip: 13

Shriver, Sargent: 26

Stein, Richard: 158

Stillman, Richard, on city managers: history, 43; role ambiguity, 50; typical day, 77–78; typology, 107, 138, 140–41

Stogdill, Ralph: 20–21

Stone, Harold: 43–44

Stone, Kathryn: 43–44

Strauss, Annette: 50

Stress: as related to time management, 156–58; techniques for dealing with, 158–59

Strong mayor-council form of city government: 37–38, 40

Structure: local government, 35, 41, 54, 161–62; organizational, 11–12

Svara, James: 52, 58

Tannenbaum, Robert: 22, 28

Task selection. *See* Time allocation by source of demands

Taylor, Frederick: 41

Taylor, A. Starke: 50

Telephone calls. *See* Time allocated by activities; Time management; Time wasters

Theory X, Theory Y: 24

Theory Z: 24

Time allocated by activities: 95–99, 110–11, 164, 179, 180, 181, 182–83, 184

Time allocated by source of demands: 86–88, 104–05, 164, 177, 180, 181, 184

Time allocated by foci of work: 88–95, 105–10, 164, 178, 180, 181, 184

Time allocation: preferences, 63–64; reasons for variation, 63–65; variations among municipal executives, 61–63. *See also* Workweeks

Time, control over: 99–101, 143. *See also* Time management

Time management: prospects for, 165–70; techniques of, 146–56, 212–13n.18

Time wasters: 144–46, 166

Tours. *See* Time allocated by activities

Trammel, Mary: 150

Tugwell, Rexford: 53

Typology: of city managers, 47, 48–49, 108; of managers, 79–80, 109; of mayors, 55–56

Unscheduled meetings. *See* Time allocated by activities; Time management; Time wasters

Washington, Harold: 26

Waterman, Robert: 11, 149

Weak mayor-council form of city government: 37–38, 40

Webster, William: 17

Welborn, David: 82, 170

White, Leonard: 42

Whitmire, Kathy: 77, 94

Wikstrom, Nelson: 53

Wilson, B. Gale: 96

Wilson, James Q.: 36, 53

Wilson, Janet: 57

Wilson, Woodrow: 35

Workdays, typical: 71–78, 162, 205n.22

Work variations, alternative explanations for: age, 132–33, 185;

education, 133–34, 186–187; experience, 134–35

Work variations, comparison with Mintzberg: formal meetings, 121–23; key variables, 117–18; managerial dyads, 126–31; managerial level, 125–26; propositions, 117–20; related studies, 135–40; size of organization, 122–25; summary, 140–42

Workweeks: 61, 71–72, 125, 162, 168, 205n.22, 210n.11
Wright, Deil, on city manager roles: 7, 33, 47, 60–69, 82, 161

Yates, Douglas: 56
Young, Andrew: 85, 93
Yuen, Lenora: 149
Yukl, Gary: 29–31